# THE CONTRIBUTION OF CARL MICHALSON TO MODERN THEOLOGY

*Studies in Interpretation and Application*

# THE CONTRIBUTION OF CARL MICHALSON TO MODERN THEOLOGY

*Studies in Interpretation and Application*

Edited by

Henry O. Thompson

Toronto Studies in Theology
Volume 55

The Edwin Mellen Press
Lewiston/Queenston/Lampeter

**Library of Congress Cataloging-in-Publication Data**

This book has been registered with the Library of Congress.

This is volume 55 in the continuing series
Toronto Studies in Theology
Volume 55   ISBN 0-88946-788-9
TST Series   ISBN 0-88946-975-X

A CIP catalog record for this book
is available from the British Library.

The Edwin Mellen Press
Box 450
Lewiston, New York
USA  14092

The Edwin Mellen Press ·
Box 67
Queenston, Ontario
CANADA  L0S 1L0

The Edwin Mellen Press, Ltd.
Lampeter, Dyfed, Wales
UNITED KINGDOM  SA48 7DY

Printed in the United States of America

# TABLE OF CONTENTS

## V. GLOBAL INTERPRETATION

## VI. FINAL INTERPRETATION

## MICHALSON: MAN & SOCIETY
### By Way of Preface

Carl Donald Michalson, Jr. (1915-1965) was born in Waverly, Minnesota, on 29 June. He was the second son of the four children of Gertrude Kathryn (Leuzenger) and Carl Michalson. In time, brother Gordon became President of The Claremont (California) School of Theology and sisters Edna and Eva became concert pianists. The family moved to Minneapolis soon after Junior was born. Here they joined Park Avenue Methodist Episcopal Church (MEC) where "Mike," as he came to be known, came under the influence of Rev. George Vallentyne. Vallentyne told Mike to go into the ministry and helped him attend John Fletcher College in University Park, Iowa. Mike graduated from there in 1936, working as associate pastor at Avery (Iowa) MEC in his senior year.

Michalson read Drew University professor Edwin Lewis' book, A Christian Manifesto; NY: Abingdon, 1934. In 1962, he wrote

> In 1935 I read this book and determined to study at Drew. Without understanding a word of the book, I nevertheless learned from it how a word can be like a hammer that breaketh a rock.

One might say this was the beginning of his 30-year association with Drew. On the basis of this book, Mike decided to go to Drew. He attended The Theological School, graduated "summa cum laude" in 1939 with a B.D. and stayed on to do an M.A. (1940). His thesis was on "Human Responsibility in the Republic of Plato and in the Synoptic Gospels." He took courses at Union Theological Seminary in New York City during the three summer sessions of 1938-1940 but went to Yale for his Ph.D. During this time he was a supply pastor at Teabo (NJ) Methodist Church (MC) and from 1940-1943, of Hillside Heights MC in Long Island. His heart was still in Minnesota for he joined the Northern Minnesota Annual Conference of the MC, as a member on trial in 1939 and in full connection in 1942. However, he received his Methodist ordination as a courtesy from the NY East Annual Conference, deacon's orders in 1941 and elder's orders in 1942.

He studied at Yale from 1940-1943 and then returned to Drew to begin his 22 year teaching career there until his death in a plane crash at Cincinnati, 8 Nov 65. He passed through the usual stages of Instructor, Assistant Professor (1945-1951) and Associate (1951-1955). In 1955, he was named Andrew V. Stout Professor of Systematic Theology, after the retirement of his teacher, Edwin Lewis. His doctorate was granted in 1945 with a dissertation on "The Problem of Revelation and Reason in the Theology of Karl Heim." In 1943, he met Janet Alyce Merrill, an artist and teacher. They were married in 1944. Their children, Karen and Steve, along with Janet, were frequent illustrations in Mike's lectures and sermons. The stories may have been apocryphal but they were true to life. Janet, now Mrs. Paul Clasper, is Honorary Chairperson of the Michalson Society. Karen and her husband Larry Bowden, and Steven and his wife Tina, were present for the first meeting of the Society. Karen designed the Society's logo - a cross on top of an outline of Drew's stone gate which stands on a lighted lamp. In his presidential inaugural remarks, the Michalson Society's first president, Dr. Michael Ryan pointed out that the three - the cross, Drew and the lamp of learning - were the primary things for which Michalson stood.

The Carl Michalson Society owes much of its existence to the continuous efforts of Michalson student, Michael D. Ryan. Ryan received his B.D. ('63) and Ph.D. ('67) from Drew and returned to the Seminary to teach in 1969. He chaired a steering committee composed of Lester Berenbroick and Russell Richey, also from the faculty, John Painter, Robert Fisher and Virginia de Veer, of the Drew staff, and Robert Goodwin and Henry O. Thompson as alumni (as is Painter). The first meeting was held 28 April 77.

The purpose of the Society is of course to perpetuate the memory of Carl Michalson, Jr. Yet it is far more. The Society's brochure says the Society was organized:

> To support the commitment to Jesus Christ and sound scholarship which characterized the life of Carl Michalson and which has been the aim of Drew Theological School from its inception in 1867.

> To promote awareness of this heritage among alumni, faculty, students and friends of The Theological School so that this living tradition may bear as creatively as possible on the current task of education for professional ministry.

> To provide financial support for special programs to serve these ends.

This relates directly to Michalson's own primary aim as teacher or preacher: to transmit the message of Jesus of Nazareth "in worldly, everyday terms so that each one who hears will clearly understand it to be a summons to obedience, to responsible personhood. To know that is to know one stands in the midst of the presence of God."[1]

The bulk of the funds raised by the Society through memberships and donations have gone into a scholarship fund. Since 1980, the interest from this fund has been given as the Michalson Fellowship each Spring. The recipient, chosen by The Theological Schools' awards committee, is a first year student whose commitment to scholarship and the Christian faith represents excellence. The first recipient was Ellen Thompson Little, followed by Eileen Freeman Visconti (1981), Suzanne Lane Harris (1982), Mary Robinson Heyne (1983), Virginia Jackson-Adams (1984), Lynda Wallace (1985), Andrea Lee Spencer and Richard Simpson (1986), Karen Ann Engleman (1987), Victoria Hanjian (1988), Colleen G. Kristula (1989), Margaret Michael (1990).

Long range plans have included a scholarship for a Japanese student to study at the seminary. Michalson spent a sabbatical in Japan and later published Japanese Contributions to Christian Theology (Philadelphia: Westminster, 1960). His books have been translated into Japanese. These include Faith for Personal Crises (1958), The Hinge of History (1959), The Rationality of Faith (1963), Worldly Theology (1967), all published by Scribner's. He edited Christianity and the Existentialists (NY: Scribner's, 1960) and The Witness of Kierkegaard (NY: Association Press, 1960). In addition, his bibliography includes over 70 articles and 125 book reviews. These, in the most complete Michalson bibliography available, are listed in The Appendix of Edward J. Wynne, Jr.'s The Implications of Carl Michalson's Theological Method for Christian Education (Lanham, MD: University Press of America, 1983). The latter publication was sponsored by the Society, which also sponsored a collection of Michalsonia which was titled Prayers for Today's People (UPA, 1982) edited by Edward J. Wynne, Jr. and Henry O. Thompson.

The Society has published a Bulletin with news of the Society, announcements and summaries of lectures, excerpts of Michalsonia and other relevant matter. The lectures were sponsored as part of an annual meeting with guest lecturers. Most of these lectures have been published in the Drew Gateway (DG), the journal of the Theological School. The lectures were given over a 12-year period.

John J. Vincent, "Christian Theology and the Challenges of Our Times," DG 47, Nos. 2,3 (1976-1977), 110-132.

John D. Godsey, "The Maturity of Faith in Carl Michalson's Theology," DG 49, No. 3 (Spr 79), 1-9.

Theodore Runyan, "Carl Michalson as a Wesleyan Theologian," DG 51, No. 2 (Wint 80), 1-13.

Lawrence E. Toombs, "The Foolishness of Preaching," DG 52, No. 1 (Fall 81), 14-20.

Kosuke Koyama, "Religion in the Global Village," DG 52, No. 3 (Spr 82), 39-48.

Paul S. Minear, "The Death of Death," DG 54, No. 1 (Fall 83), 17-25.

James Carse, "Mythic Resonance: Towards a Theory of Interpretation" [unpublished]

Bernhard W. Anderson, "Cosmic Dimensions of The Genesis Creation Account," DG 56, No. 3 (Spr 86), 1-13.

Howard Kee, "A Sociological Approach to New Testament Interpretation" [unpublished]

Karlfried Froehlich, "Paul The Theologian?" [unpublished]

David M. Graybeal, "On Adopting the Orphan Named Justice," DG 58, No. 2 (Fall 88), 51-61.

xii

## ENDNOTES

1.     Gordon E. Michalson and Olin M. Ivey, eds., <u>The Witness of Radical Faith</u>; Nashville: Tidings, 1974, pp. 14-15. Quoted by Edward J. Wynne, Jr., "Introduction," unpublished.

## ACKNOWLEDGMENTS

The material reprinted from the <u>Drew Gateway</u> is published by permission. Special thanks are extended to Janet Fishburn for facilitating this portion of the work. Permission for reprinting Michalsonia was granted by Janet Michalson [Mrs. Paul] Clasper. Each author has also granted permission to reprint or publish and their cooperation is gratefully acknowledged. Their moral support and encouragement in this venture is deeply appreciated.

Michalson, like many clergy, and perhaps especially Methodist(?) clergy in particular, and teachers and politicians and other public speakers, was fond of using illustrations from his home life. The editor has done the same but the scene has shifted from children to grandchildren so it is with a sense of the appropriate that this volume is dedicated to the latter. Gilbert, William, Philip and Paul are the sons of Elizabeth (Nestor) and Howard Orrin Thompson, musician and J.D., while John is the son of Mary (Lenzi) and Warren Gerald Thompson, Ph.D. (philosopher) and M.D. respectively.

In a larger sense, the book is IN MEMORIAM of Carl Donald Michalson himself, in appreciation of his contribution to scholarship and worship and his inspiration of both in others. It is appropriate to add here, too, the Michalson Society which honors his memory and continues to promote not merely his contributions but those of others, not in some carbon copy but in continuing growth and moving beyond to new frontiers of faith and knowledge. The support of President Jenny Jackson-Adams and Financial Secretary David J. Bort are especially noted.

# INTRODUCTION

A dozen lectures over a dozen years were given independently by a variety of scholars on biblical and theological themes. While the lecture series was established in the name of Carl Michalson, a theologian of the modern world, the speakers were not under any obligation to speak in his name or continue his thought. Indeed, there was wide agreement that had he lived, Michalson would have changed and expanded his own thinking. He sought the cutting edge of the discipline. Speakers were free to do the same.

The results, however, are interesting for the vector from Michalson's work with the Bible, theology and preaching. We begin with Michalson himself in revolutionary terms for many saw him as a radical Christian, or at least his was a radical faith as witnessed by his brother Gordon and student Olin Ivey, and many more. Radical, of course, means coming from or getting back to the root of things and he did. He sought the real reason(s) for what we do, or should do. Thus the presentation here is not from his considerable collection of theological treatises but his practical communications.

I have an existential appreciation for this. While a student, I stood in awe of the man's power of thought. Yet, he was by some legerdemain of the mysterious inner workings of the school administration, my faculty advisor. Faced with a problem in my field work, I could only turn to him. While the problem seemed insurmountable to me, he solved it in less time than it took me to explain the matter and left me breathless while he went on to other things.

That bit of problem solving involved direct interpretation on Michalson's part. Thus it seems fitting to follow his interpretive effort presented in these pages with an interpretation of him, and move out, and beyond him, as Godsey notes he encouraged people to do, to interpretation in the broader scheme of things in the thought of Runyon and Carse. In Michalson's lifetime, I doubt many people recognized him as a <u>Wesleyan</u> theologian. But since Runyon pointed it out, there is the 20/20 vision of hindsight. Michalson was forever telling stories, sometimes stories within stories. Sometimes we understood and sometimes we did not. Sometimes we <u>thought</u> we understood but whether we understood <u>correctly</u> or not, is another question. Mythic resonance is pure Michalsonian but "The Life Story as the Search for Story" is James Carse's story... and perhaps Everyone's story...

Bernhard Anderson gave the greetings when the Michalson Society was founded. He noted

> I think it is somewhat surprising that many of the impulses in Carl's theology are now finding expression today in theological discussion. Many students took Carl's course "Theology as History" not because it was a curricular requirement, but because it was a personal necessity. I believe that the general tenor of that course is being re-expressed today in the movement known as "story theology," or "theology as story." So Carl's understanding of the theological problem was conditioned by the time in which he lived and yet his imagination leaped ahead into the future - the future into which we are moving.

Michalson had a way of circling around in his thinking but always coming back to the Bible, as the touchstone of his thought. While more and more Roman Catholics make awesome contributions to biblical scholarship, some would see Michalson's "touchstone" as the Protestant in him. Protestantism has focused on the biblical tradition, sometimes to the point of making the Bible a paper pope. He never did that, however, and neither do Anderson, Kee and Froehlich who move with the times in biblical interpretation.

Of course, interpretation of the Bible is not just a matter of doctrine or seeking its meaning in its own time. What do we <u>do</u> with the good Book or perhaps one should ask what <u>should</u> we do? The Judeo-Christian tradition has produced great preachers throughout the ages - the Prophets, John Chrysostom, Bernard of Clairvaux, Martin Luther, John Wesley, Stephen Samuel Wise, Fulton J. Sheen, Billy Graham and many others. Those who heard Michalson in the classroom, exploring the nooks and crannies of theological thought, were often surprised that he was a preacher, and not just a preacher, but one who communicated in the pulpit. The Toombs paper comes from another who is equally at home in the pulpit or behind the lectern. Like the veritable embodiment of the biblical prophets, Graybeal notes the extension of the Word of justice and judgment into the real world. Vincent does also in the practical, working day world of a modern industrial society. All three speak not only as scholars of the first rank but out of years of practical experience.

Koyama then carries the whole concern of faith into the world. In the tradition of Michalson and his spiritual ancestor, John Wesley, the world is our parish. Faith was never meant to be hoarded in anyone's pocket or even in a local society. It is to be broadcast around the globe. That, of course means, that faith cannot be limited to a one dimensional articulation or to one cultural explication of the faith, as Michalson knew all too well from his own experience in Europe and Japan.

Death ends it all, for some thinkers. But faith faces death and sees beyond. Minear's work is placed last here, though some think it should be first for until we come to terms with death, they say, we cannot live. There is much truth in that. But the arrangement of material here focuses on faith in revolutionary times for individuals, for society and for the world.

4

In the end, people must do their own dying, but there is a cultural context for that, as well as a global one.

Thus we move from faith to faith, from Michalson's <u>The Hinge of History</u> (1959) via his <u>Rationality of Faith</u> (1963) to <u>Worldly Theology</u> (1967). We move from <u>Faith for Personal Crises</u> (1958) to <u>Japanese Contributions to Christian Theology</u> (1960) and we move in existential involvement which is hardly coincidental (<u>The Witness of Kierkegaard</u>). While we each must die, we face global death as a human civilization, whether from the nuclear "Big Bang" that may take us back to the beginning, or the slow strangulation of a polluted environment that will take us out, not with a bang but a whimper. In any case, whether from beginning to end, from birth to death, from individual to society to the world, we move from faith to faith.

Henry O. Thompson
Editor

I.


THEOLOGIAN OF THE MODERN WORLD

# FOCUS ON A REVOLUTION[1]

## Carl Michalson

I have about three very small questions I'd like to raise, though I have no expectation of answering them, save possibly one. And I must say also that I am greatly embarrassed about my involvement in this particular situation, because I enjoyed the whole thing so much. I think I would rather face the southern whites than the Drew theologians in my classes. So I left my tape recorder and went off to Montgomery, but I had to confront myself with three questions: One, "Why did I go?" and another, "Would I do it again?" and a third, "What will we all do when we have further occasions like this?" (I assume this third question is a big open question which I know I am not going to be able to answer, but which ought to occupy some discussion.)

I think I went, not because I expected to integrate Alabama. I couldn't have gone to integrate Alabama, because that is a work of Sisyphus, and furthermore, it's something we have not even completed in my own community of Morristown. So I might rather have stayed home if that had been my motive. I think I went mainly to demonstrate on behalf of the freedom to demonstrate. I think that was the occasion that really called us there. And it is an important thing, because the hope of civil liberties everywhere will depend upon our continued freedom to demonstrate on behalf of just causes.

Then I ask myself, "Why a theologian in a situation like that?" "Why not better at home with my books?" And that is even harder for me to answer. One might say, "I didn't go as a theologian, I went as a man." But that is a bifurcation I do not accept. I pat my neighbor's dog as a theologian. I kiss my wife as a theologian. (That's why theology is so crucial!) And when I demonstrate on behalf of civil liberties, I do it as a theologian.

As a matter of fact, I understand that the very existence of God is at stake in what people do in history. I got a little advance clue to that last night when reading a poem by Robert Frost:

> I turned to speak to God about the world's despair,
> But to make bad matters worse, I found that God wasn't there.
> God turned to speak to me - Don't anybody laugh.
> God found I wasn't there, at least not over half.

I am sure that one cannot do theology today without involving God in just such historical causes as the present civil rights enterprises give us a chance to do.

But then, "Would I do it again?" That all depends on whether what we did there was like a baptism, which is unrepeatable, because so indelible, or like pastoral calling, which is infinite in its demands upon us. It seems quite obvious that many aspects of this experience were like a baptism. (We just will never be able to shake the memory of it from us. I have been baptized! We will say that over and over again, because of this experience.) At the same time we know that it was not just something that happened once, but it was an invitation to repeated acts of responsibility.

So that leads me to my third question, "What will we do when we have these repeated opportunities to leave our immediate responsibilities and go off in this way?" I just do not know. (Here's where I do not think I have any answer at all, but I will be very eager to participate in discussion about it.) You see, one cannot be a theologian without being involved in just such causes, but can one remain a theologian if all he does is get involved in such causes? That is the difficulty I face.

As I understand the situation in the first century church, as reported by the apostle Paul, there was mainly one big opportunity for the expression of faith - the contest against legalism. And why could it not be just as true today, that there is one main opportunity for the expression of faith, the contest against racial injustice? That could be the case. It could be so much the case that we'd rewrite our curriculum. We would have a core curriculum in which everything we discussed would be built around the question of racial inequity. We would have civil rights as an epoch in Heilsgeschichte. And we would have field work in which we would not just do everything in general under District Superintendents, but we would do one thing in particular. We would train ourselves for efficiency in seeing to it that in every one of our communities, civil liberties were increasingly respected. And we would have a varsity team to go off to remote places like Selma and Montgomery to carry on these contests on our behalf, on the front lines. But in doing it all, we would have a sense that in fulfilling our human responsibility, we were giving God a chance to be born again.

## ENDNOTE

1.    Early in 1965, Bernhard Anderson, Carl Michalson, and Howard Clark Kee represented the Drew Theological School faculty at a civil rights march in Montgomery, Alabama.  Upon returning to Drew, they addressed a Theological School assembly that attempted to "Focus on a Revolution."

For several generations of Drew students, Michalson represented an incomparable teacher of theology, and a fine churchperson, who proclaimed a relevant and responsible faith. With the publication of this address, transcribed and edited from recording tapes in the Drew University archives, Michalson continues to preach a Gospel that is responsible to God, and responsible for the world. And he does so in a surprisingly timely way.

This essay was transcribed and edited by Sam Roberts (Ph.D. '85) in connection with research done for his dissertation "Carl Michalson's Contribution to Christian Ethics: Faithful Responsibility in the World."

THREE SERMONS ON PRAYER

Carl Michalson

I. Christians Don't Have to Pray

Scripture: Mark 14:26-42;  Text: Hebrews 5:7

Suppose you were commissioning an artist to do a painting for your church.
Your congregation has decided it wants to depict Jesus with his disciples.
What would you expect to be the content of the picture?  When I put this
question to my wife, who is an artist, she suggested a scene with the
disciples arguing over who would be first in the kingdom. Two things seem
wrong with that answer.  For one thing, it was too cynical.  Furthermore,
whenever my wife does paint those disciples they are huddled around their
Lord in a very pious expression of devotion.  My guess is that most church
committees would want a similar scene, of having the disciples with Jesus in
a kind of prolonged prayer meeting, reminiscent of a medieval monastery.
The picture would then stand there in judgement upon the congregation,
because most red-blooded Christians do not do a lot of praying, and do not
even care to, even though they nurse a sense of guilt over the omission.
Most people believe that the proper way to be pious is to pray.

Let me propose a different theme by something I believe is closer to the Gospel intention: No praying at all - just eating and drinking. The concept might not conform to just this image exactly, but it would be historically accurate (Lk 5). The Gospel of Luke reflects how the religious people in Jesus' time had noticed a strange lack of conformity in the disciples to what is customarily expected of the religious. They called this discrepancy to Jesus' attention, expecting him to change his disciples. They said, "The disciples of John the Baptist pray, and the Pharisees pray, but your disciples only eat and drink!" (Lk 5:33ff). How would that picture look in your church - the disciples eating and drinking, but not praying at all?

Was this a charge against which Jesus felt he must defend his disciples? Did he say, "But they pray! They pray without ceasing! They pray privately! It's only that I've taught them to pray in secret! So let no man judge them!" The truth is he did not defend them. He had no basis for defense. He said, "When the bridegroom is among you, you want to eat and drink." Besides, the disciples are not reported to have prayed to any conspicuous extent. It was Jesus who did the praying, but usually alone. And in the most crucial moment of Jesus' career, the moment in the garden of Gethsemane just prior to his arrest, when Jesus went off to pray he instructed the disciples not to pray but simply to remain there and watch and stay awake. That seems to indicate that Jesus turned the would-be-criticism of the crowd against them. What they expected to see in the disciples in the way of prayer and fasting was "old hat," passe, an old garment. What the disciples were to do in the footsteps of Jesus was something wholly new, and one does not put a new patch on an old garment.

What was this new thing, and how did it relate to the joyful prayerlessness of the apostles? Did not the British preacher, P.T. Forsyth, warn us that "The worst sin is prayerlessness?" In the appearance of Jesus of Nazareth in human history, mankind has, so to say, tuned the corner of prayer (Dylan Thomas). Jesus prayed the prayer to end all prayer. When he prayed, he was heard. Henceforth, to be a Christian is to know it is true for us - that the prayers of Jesus have been heard. He prayed for us. People no longer have to pray.

Now we know that the Christian faith has claimed Jesus died for us (although we have a hard time any longer saying what that means). Because Jesus died for us, we believe there is a sense in which we no longer have to die (although we are not sure precisely what that means, either). But have we given sufficient consideration to the New Testament belief that Jesus also prayed for us - that is, prayed not simply on our behalf but in our place, so that we no longer have to pray?

You may respond to that claim by wondering, "How, then, will a person find God if one does not seek, and how does one seek who does not pray?" In the world which Jesus inaugurated, we know it is God who seeks for us, so that we no longer have to seek for God. "But did not Jesus pray? Ought we not also pray as he did? Ought we not follow Jesus? That is just the point - because Jesus prayed, we no longer have to pray. He prays in our place and puts an end to the necessity for us to pray. One who sees Jesus is not to see Jesus but the One who sent him (Jn 12:45). To follow him is not to imitate him but to live the life of obedience to God that his life has made possible.

"Are we then to conclude that we can stop our praying and even end our sense of guilt over not praying?" You may end your sense of guilt over not praying, because you live in the epoch in which we no longer need to pray. But you need not stop praying. You need only stop praying out of a sense of obligation to pray. Because Jesus prayed the prayer to end all praying, prayer is now permitted rather than commanded.

In what way does Jesus put an end to our praying? To know the answer to that, we need to know two things first: (1) We need to know why most people pray. If we could see that Jesus' ministry puts an end to those reasons for praying, we would see that the effect of Jesus' ministry is to put an end to that kind of praying. (2) Then we need to know how Jesus himself prayed. If we could see that Jesus' prayer was the perfect and complete prayer, not just one prayer among many, we could see that the prayer of Jesus is the prayer that converts all our praying into mere watchfulness, mere attendance upon the prayer of Jesus.

Why do most people pray? They believe that the life of prayer distinguishes them as decent and committed Christians.

There is much that is true in that belief. While one must not pray "to be seen of men," there is a sense in which a praying Christian is a witness to the truth of faith. When you look out your window and see a man blowing on his hands, you can usually conclude that the weather is cold. When you look out your window on Sunday morning and see your neighbors dressed up and getting into the family car at about 9:45 or so, you can usually conclude they're on their way to church. When you look through a window and see a woman with her head bowed in prayer, you yourself are confronted with the possibility of a reality named God toward whom some people make meaningful gestures. A man or woman of prayer is a witness whose acts have the effect upon our wistfulness for God that signposts have upon the goals of travel. I think I have never been so filled with the sense of reality of God as in one hotel in Cairo, where my family and I could see people in the street down on their knees, and in windows across the street, bowing in prayer at the appointed hour, as one does in Islam.

The difficulty of concluding anything from such analogies is that a life of prayer is so ambiguous. That family getting into its car could be getting an early start at the World's fair. The man with hands folded and eyes closed could be engaging in luxuriant dream fantasies. I have even heard of a pious young married man who knelt in prayer every evening before retiring. At first, his young wife was impressed with his piety, until the night she saw that his eyes were focused on a window across the court from their apartment. Thereafter she lowered the shade of their window every evening before prayer, and then observed the gradual corruption and decline of her husband's prayer life.

If Christians think prayer is a sign of devotion, they may be blemishing the distinctiveness of their faith. All religions pray, just as all people at their wit's end pray. But where among the religions do you find it the hallmark of faith that people eat and drink because they do not have to pray, because they can trust that God has already answered Jesus' prayer? Luther with his glass of beer and his noisy companions around the table is closer to the confidence of answered prayer than all of medieval Christianity with its thin-lipped priests and their memorial bread and wine, and their monotonous repeated scholastic intonations.

Some pray because they believe God requires them to pray. But Jesus came precisely to put an end to a religious life based on commands. Why then should it be thought that he requires even prayer?

Sometimes it is believed that Christianity simply changes the commandments from negative to positive requirements - all "thou shalt nots" are converted into "thou shalts." Nagging, sniping prohibitions are translated into benevolent, wise guidance. Instead of "don't covet" we hear "give." Instead of "don't kill" we hear "let live." Instead of "don't commit adultery" we hear "love." As if Jesus did to the ten commandments what a painter in the Thomas Hardy novel does. He was hired to letter the ten commandments on the wall of the sanctuary, and on the following Sunday the people gathered in solemn worship only to discover to their horror that the artist had omitted every "not" from the commandments! But, "fasten your seat belt" is just as commanding as "No Smoking," despite its being positive and the other negative.

Positive commandments, however, are as alien to a Christian's faith as negative commandments. "Tithe," "be good," "go to church," "love your neighbor," "be ye perfect," "pray!" What a beast of burden God seems to have made of his children when seen from the standpoint of a religion of commandments.

The truth about Jesus' ministry is not that he changes prohibitions into positive requirements, but that he changes the basis of our life with God from commandments to promises. Since the time of Jesus, the test of faith is how one <u>hears</u> God's word. It is true that God says, "Thou shalt." But how do you hear those words? Usually as a command. But what if you heard them as a promise? The Christian life is not a corral which fences us in. It is an open range with limitless possibilities. Freedom, not law, is its hallmark. Wesley made this case dramatically when he retranslated the words of Jesus in the Sermon on the Mount. Where we are accustomed to read, "Be ye perfect," and to shudder at this tyranny that might be imposed, Wesley perceived it should be rendered, "Ye shall be perfect!" And when your tender conscience poses for you what is one of the least minimum expectations of a devout life, "Thou shalt pray!," how will you read that? As a command? No - as permission and promise. "Now prayer is the kind of possibility never before realized!"

Many people pray because they feel they need to pray. Prayer is like breathing. No one needs to tell you to breathe, let alone permit it. We pray because we need to, and if we do not pray, something suffocates our spirit.

The real truth about the Gospel is, however, that Jesus has robbed us of the need to pray. He kicked away the crutch of prayer as Salk vaccine has kicked away the paralytic's crutch. Why would he do that? Because a religion based on need for God lasts only as long as the need, and nothing so ultimate as the God-relation should be subject to that kind of erosion. When a child fears the dark, he needs his parent's hand. What happens to that need when he discovers how a flashlight works? When the primitive man falls to his knees in awe before the thunder, he needs an altar to some god like Thor. Who will pluck the weeds from around that altar when the primitive man begins to study meteorology?

We have learned today what a dreadfully short step it is from an African jungle to a university. Parents are always learning what a short time it takes a baby to grow into a child, then into a fully mature person who discovers he or she has no need for a parent. Gods based on human needs are dying all around us, all over the world, whereas Jesus did not come to bury God but to give him a resurrection. A God who contracts as human life expands is a fictional God based on human invention. Jesus came to announce the presence of God, the God who really is, and who reveals himself. At this late date in the history of the Christian faith, we must not allow ourselves to get jockeyed into the place of the hermit Nietzsche writes about. Zarathustra came upon an old man praying and singing praises in the forest. "Is it possible," he cried. "Can it be that this old hermit lost in the forest does not yet know that God is dead!"

Jesus counsels us to pray in _his_ name, not in ours. He teaches us to pray to "our Father who art in heaven," because it is his kingdom which comes through prayer, not our utopia. The time in which to pray is not the time of our need, but the time of God's revelation of his will. That is why I would not want to be seduced by the suggestion in Bishop Robinson's Honest To God. He says, suggestively, that we have been wrong to structure our prayer chronologically, in morning prayer and evening prayer and Sunday prayer. We should pray not in _chronos_ but in _kairos_, he says. _Kairos_ is "right time," crisis time, "the moment that drives us to our knees." But according to the New Testament faith, the one thing that drives a Christian to his or her knees is not the calendar or the clock (although Montaigne has a cute story about a prostitute who every time she heard the angelus ring would stop what she was doing and fall to her knees at the side of her bed). Nor is it even the human predicament that forces us to our knees (although a thief cannot suppress a prayer for deliverance upon the arrival of the law). When Jesus teaches us to pray, it is for the presence of God in the coming of his kingdom. "_Thy_ kingdom come," we pray; "_thy_ will be done."

How, then, did Jesus pray? He prayed in such a way as to make our prayers superfluous. He prayed the great prayer in the light of which all our prayers are little ones. His prayer ploughed a furrow in the sea of life through which our prayers trail in the wake. "Jesus offered up prayer and was heard" (Heb 5:7). Is it not enough for a man or woman of faith that God has heard the prayer of Jesus?

When Jesus prayed, he was so wholly attentive to God's will that because of him God's kingdom has come.

That is not to say he had no struggle maintaining this concentration. The history of Jesus' ministry is a history of the efforts of the multitudes to tempt Jesus into advancing their causes. That is why, when the crowds pressed upon him with their demands, so frequently he pushed off in a boat to separate himself from them and went off by himself to pray.

The cardinal instance of this contest to know God's will was in the garden of Gethsemane. Would he capitulate to the demands of the crowd for a movement of violence which would restore Israel as a political entity, or would he continue to speak on behalf of God's kingdom alone, which comes in judgement upon all the kingdoms of this earth? Escape from death was possible to him if he came over to the popular side. Death was inevitable if he remained adamant for God. "Thy will be done," he prayed. Precisely that prayer makes sense of his death on the cross. There on the cross he is lifted up in such a way as to draw all men and women unto him, not for his human courage, not for his being some sacrificial lamb who atones for the sins of the world, but for his total obedience to God in prayer through which God's intentions become the basis for the world's life.

Jesus's praying in the wilderness participates in the same kind of victory for God as his praying in Gethsemane. For forty days and nights he prayed, yet there he met with his temptations. Now you can understand why a person who doesn't even pray would be liable to temptation. How do you explain that Jesus is tempted right in the midst of his praying? He wasn't studying The Wall Street Journal as if he had funds to invest; he wasn't leafing through Playboy, a magazine even for those whose funds are running out! He was praying. What kind of temptation comes to one who prays? The wilderness in which Jesus was tempted resembles the garden in which the first human beings were tempted. "Ye shall be as God," said Satan to Adam. And now the tempter says to Jesus, the second Adam, "Throw yourself down from the pinnacle and escape injury; the people will worship you. Change these stones to bread and the people will worship you." Jesus was so powerful in prayer that he could conceivably be confused with God himself and made the object of human worship.

In his praying, Jesus seeks God so importunately that God has found us. Thereafter, any prayer in which we think we are seeking God is prayed in misunderstanding. God has found us in the praying of Jesus.

As Albert Schweitzer has said, Jesus is the first religious figure to have attempted to precipitate God's kingdom by a word alone. Without exploiting social, political, or cosmic catastrophes, as many leaders did who warned of the coming kingdom of God, Jesus simply prayed for the kingdom of God, and the kingdom came. As the Gospel of Luke comments about the incident of the baptism of Jesus, when Jesus prayed, the heavens opened.

The power of Jesus' prayer to open the heavens and make the face of God appear - not for us to see, but to see us - is the occasion for the many descriptions of our Lord as the one through whom God seeks us. He is the shepherd who leaves the ninety-nine sheep to go after the one lost sheep. He is the one who leaves the company of the self-styled righteous people in order to eat and drink with the publicans and sinners. He is the pearl of great price which, when it appears, reduces the lustre of all our lesser jewels and presents itself as the goal of all our questing. Most astounding of all, he is the importunate widow (Lk 11:8). He is the righteous man whose fervent prayer "availeth much." By his importunity, the God whom all people seek in more or less conscious ways is made present to us.

Now because of Jesus' prayer in which the lost are found by God, the journey of the Christian life is like the journey of St. Christopher. Christopher is the man who went out in search of Christ. He searched and searched until the day he found that the little child he was carrying across a stream on his shoulders was the Christ child. We will continue to seek for God in our own way. But when we find him, we will know it is because he has found us.

The full truth of the way Jesus prayed, then, is not simply that he prayed for others, which is what we call intercessory prayer. He prayed so obediently and so importunately that through his prayers God becomes present. He prayed, that is, in such a way as to take our place in prayer. No one again need pray as Jesus prayed, because, since Jesus, all our praying presupposes his.

In that light, some of Jesus' puzzling prayers are more understandable. At the raising of Lazarus he prayed (Jn 11:42), but he explained that his prayer was not for his benefit but for the benefit of those around him. Traditionally, theologians have interpreted that to mean that Jesus, being God, would surely not need to pray for himself. Now it can be seen that Jesus, being the importunate widow, the second Adam, the righteous man with fervent prayers, prayed not in his own stead - as ordinary men pray - but our stead. After his triumphal entry expressed his intent, Jesus faced a critical decision. "What shall I pray for?" was his question. The problem was whether to pray for God to rescue him from his hour of death, or to pray for God to be glorified even in his death. Jesus prayed the prayer of obedience which led to his death. When he died, angels are said to have spoken - not for his benefit, but as the Scriptures say - for the sake of "the crowd standing by." In one way of seeing this, Jesus was using prayer as a charade - to be seen or heard of men. When we understand Jesus as the one whose prayer is in our place, the concept of charade vanishes into a drama of salvation.

That is why the work of Christ for us and our salvation is referred to by the Epistle to the Hebrews as Christ's high priesthood. He is at the right hand of the Father in heaven, continuing to do what he did on earth - making intercession for us.

And what does he say for us to do? "Sit there and watch," he says, "while I pray." Jesus' praying ends our praying by reducing all our prayers to the status of watchfulness.

Are we, then, no longer to pray? Will there be no prayer to end this sermon today? Will there be no mumbling over the plate at mealtime this noon? No hands clasped in whispered petitions at our bedsides nightly, no praying together in this sanctuary next Sunday? That conclusion would very badly miss the point.

F.W. Robertson, a great preacher in England during the last century, used to make the point that we should "pray as Jesus did, till prayer makes you cease to pray." I would not say that. I would say that no one can pray as Jesus prayed, because his prayer has ended our requirement and need for prayer. But neither would I say that we should cease to pray. The Japanese theologian, Seiichi Hatano, made this clear to me. During an epoch in Japan when the Emperor was trying to stamp out the Christian religion, the Meiji era, the Emperor said to the people, "Lead good lives and your God will love you without your prayers." Hatano's reply to the Emperor is precisely my proposal to you: "It is precisely because God loves us without our prayers that we pray."

What shall we propose, then, for that picture to be painted for our sanctuary? Show the disciples eating and drinking. Don't let them be tense with uncertainty about the future, as if Jesus hadn't prayed for the kingdom, and been answered. Don't let them cringe with guilt for their prayerless lives, as if there is something they should be doing though they are not, as if we had no high priest as intercessor with the Father even while we sleep. Don't let them be sensitive or apprehensive and condemned like children at summer camp or college who haven't written letters home and know their parents are expecting it.  It is enough for the man or woman of faith to realize God is satisfied that he has heard from Jesus.  Amen.

## II. How Working People Can "Pray Without Ceasing"

Scripture: Luke 10:38-11:1a; 14:25-35;  Text: I Thess 5:17

How would you like to have working for you a person who prays without ceasing?  An occasional coffee break, yes, or maybe even two days of prayer now and then, like the Buddhist monks in Saigon last week.  But non-stop prayer seems pretty hard to combine with the ordinary course of commercial life.

The New Testament has given us a preview of such a possibility in the person of Martha's sister, Mary.  Martha, busy over many things, is the Biblical prototype of free enterprise.  When Jesus comes to visit, it is Martha who greets him at the gate; Mary just sits.  When Jesus needs to be fed, it is Martha who serves him; Mary just watches.

Nevertheless, notwithstanding our modern activistic predisposition toward Martha, Christendom has tended to endorse Mary - and to take with literal seriousness the apostolic injunction to "pray without ceasing." In some ways, even the command to "Love thy neighbor" has become subordinated to the command to pray.  At least the church has never worked out a satisfactory rationale whereby our neighbor could be loved without ceasing. But it has designed ingenious styles for unceasing prayer.  Monasteries and convents have been set up mainly for the purpose of around-the-clock prayer. Breviaries and prayer books have been printed to supply more than enough content for that prayer marathon.  Strings of beads have been used as a kind of non-stop watch which keeps prayer going on and on endlessly, even despite lapses of prayer into unconsciousness or even sleep.  Moreover, one breathes when one is asleep - that doesn't render the breath any less vital. Why should unconscious prayer be thought insignificant? This kind of uninterrupted prayer has been the church's interminable filibuster against the vetoing power of the devil. Like the boy with his finger in the dike, it is believed that, if the church stopped praying, torrents of evil would inundate us. The continuous insurance of the church's prayers is to the Christian what the continuous power of the motors is to a passenger on a plane aloft.

Now ceaseless prayer is no medieval invention. Jesus endorsed it in endorsing Mary - she had chosen the better part. John Wesley endorsed it in his commentary on I Thessalonians 5 when he said of it, "This is Christian perfection. Further than this we cannot go...Prayer must be said to be the breath of our spiritual life. He that lives cannot possibly cease breathing" (Explanatory Notes Upon the New Testament, p. 762). The difference between Wesleyan constancy and medieval constancy is that the medieval church expected such perfection though prayer only of the few Christians who had taken vows to perfection, like the monks. Wesley held it out as the privilege of every Christian. Our problem today is, how can we do it? How can we busy workers "pray without ceasing" and still keep our minds on our work?

If we could do it, I think you can see there would surely be some excellent advantages.

For one thing, to pray while you work would introduce a much needed singleness of perspective into our preoccupations with many things.

Suppose you had just completed a manuscript of a half million words, requiring a truck to ship it off to the publisher. One hazard you face is, of course, its destruction before it gets there. Carlyle's manuscript on The French Revolution was destroyed by fire - the maid used it to start a fire in the fireplace! But a worse hazard would be to have it published, and then discover the whole thing had been written from the wrong perspective. Our own work seems to suffer from this lack of proper perspective. If you ask the reason why most people are in their present vocations, the usual answer is, "We don't really know why we have done what we have."

Consider the attitude of the pilot and the tail gunner in war toward the navigator. The navigator can't fire a gun, and doesn't know how to pilot the ship. He just sits there - like Mary, or perhaps more like a big silent Buddha - taking his directions from the heavens and chartering one course so that the enemy fighters can be accurately engaged!

Jesus cautioned his hearers that, before building a tower you first sit down and make plans (Lk 14:28), or when a king fights a war he "first sits down" and plots his strategy and estimates his resources (31).

What if you are spicing your life with a salt that loses its savor? But as you go through the motions of sprinkling the salt, somehow there will be that tedious and tasteless flatness to remind you that somewhere you have missed the one thing of importance. Work without perspective is like salt that has lost its savor.

For another thing, to pray while you work would introduce a much-needed freedom into our work.

It was the poet Rilke who said, "Man is a goblet which shatters in the ringing," so brittle is human nature and so jarring the effects of life. The customary antidote to the shattering effects of work is leisure. We call it "free time" or vacation. Yet during our vacations most of us illustrate our tensions rather than soothing them. There is a growing trend of retired men to reapply for work, but not out of any economic need. As Pascal put it, "All the unhappiness of men arises from the fact that they can't stay quietly in their rooms." This reminds me of the young college sophomore home for semester break in a busy household who complained, "What are you running away from? Why is it you can't stand just to be alone with each other?"

We seem to be "at sixes and sevens" because we don't know the one thing needful. As Wesley said of Martha, "The Greek word properly signifies, to be drawn different ways at the same time, and admirably expresses the situation of a mind surrounded (as Martha's then was) with so many objects of care, that it hardly knows which to attend first" (Notes, p. 242). The hymn writer admonishes us to "take time to be holy." That doesn't even allow for a coffee break. But the point is that time is not to be taken from work, but to be given in work. "Free time" is the sense of freedom which comes from knowing what it is you are really about. In that sense, you wouldn't need a vacation - you could find your leisure, your free time, right in your work - the kind of time that is really free.

"Pray without ceasing." We can do it, but not in ways customarily proposed. One suggestion offered has been to do it alternately - worship and then work. The usual recommendation is to pray in the morning, or in the evening, or at mealtime, or when facing issues. But that's not praying without ceasing. That's a compromise in the direction of realism which means, "We'll work it in wherever we can!"

Another recommendation has been to write a book of prayers for individual situations: "Before entertaining your boss," "Before signing a contract," "Before scolding your children," "When someone has criticized you," "Upon sending your daughter off to college," "When you feel inadequate," etc. But it is impossible to anticipate every text for a situation. Can you imagine Peter in his fishing boat when a storm comes up, running around demanding, "Where's my prayer book?"!

A second suggestion offered has been to pray and work simultaneously, assuming a person can do two things at once. Augustine called prayer "unceasing longing for God." Luther spoke of it as "joining the thought of God with any thought of importance that occurs to us...even in the most mirthful hours to remember his all-seeing eye." F. W. Robertson put it similarly, "joining every thought with the thought of God."

Someone recently made the news when he said he watched two baseball games at once on his TV. I really can't understand why that is so newsworthy. After all, I have been known to grade papers, watch a TV ballgame, and listen to stereo all at the same time! It's possible to do this, not because you have two ears in your head, but because you have the mental capacity to hold two programs in your attention at the same time. But not adequately. Something suffers - either the work or the worship. There's something wrong with that - as wrong as thinking about God when kissing your wife. A person can only do two things simultaneously if he or she is a spectator in at least one of them. You can't be a spectator in prayer, but neither can you be in kissing your wife or in performing your vocation. J. D. Salinger tells of someone in church busy robbing the poor box, but saying his prayers while he did it. You get the impression he is really only greatly involved in one of these two enterprises. It's obvious he wasn't equally committed to both. His heart was obviously not in both these enterprises simultaneously.

We can only "pray without ceasing" if it is true that "to work is to pray" (laborare est orare). This does not mean "to pray is to work," although that is true. You could always install a monk in a cell outside your office to pray on his knees around the clock for your success. It is not that any work is prayer. Most men who have made prayer their work have been mendicants. Mendicant monks are those who pray, but require to be fed by those who don't pray. What we do mean is this: the very meaning of life is "praying without ceasing" (Ebeling). You don't rob time from life to be holy. Life as it is meant to be lived is itself an act of prayer. How do we understand that? An act of prayer is every act in which we are receiving the world from God as our responsibility. That's not something you do verbally, but rather actively. As Ellison says in The Invisible Man, "That's the trouble with the world today: too damn much praying," by which he meant the kind of prayer which robs time from action, or substitutes for action, or delays the time of action. Wesley was run out of town because his prayer meetings took men off the job.

"Pray without ceasing" is not the endorsement of a compromise with life, but a way of identifying prayer and life. Prayer is a <u>way of being</u>. As such, if we do it at all, we never escape doing it.

Cleanth Brooks once asked of a dancer, "When the dance is completed, has not the dancer ceased to be a dancer? How can we know the dancer from the dance?" The point is that a dancer is not a person who does dances, but is a dancing person. As Napoleon put it: "I don't have ambitions; I am ambition. I don't have progress, but I say I am progress." It was the Apostle Paul who claimed: "For me to live is Christ" (Phil 1:21). Kierkegaard's point was: "You ought not pray in a temple and live in a dog house. Pray as you live; live as you pray." That is the meaning of "pray without ceasing."

You don't just pray now and then, thinking that a little prayer indicates a praying man. You pray all the time. But you don't pray all the time as if your life and work had to stop while you pray. You pray all the time as you breathe all the time - constantly, knowing that constant living makes a praying man or woman.

I started this series of sermons by saying you don't have to pray at all. Now I'm telling you to pray without ceasing, which means in the freedom of the praying life. I began by saying that prayer is a verbal phenomenon like poetry. That is, it is not communicating knowledge to God, but is invoking Gods's presence. Now I'm telling you prayer is not so much a speaking but a being - a silent perspective, but you can tell where you are going.

Not that prayer is silent in the sense that it has no verbalizable content. A silent prayer without content could be the sign of a spiritual disease called aphonia (speechlessness). Prayerlessness is aphonia at its most critical level. Aphonia is not just refusal to speak, but refusal of the other. Silent prayer could be refusal of God.

What then would it mean to exist continuously in prayer, to be a praying person - to pray without ceasing? There would be the prayer of thanksgiving, not as flattering utterances directed toward God, but as a human life converted into a gothic structure - always open upwards toward God. There would be the prayer of confession, not as a seriatim delineation of the flaws in our character, but as a life porous and transparent - nothing hidden from God or ourselves. There would be the prayer of petition, not as a verbal nagging of God for divine concessions, but as a persistent will that the goals of God's kingdom may come to pass. Intercession is there, not as a kind of celestial gossip, but a spiritual stance equivalent to a faithful pointer dog - holding human wretchedness up to the attention of God, sighing for that wretchedness, but not shunning the wretched, hands outstretched toward a situation too heady for you to cope with, but nevertheless chosen by you as your responsibility.

What Wesley failed to notice about life was that often his understanding of perfection was less than perfect. He wrote: "Only a Christian can be happy." He was happy because of people in general in the street merely living while he was inside praying without ceasing. His defense: "I am happy; they are only mirthful."

Do you recall the story of Wesley on board ship coming to America when a big storm came up? Everyone was terrified except for two groups. One group was huddled together in prayer, singing hymns, and looking heavenward - the Moravians. The other group was the sailors who moved swiftly about the ship performing their duties with no sense of being in danger. Wesley endorsed the Moravians who looked so monk-like, like Mary, while he had nothing good to say about the sailors who acted like Martha. Whereas I would say more prayers are wrought by responsible work than this world dreams of.

There is a real question as to who in fact really did the praying. But the sailors were busy over many things! Yes, but with one firm perspective - ensuring their safe delivery. Could it be Martha, busy over many things, who provides us the motivating spirit of the worker?

Just about the time of the Reformation, the German mystic, Meister Eckhart, judged Martha to be superior to Mary as a pattern for Christian piety, for he developed the vision of a Martha who had all that Mary had but more. What would be this "more?" His Martha was not the picture of a person who steals time from life in order to pray, nor of a person who steals from prayer in order to live, but of one in which prayer and life had become one - indistinguishably fused. Amen.

III. Does God Really Answer Prayer?

Scripture: Mark 11:15-26;  Text: Mark 11:24

For several weeks now I have talked with you about the limits and the language of prayer, about what God encourages us to seek in prayer, and about how we should seek it. But not once have I spoken directly to the one most agonizing question of all, "Does God really answer our prayers?" Well, the clear promise of the Scriptures is given for us in Jesus' words to his followers: "Whatever you ask in prayer, believe that you will receive it, and you will" (Mk 11:24). Every pious Jew knew that was the difference between the God of Abraham and the god of the pagan. "If one cries to it," said Isaiah, "it does not answer or save him from his trouble" (Is 46:7b). Whereas Yahweh and the Father of our Lord Jesus Christ is held before us as a God who hears and answers prayer.

Yet, the plain fact of the Christian life is that our prayers often do go unanswered. That is not a fact we can easily absorb. The road to unbelief is paved with unanswered prayers. How long would you keep a pen pal who never gave you the courtesy of a reply? How often would you invite to your home a person who never acknowledged your R.S.V.P.? How long, then, are we expected to go on praying to a God who does not seem to answer our prayers? As C. S. Lewis says in his posthumously published treatise on prayer, called Letters to Malcolm, "Every war, every famine or plague, almost every deathbed, is the monument to a petition that was not granted." Can faith survive the test of unanswered prayer?

Conscientious and thinking Christians are not apt to make wildly exaggerated claims for prayer. Usually it is the pagan who taunts the Christian with the failure of faith which is implicit in exaggerated claims. One who knows and loves God as he has been revealed in Christ does not press extreme claims. Prayer does not admit us to just anything we ask simply because we believe hard enough. The human will is not so powerful that it can control the universe. And God's will is not so powerful that it can create new worlds to accommodate the petulant and contradictory wishes human beings are capable of conjuring up.

Much of our inadequate expectation of prayer has to be seen against the background of a practice popular in the ancient Middle East. In the world surrounding ancient Israel it seems to have been an accepted practice for kings to present tokens to their favorites. On demand, any request of the favorite possessing such a token would be granted by the king. The procedure seems extreme and implausible, yet how else do you explain that Ahasuerus gave half his kingdom to Queen Esther, and Herod gave the head of John the Baptist to the daughter of Herodius? Now if oriental kings knew how to give just anything to favorites who asked, how much more ought God to give what his children ask? That simple oriental logic still makes pagans out of modern Christians. Would you like a fine day tomorrow for your trip to the shore? Well, God has promised to give you what you ask, if you believe hard enough. Go ahead and demand it. See what happens! Would you like a beautiful new automobile in your second garage? But would God draw the line at that, when he has promised to give you what you ask? Isn't Jesus' promise of answered prayer a kind of universal token from God which binds him to our requests?

No, that kind of praying rarely occurs to a reflective Christian. With God, nothing is impossible, to be sure; but our Father knows how to give good gifts to his children when they ask. We will not turn prayer into a blank check for supporting every whim. John Updike has a little story that comes convincingly to that conclusion. A young son is helping his father put chains on their car in a severe snowstorm. At the outer limit of his endurance in his effort to get the catch to close, one knows in his bones that he's either got to swear or to pray. The boy beseeches God to make just one "microscopic concession," involving "no apparent sacrifice of principles" in the universe. But the prayer fails. "Matter is obdurate." "The catch fails to close." We will not presume that God is in a position to create "a whole new universe" (F.W. Robertson) every time we happen to want something!

Do you know how Italian spaghetti manufacturers cut those long noodles for packaging? They use diamonds! Diamond needles to play high fidelity stereo you can understand - but diamonds to cut spaghetti, no. Some Christians use prayer as a device for cutting through problems wholly unworthy of prayer. As C.S. Lewis said, we are "deterred from small prayers" not alone by a sense of God's dignity but "by a sense of our own dignity." The fifth century mystic, Dionysius, settled that question. Prayer, he observed, is like a chain to heaven which seems to pull heaven to earth when you draw on it. But it is really only like the situation of a boat chained to the shore. When you pull on the chain, you seem to be drawing the shore to the boat, even though actually you are only pulling the boat toward the shore.

All we really hold out for as Christians is some assurance that our most cautious and considered prayers, our rarest requests, have some likelihood of being honored.

On rare occasions, occasions of great stress, when no sacrifice of principle is involved in the request, will God be moved to do what we ask? We will refrain from storming God with petty requests. We will not cry, "Wolf! Wolf!," so that when we do need help, he will know our request is in good faith. We will devote the bulk of prayer to thanksgiving and confession, and if we ask for anything in petition or intercession, we will make our prayers so vague and so likely, that God will not be brought to any serious test. We will pray for daily bread when we know it is already in the pantry. We will pray for the kingdom of God to come when we know most people wouldn't know how to recognize it anyway. And just for suffering's sake, all our petitions we will make permissive, praying, "if it be thy will," or "in thine own time and in thine own way."

We will save the promise of answer to prayer only for urgent requests. We will be like the rare child who has forgone almost every hasty desire in acts of virtuous caution in order to save his money for one big worthwhile purchase. We will make no quixotic or ill-advised request of God. Then one day we will break open our prayer-bank and invest all our faith in one possible request. Will God keep his promise then? "Oh, God, if ever I needed you, I need you now!" That will be the spirit of our prayer. After a drought, when all human resourcefulness is at its end, and your life's holdings are withering on the vine: "Oh, God, send us rain!" After seven years of disciplined study in college and seminary or professional school, and one last examination stands between you and the fulfillment of your vocational privileges: "Oh, God, let me pass this exam!" After twenty years of marriage, alternately bitter and sweet, when the bitterness seems to have overtaken the sweetness, and the final rupture seems inevitable: "Oh, God, save our marriage!" After an accident for which you are responsible, and in which your close friend has been critically hurt: "Oh, God, don't let her die!" "Whatever you ask in prayer, believe that you will receive it, and you will." Is not that promise our oriental token from God? What if we save its claims only for these obvious urgent emergencies? What if we narrow the expectations in prayer down to their reasonable minimum? Will God answer?

In the light of our text we seem to drug ourselves if we use that old soporific which says there are two ways to give an answer, not one: God can say "No" as well as "Yes." That is not what the oriental king told the daughter of Herodius. He did not say, "You can ask what you will, and, if

I will, I'll grant it." He said - and our text repeats it - "What you ask you will receive." God has promised to give us what we ask for. Has not God bound himself to a promise like that?

Either this verse summarizes all we have said in the past several weeks, or we have run the risk of turning it into an oriental token which makes prayer something non-Christian. Actually, notwithstanding its apparent endorsement of excesses in praying, this verse collects and affirms all the major claims about prayer that I have been making during this series. A closer look at the text should help us see that. The words I have been citing are from the Revised Standard Version of the New Testament. They burden the interpreter less than the more incautious rendering of the King James Version: "What things soever ye desire, when ye pray, believe that ye receive them, and ye shall have them." The original Greek text, however, is much more explicit than either version: "Whatever you pray for and seek, believe that you are receiving it, and it will be yours." The accent in the verse is not on human desire but on prayer, and, in the New Testament, prayer is a highly defined reality, not just any old form of seeking. That has been the burden of my discussions in these last weeks. What if you really pray - will God answer the requests of well-tutored prayer? That is the only valid question to be asked.

What, then, is prayer for the Christian? It has four characteristics. The criterion of prayer is seeking what God has promised to give. Jesus' prayer in the garden, "Not my will, but thine," makes Queen Esther look like a cheap power broker, and the daughter of Herodius a racketeer. Christian prayer does not bind God to human desires; it purifies human desires by the announced will of God. The Johannine writings make this quite explicit: "If you abide in me, and my words abide in you, ask whatever you will, and it shall be done for you" (Jn 15:7). "And this is the confidence which we have in him, that if we ask anything according to his will he hears us" (I Jn 5:14).

The <u>context</u> of prayer is the prayer of Jesus. We pray in the context of God's answer to Jesus' prayer. Jesus prayed for the coming of God's kingdom. God answered the prayer of Jesus by making himself present decisively in the preaching of Jesus. Hereafter, all Christian prayer is prayer in Jesus' name. To pray in Jesus' name is to pray within the understanding of God that his prayer and preaching have made available to us. Probably nowhere in contemporary literature has that come more clear than in J.D. Salinger's story about <u>Franny and Zooey</u>. Franny has learned a prayer which involves her in the mere repetition of the name of Jesus, and it is making her sick with unfulfillment. Zooey says to Franny, with brotherly tenderness and theological accuracy:

> How can you pray to a Jesus you don't even understand?....If you're going to say the Jesus prayer, at least say it to <u>Jesus</u>, and not to St. Francis and Seymour and Heidi's grandfather all wrapped up in one. Keep <u>him</u> in mind if you say it, and him only, and him as he was and not as you'd like him to have been....If you don't understand Jesus, you can't understand his prayer - you don't get the prayer at all, you just get some kind of organized cant.

The <u>character</u> of prayer is its power, like poetry, to create a situation, a situation in which God is present in the way he has promised through Jesus of Nazareth that he would be present. Gerard Manley Hopkins, the Irish poet, once despaired of the possibility of prayer to reach God: "No human words can reach a God who has withdrawn to an infinite distance." Possibly he had in mind the phrase, "Our Father who art in heaven," and how do words provide the chain-like strength to draw the heavenly Father to earth? Well, as Gerhard Ebeling, the German theologian, has cleverly observed, heaven is where God is. Jesus of Nazareth has revealed that God is among us, on earth. Therefore, when we pray, "Our Father who art in heaven," we actually mean, "Our Father who art on earth."

The <u>content</u> of prayer is that God gives us the world as our responsibility. In his <u>presence,</u> God turns the world over to man. Your Father knows what you need before you ask. God's answer to our prayers has been given before we have sought him. The Christian is not like the pagan who cries to his god and his god does not answer. Nor is he like the child, driven by habit, who, hearing the bells of the ice cream wagon, runs toward his father's room, crying, "Daddy! Daddy! Can I buy some ice cream?," and then stops in his tracks embarrassed by the recollection that his father has been dead now for nearly a month. The pagan gods who never answer, or who inhabit a fortress built merely upon our wishes - these gods are all dead. The Christian is one who prays to a living God who has already answered our prayers in giving us the world as our responsibility. The French Jerusalem Bible's version of our text best summarizes the gospel message about prayer: "All that you ask in praying, believe that you have already received it, and it will be given to you."

If prayer is definable as the act in which God turns the world over to us as our responsibility, then the really querulous question about prayer is not, does God answer prayer, but do you? God has moved; the next move is yours.

Our role, therefore, in answer to prayer is to receive the responsibility. Prayer is like the vote which is untrue unless the voter is behind it. Kierkegaard had this to say about the two men who went up to the temple to pray - to pray to God without passion is more false than one who prays to a false god but with all his heart.

At Ebenezer, the Israelites fought against the Philistines and lost the first battle. So they brought the Ark from Shiloh to guarantee the presence of their God in the second battle. While it sounds like an act of primitive superstition, the carrying of the Ark to camp meant that the whole society of Israel was being deployed against the Philistines. Prayer is our Ark of the Covenant which signifies not only that God is in this place, but that we are too.

Let's test this concept of prayer out on two phrases from the Lord's Prayer:

1. "Give us this day our daily bread." This is not like manna from heaven in the wilderness, but like the act of receiving the world from beyond ourselves. How many of you could find it possible to pray that prayer over a meal your money has bought, and you have prepared with your own hands? The point is that you are not requesting something you already have, you are receiving it from God in an act of cooperation.

2. "Thy will be done." It is God's will that negroes and whites worship together. "There is neither Jew nor Greek, there is neither slave nor free, there is neither male or female; for you are all one in Christ Jesus" (Gal 3:28). How many of you will invite a negro to come to church with you next Sunday? "Whenever you stand praying, forgive, if you have anything against anyone: so that your Father also who is in heaven may forgive you your trespasses" (Mk 11:25).

In the new Catholic liturgy, when mass is conducted and the wafer is given to a communicant as the priest says Corpus Christi ("This is the body of Christ"), formerly the priest said "Amen." But now the communicant says it. Prayer is not an act of recognizing what God has done, but is our response to what God has done.

Now, how are you reacting to what I have said? Some of you are saying, "If this be prayer I have lost all I prized. It is sad and depressing to think prayer will alter nothing and bring nothing that I wish. All that was precious in prayer was struck away from me." And Robertson answers: "And will you dare to say that prayer is no boon at all unless you can reverse the spirit of your Master's prayer and say, 'Not as Thou wilt, but as I will'?" Amen.

# II.

# INTERPRETATION

# THE MATURITY OF FAITH IN CARL MICHALSON'S THEOLOGY

John D. Godsey

I must begin this address with a confession. To return to Drew to lecture on the theology of Carl Michalson is at once thrilling and terrifying: thrilling because of the honor and pleasure of being among so many friends in a place which is so bound up with my own life, and terrifying because I find it exceedingly difficult to take the measure of the thinking of a man to whom I was so closely related and am so deeply indebted. It was Michalson who introduced me to theology, Michalson who encouraged me to go to Basel for graduate study, Michalson who had much to do with my return to Drew as teacher and colleague. Is it any wonder, then, that I have an awesome respect that makes me reticent to assess Michalson's theological contribution?

Nevertheless, I must. But I do so in the same spirit in which Michalson once wrote of his own teacher, Edwin Lewis:

> Many people had expected Edwin Lewis to live forever. They had wrapped an eternity about him like a mist of myth. Myths are memories dilated by time and affection. In his case the time was thirty-five years as teacher of Drew. The affection was based on personal contacts with the rarest spirit most of us will ever know. The aura surrounding the name of Lewis is always intended in his honor, but it really obscures him. His achievements have been elevated so high, they discourage emulation. The realism in the route he travelled has been blurred.[1]

For Michalson's own sake, we must not allow the "realism in the route he travelled" to be blurred. Moreover, Michalson and Lewis both knew, as did Nietzsche, "that a student's highest compliment to a teacher is to go beyond him, if he can."[2]

Let me begin my wrestling with Michalson's theology by stating a thesis, or at least a suspicion, namely, that Carl Michalson's theology is a sophisticated elaboration of an evangelical piety typical of much of American Methodist thought, and certainly not foreign to what he experienced in his Minnesota homeland. By evangelical piety I mean a Christianity which emphasizes the converting power of the preaching of the gospel and a personal response which is experientially and morally meaningful. This type of Christianity is characterized by an urgent sense of mission, but the focus tends to be on the individual rather than society, on inner rather that outward events. It is a Methodism that was more affected by revivalism than by the social gospel movement, so that its social outreach was more philanthropic than political.

That Michalson should have been reared in an atmosphere of evangelical piety is not at all unusual. The interesting question is how he developed in terms of this early conditioning. We know from his brother Gordon that John Fletcher College was a "Wesleyan oriented school" where education was "a very serious junction of piety and learning."[3] We also know that in his first year of college he began to serve a small rural church, where, according to his college roommate, he was "a flaming Evangelist" as well as loving pastor.[4]

Nothing in Michalson's further education would have dampened his evangelical ardor. On the contrary, his basic orientation was broadened and deepened under the impact of the neo-orthodox movement, which was then overrunning the bastions of liberalism and its gospel of social progress. Michalson entered Drew in the fall of 1936, only two years after Edwin Lewis had published A Christian Manifesto, that ringing challenge to the church to renounce the apostasy of modernism and to recover the faith of "historical Christianity."[5] Although Edwin Lewis and Harry Taylor and Lynn Harold Hough, three of his influential teachers, were unable to agree theologically, they all believed preaching to be the central task of the minister. They guided their gifted student into the realms of philosophy, literature, and theology. Their orientation was mainly British, but Lewis was increasingly being influenced by the Barth-inspired dialectical theology of the Continent, especially in its Brunnerian form. These winds from the Continent were to determine Michalson's future course.

One further point needs to be recognized regarding Michalson"s education at Drew. Along with the emphasis on the evangelical message came an ethical thrust toward the demands of Christian living. Under the stimulus of Lewis, who taught a course on Platonism, Michalson wrote an M.A. thesis on "Human Responsibility in the Republic of Plato and in the Synoptic Gospels." The influence of Emil Brunner, three of whose books are listed in the bibliography, is unmistakable on Michalson. At one point in his Conclusion he approvingly quotes this statement from Brunner's Man in Revolt: "The Christian doctrine of man is simply a doctrine of responsibility."[6] Of course, the cutting edge of evangelical pietism has always been moral living. The question is only how that morality is understood and practiced.

In the fall of 1940 Michalson began his doctoral studies at Yale, where the broadening of his intellectual horizons, begun at Drew, was extended further, particularly in the direction of Continental theology. Two teachers were especially influential. Robert L. Calhoun broadened his historical knowledge of both philosophy and Christian doctrine, and also provided a model of lecturing which Michalson would endeavor to emulate. But theologically more important was the influence of H. Richard Niebuhr, whose distinction between inner history and external history was to be decisive for Michalson's theology from that time onward.

In his book <u>The Meaning of Revelation</u> Niebuhr insisted that a revelational theology must be confessional and employ a historical method which distinguishes between inner and outer history, that is, between history as lived by participating subjects and history as seen as contemplated objects. This accords, of course, with Buber's differentiation between "I-thou" and "I-it" relationships, and Kant's distinction between the realms of the practical and the pure reason. Niebuhr taught that Christian revelation occurs fundamentally in inner history, which in turn is always an affair of faith. Revelation, he said, is "that special occasion which provides us with an image by means of which all the occasions of person and common life become intelligible."[7] That special occasion is, for Christians, Jesus Christ, who reveals God, not in an objective manner, but as the one who knows us from beginning to end, who judges us and values us and gives us a new faith.[8]

Michalson learned well from Niebuhr that revelation is not to be found in nature or objective history, but in the inner life of the self; not in the externalities of miracle, scripture, or sacred events, but in faith. However, it seems questionable whether he learned, or at least accepted, Niebuhr's teaching that internal and external history are necessarily related. True, the relation is paradoxical, but the fact that revelation for Christian selves occurs in the realm of inner history does not relieve the church from taking seriously its own external history, as seen by itself and others. Furthermore, those who in faith apprehend the divine self in their own history, "can and must look for the manifestation of the same self in all other events."[9] Finally, since internal life does not exist without external embodiment, knowledge of its external history remains a duty of the church. These teachings, in which Niebuhr insists on the interrelation between inner and outer history, would appear to oppose Michalson's sharp cleavage between history and nature, which he claims are immiscible structures of realty which have nothing in common.[10]

In 1945 Yale accepted Michalson's doctoral dissertation on "The Problem of Revelation and Reason in the Theology of Karl Heim." The study of Heim, who was professor of systematic theology at Tubingen from 1920 until his retirement, was not calculated to change Michalson's general orientation, for Heim was well-known as a representative of Swabian evangelical piety.[11] However, the study seriously introduced Michalson into the labyrinth of Continental theology, which was to form the chief context for his theological dialogue during the remainder of his career. Through Heim he came into contact with Husserl's phenomenological method, the existentialist insights of Kierkegaard and Heidegger, the hermeneutics of Bultmann, and the dogmatics of Barth. Moreover, Michalson was impressed by the priority of faith in Heim's theological method and the category of "dimension" which Heim employed to speak of transcendence. The latter subsequently became useful when Michalson chose to delineate four "dimensions" of history: worldly, existential, biblical, and eschatological.[12]

Despite the fact that he learned much from Karl Heim, Michalson concluded from his study that Heim was not of the stature of Barth or Bultmann and that Heim"s "positive apologetics" did not represent the wave of the future. Michalson later explained it in this way:

> Barth, by his exclusive preoccupation with the Christian gospel in its own terms, has run the risk of moving parallel to modern culture, although he himself understands that the connection between God and the world is a circuit which God, not the theologian, completes. Bultmann, with his concern for the meaning of human existence, has run the risk of changing the traditional form of the gospel, although not the gospel itself. Heim has run no risk. He has attempted to reach the world without jeopardy to the traditional form of the Christian gospel.[13]

Michalson accepted a teaching position at Drew in 1943, two years before he received his doctorate from Yale. When I entered Drew in 1950, he was philosophically committed to existentialism, but, so far as I could tell, theologically he was open equally to Barth and Bultmann, and even to Brunner. When I was considering my own doctoral work, he advised me to study with Barth. By the time I returned to join the faculty in 1956, however, his commitment was to the hermeneutical theology represented by Bultmann. I think he liked the fact that, although we both were utterly committed to a theology grounded in the gospel of Christ, we did not see things in exactly the same way. While the question of differences is too complex to allow simple formulation, Michalson's own perception of the issues between Barth and Bultmann are illuminating for our own differences. First, he said, they differ on how to interpret the Bible. Bultmann insisted that the theologian must distinguish within the Bible those answers which are meaningful for human existence and those which are not, that is, between kerygma and myth. The proper method of interpretation, then, is to approach the Bible with the right questions, which are helpfully raised by existential philosophy. Barth, on the other hand, eschewed the necessity for a particular preunderstanding and asserted that the Bible provided its own questions as well as its own answers.

The second issue mentioned by Michalson concerns what is meant by the historical character of Christian truth. For both Barth and Bultmann, claimed Michalson, Christian truth had to do with an event in history, but Michalson asserted that Barth defined the event primarily from the standpoint of God's participation in it, i.e., trinitarily, whereas Bultmann defined it from the standpoint of human participation in it, i.e., existentially. Michalson elaborated this important distinction in these words:

> For Barth, revelation is not true unless it is <u>theologically</u> meaningful, that is, unless it involves God himself. For Bultmann, revelation is not true unless it is theologically <u>meaningful</u>, that is, unless it involves man himself. For Barth, Christian faith has to do with God <u>and</u> his relevance for the here and now, not with God <u>in</u> his relevance for the here and now. That is the characteristic Barth decision in theology today which separates him from those for whom the reality of God is in some sense at stake in history, in acts of interpretation, and for

whom God's reality is not event simply, but historical event, or, event inseparable from man.[14]

This is not the time to argue about the adequacy of Michalson's interpretation of the issues between Barth and Bultmann, but only to indicate his own decision to adopt Bultmann's perspective. Once having set his course, Michalson's development was spectacular and his contribution to theological literature amazing. Within a ten-year period he wrote five substantial books, edited two others, and helped translate a third. And all of this in addition to a large number of significant articles and reviews! Moreover, his writing is characterized by an erudite examination of the most profound issues in a literary style of the highest quality.

Gordon Michalson has written that his brother "moved from Lewis to Heim to Barth to existentialism and Kierkegaard to Husserl phenomenology to Heidegger and hermeneutics,"[15] and, chronologically speaking, I think he is correct. From the standpoint of his mature theological position, however, his lineage might be better run from Kierkegaard (subjectivity is truth) and H. Richard Niebuhr (revelation occurs in inner history) to Bultmann (existentialist interpretation) to Gogarten (theology as history) to Fuchs (Jesus' words interpret his conduct) and Ebeling (revelation as word-event). The linkage backwards would run through Wilhelm Herrmann (Jesus as ground of faith) to Friedrich Schleiermacher (theology as Glaubenslehre) and perhaps to Melanchthon (to know Christ is to know his benefits). In philosophy his chief mentors were Dilthey, Husserl, Heidegger, Sartre, Gadamer, Merleau-Ponty, and Ricoeur.

Merely to determine influences and trace developments, however, fails to do justice to Michalson's own genius. For the sake of the preaching of the church in the present, Michalson pursued a theological methodology in which faith is interpreted as the historical event in which meaning is conferred upon human existence by the performatory Word of God's eschatological action in Jesus Christ. The radicality of this method is envisioned only when one grasps Michalson's intention to produce a non-supernatural, non-ontological, yes, even non-theistic, theology within the realm of history alone, where history is defined as an "interworld" (or Lebenswelt) of human meaning in which the subject-object cleavage is overcome and God is present to the human and the human to God in an event of speaking and hearing. The task of this theology can no longer be defined simply as "faith seeking understanding" or even "faith seeking (or conferring) self-understanding." Rather, it is "faith constituting history," where history is the basis for a meaningful life.

In Michalson's theology as history, questions of meaning and function displace those of being and truth. Revelation is not primarily the revelation of God, but the revelation of the meaning of one's life, that is, the conferral of a new history. Creation has nothing to do with nature, but is the act in which one receives the world from God. Christology does not involve making direct statements about Christ's person, but speaks of Jesus of Nazareth as the one who speaks for God in calling the world to obedience. The work of Christ is not primarily to forgive us for our sins, but to inaugurate the age of faith in which humans assume mature responsibility for the world. Sin is no longer simply rebellion against God, but is the refusal to accept Jesus of Nazareth as the source of one's history. Thus it is the anachronism of living by the framework and standards of the old age after the new age has come. Christians are those who by definition are free from the sin of anachronism because they have adopted God's call in Christ as the form of their existence. Evangelism is not converting people to Christ, but announcing the eschaton and thus bringing the world to expression as creation. Eschatology is not about an apocalyptic end to history, but the horizon which continues to bring our finitude to light as final. Eternal life is not deliverance from finitude, but obedience to God even unto death and the realization that God can be glorified by an obedient death.[16]

This is indeed a bold theology. Some might even say "reckless." Michalson was willing to risk tradition for the sake of relevancy. Or, better, he was convinced that certain past ways of presenting the Christian message were counter-productive for today's men and women, in that they prevented understanding and thus thwarted the hearing of God's call to obedience. Thus direct claims about the person of Christ and even the traditional emphasis upon the forgiveness of sins are to be subordinated to the call to mature responsibility for the world. In a real sense Michalson's earlier existential approach to the Christian faith, guided by Bultmann and the "early Heidegger," has given way in his later theology to a vision of "worldly faith" more akin to Gogarten's theology of secularization. The intention of God's act in Jesus Christ is to turn the world over to humankind and to have them assume responsibility for it as mature sons and daughters. They have to be responsible to God for the world. This, in the end, is the vision of the maturity of faith which Carl Michalson has bequeathed to the church.

One can only speculate about how Michalson's theology would have developed had he lived longer. Having settled methodological questions, he was only beginning his more constructive theological efforts. His wider experiences, as witnessed by his encounter with Japanese theology, were beginning to have an effect on him. My own conviction is that he would have had to give much more attention to the social and ethical implications of his theology if that theology were to be truly "worldly." But whether he could do this without changing some of his presuppositions is a serious question.

Michalson's theology, brilliant as it is, has been adversely affected by the astounding demise of hermeneutical theology in the last decade. All theology linked to Heidegger, whether existentialist or linguistic, has been overshadowed by the rise of futuristic theology, which is an umbrella term covering the theology of hope, the theology of universal history, political theology, and liberation theologies of various kinds. There is no time to delineate the differences, but suffice it to say that the contrast between Michalson's theology and futuristic theology is stark. Not presentistic eschatology, but futuristic or apocalyptic eschatology; not faith, but hope; not words, but deeds; not history as personal meaning, but world history; not church as herald, but church as servant; not personal decision, but social praxis; not theology as history, but theology of history; not Word-event, but the Kingdom of God; not hermeneutical theology with a primary interest in applying the meaning of Scripture to the individual believer's subjectivity, but political theology primarily interested in applying meaning to the structures of political life; not primarily an interest in the manner of our existence in the world, but an interest in the responsibility inherent in our hopes for the world.

The contrast, I repeat, is stark, but it is not absolute. The hermeneutical task and the task of restructuring society according to the vision of the Kingdom cannot be separated. The church needs Michalson as well as Moltmann. I said at the beginning that Michalson's theology was an elaboration of evangelical piety. In my judgment his move to a worldly theology signalled a break with the piety that is closely associated with existentialism, with its focus on individuality and subjectivity (which often becomes individualism and subjectivism).

Those who would carry Michalson's banner today must advance his cause by developing the structures of a worldly faith for mature Christians. Here Michalson has provided some hints, but often his talk of "world," like Gogarten's, seems too cerebral. At this point we need help from Bonhoeffer, with his passion for the concrete, from Reinhold Niebuhr, who understood the realities of political power, and from current liberation theologians, whose social analysis and ethical praxis stem from the experience of oppression. We need to be open to and learn from the secular disciplines, so that our decisions may be informed and pertinent. We need to make common cause with all those who are working to keep human life human and who are practicing responsible stewardship of the earth.

Further, it is my conviction that a worldly faith requires the recovery of the Old Testament as Word of God. Even if we grant Michalson's view that for theology as history the Bible is more a frame of reference than a normative authority, that frame of reference rightfully entails the whole dramatic narrative, including the story of Israel, of Jesus, and of the church. Contrary to Michalson, I believe the Old Testament is not simply historically important for the New, but is theologically crucial. To paraphrase Bonhoeffer, we live in the Old and believe the New.

Finally, a worldly faith will have to take more seriously the sociality of the church. The church is not simply the church of the Word, if this implies that everything revolves around the preacher. The church is a pilgrim people of God called to an existence for others, a community of which has caught the vision of the Kingdom and presses forward toward its realization on earth. With the Catholics we may even understand the church as a sacrament, that is, a sign of the redeeming grace of Christ in a historically tangible form. In any case, thinking from the concreteness of the community will save theology from the temptations of individualism and clericalism, and will at the same time remind it of its solidarity with and responsibility toward the universal human community.

No one can know, of course, how Michalson would have developed the social and ethical elements in his emerging "worldly theology." It is enough to note that he was moving in this direction. What we can be certain of, however, is that his elaboration of the structures of responsible life would in no sense have lessened his passion for the preaching of an understandable gospel. In terms of his life-long evangelical concern, Michalson was, as his brother said, "a Wesleyan of an increasingly higher order."[17] Those who would carry Michalson's banner today dare not fail to utilize the obvious hermeneutical riches with which they have been so generously endowed.

Why was Carl Michalson such an incomparable teacher for us all? Why is he deserving of having a Society such as this bear his name? Is it not because of what he stood for, something he found in the Drew tradition and then embodied in a unique way? I close with some words that Michalson penned about his own teacher, but which are equally true of him. I take the liberty of substituting his name for that of Edwin Lewis:

> It is inconceivable that the memory of Carl Michalson will ever fade in this place. One highlight in his portrait is least likely to grow dim. Do not look for it in some turn of phrase, some exclamation, some doctrine or concept, some glowing personal trait. Seek it in the question he has put - the question implicit in his whole life and work - a question more than anything the norm of theological authority for him - a question whose genius inheres in the fact that it can be asked forever without loss of force: "Can this faith be preached?"[18]

In the final analysis, I can assert one thing with certainty: Michalson's faith can be preached, and Michalson preached his faith. Thanks be to God who gave us this witness!

## ENDNOTES

1.    "The Edwin Lewis Myth," The Drew Gateway 30, No. 2 (Wint '60), 102.
2.    Ibid., p. 106. Italics are Michalson's.
3.    Gordon E. Michalson, "Introduction," in "Hermeneutics and the Worldliness of Faith," The Drew Gateway 45, Nos. 1, 2, 3 (1974-1975), x.
4.    Ibid.
5.    Edwin Lewis, A Christian Manifesto; NY: Abingdon-Cokesbury, 1934, p. 29.
6.    Carl Michalson, "Human Responsibility in the Republic of Plato and in the Synoptic Gospels," Drew University M.A. Thesis, Madison, NJ, 1940, p. 71. The quote is from Emil Brunner, Man in Revolt; NY: Scribner's, 1939, p. 209.
7.    H. Richard Niebuhr, The Meaning of Revelation; NY: Macmillan, 1946, p. 109.
8.    Ibid., pp. 152-154.
9.    Ibid., pp. 86-87.
10.   Carl Michalson, The Rationality of Faith; NY: Scribner's, 1963, pp. 24ff.
11.   Carl Michalson, "Karl Heim," p. 279 in A Handbook of Christian Theologians ed Martin E. Marty and Dean G. Peerman; NY: World, 1965.
12.   Carl Michalson, The Hinge of History; NY: Scribner's, 1959, pp. 24ff.
13.   "Karl Heim," op. cit., p. 293.
14.   Carl Michalson, Worldly Theology; NY: Scribner's, 1967, p. 38.
15.   "Introductions," p. xiii.
16.   Ibid., pp. 110, 174-175, 201ff, 206, 215-216.
17.   Ibid., p. x.
18.   "The Edwin Lewis Myth," p. 106-107.

# CARL MICHALSON AS A WESLEYAN THEOLOGIAN
## Theodore Runyon

To suggest that Carl Michalson was consciously a Wesleyan theologian is risky. As far as I know there are no documents in which he ruminates about the impact of his Wesleyan heritage on his own theologizing. If theology, as he says, "is the process of patterning the mind with the logic of the Christian faith,"[1] we would have to be able to demonstrate an implicit or explicit Wesleyan pattern in Michalson's mind. Michalson illustrates the importance of such patterning with an example:

> Even silence which does not presuppose a patterned mind can be confusing. A young man and a young woman may be sitting together on a sofa. There may be utter silence between them. If he has no pattern on his mind, the situation can be oppressively dull. If he has a patterned mind, notwithstanding the silence, the moment can be electrically significant.[2]

In this essay what I am in effect proposing to do is to note Michalson's proximity to Wesley and claim that Michalson's mind was patterned by the presence of Wesley, even though Michalson did not say a great deal about the matter.

The claim is made even more risky by the fact that almost none of the figures who had a determinative influence on Michalson's mature thought were Wesleyans - figures such as Calhoun and Richard Niebuhr, Barth and

Brunner, Bultmann and Heim, Kierkegaard and Heidegger, Fuchs and Ebeling, Merleau-Ponty and Gadamer, Bonhoeffer and Gogarten. Nary a Methodist among them! Indeed, we have to go back all the way to Michalson's student days at Drew, to Edwin Lewis, to find an avowed Wesleyan among his mentors. Nevertheless, I would propose that there are certain theological moves made by the mature Michalson that can best be understood as arising from affinities bequeathed him by his Wesleyan heritage, moves which put some distance between him and the continental theology that otherwise played such a dominant role in his thought. Moreover, had he had the opportunity to persist in a Wesleyan direction, he might have avoided some of the limitations in his theology now evident when he is viewed from the perspective of recent Latin American liberation theologies.[3]

Michalson's origins were in pietistic Methodism. He grew up in Park Avenue Methodist Church, in Minneapolis, a congregation noted for its self-conscious Wesleyanism and continuity with the holiness wing of Methodism. He attended struggling John Fletcher College, named after Methodism's first systematic theologian who codified Wesley's doctrine of holiness. The college is described by Michalson's brother Gordon as "an unendowed Asbury College," which not long after Carl graduated went under, the victim of the depression and the Second World War. Thus we can be sure that the standard holiness vocabulary of "religious experience," "sanctification," and "Christian perfection" was familiar terminology in the world young Carl Michalson inhabited. I have not found in Michalson's writings any direct and explicit discussion of this holiness heritage, but I suspect that some of his later preoccupations cannot be understood apart from his reactions against it as well as his appreciation of it. I am not about to propose an Eriksonian treatment of "The Young Man Michalson," yet there is little doubt that his sensitivity to the issues of the relationship of law to faith and the resistance against coercion in faith can be traced back to questions of authenticity which he must have raised as a youth exposed to the high-pressure methods of revivals and the nagging demands of perfectionism. The brand of pietism practiced within the Michalson family seems to have been positive and healthy, however, and may have been a conscious effort to counterbalance the compulsion to deprecate the human which characterized so much of nineteenth century holiness theology and preaching. The pietistic negation of the self and the world was what Michalson later was to find least attractive in Wesley.

> When Wesley is tempted to admit the poise and success of a British statesman, he interrupts his reverie to say, "What is a lord  but  a sinner born to die?" In a moment in which he seems thoroughly to relish the beauty of the Irish landscape, he checks himself by saying "The eye is not satisfied with seeing till it see God".... When young people fall in love, he insinuates that the Holy Spirit has left them...He could rarely enjoy the company of friends because of his compulsion to go out to preach.  He was uncomfortable in the presence of genteel people because he had only one subject of conversation.[4]

As a lover of good company and good conversation, Michalson was ever grateful for his liberation from the dour side of Wesleyan perfectionism. Genuine Christian faith exudes a joie de vivre which Wesley also knew but somehow felt guilty about practicing. Michalson had no guilt at that point; his zest for life was infectious. And he refused to give legitimacy to any reading of Christianity that did not include a profound sense of release and joy.

Precisely this insistence that Christian faith is freeing and existence-transforming is also traceable to Michalson's Wesleyanism, however, and is one of the factors that made him prefer Bultmann to Barth, in spite of his profound appreciation for, and indebtedness to, the latter. Michalson quotes Wesley as saying "No man can be justified and not know it!"[5] which is the substance of one of Bultmann's objections to Barth.[6]  This is because for

Barth the significant change is the change in status of the sinner in the eyes of God. But for Bultmann and Michalson what is involved in salvation is not just a change before God but a new history in which the Christian knows himself reflexively as the beneficiary of divine reconciliation. A recurring quote in Michalson's writings is Melancthon's formulation of this truth: "To know Christ is to know his benefits."[7] For Michalson, if this is subjectivism it is that variety of subjectivism which is appropriate to Christian faith, and is therefore not to be bartered away for the false security of objective assurances. This concern for existential participation is something shared by Michalson with the whole Lutheran wing of neo-Reformation theology, however. It can be found in Heim, Brunner, and even Gogarten, as well as in Bultmann, and therefore cannot be said to come from distinctively Wesleyan sources.

Faith as existential transformation is typically couched by Michalson in terms of a change in meaning as a result of an event of communication. This is essentially what is involved in his notion of "history," the hallmark of his whole theological enterprise. John Godsey points out that Michalson's understanding of history roots back to his appropriation of H. Richard Niebuhr's distinction between "inner" and "outer" history.

> Niebuhr taught that Christian revelation occurs fundamentally in inner history, which in turn is always an affair of faith. Revelation, he said, is "that special occasion which provides us with an image by means of what all the occasions of personal and common life become intelligible". ... Michalson learned well from Niebuhr that revelation is not to be found in nature or objective history, but in the inner life of the self; not in the externalities of miracle, scripture, or sacred events, but in faith.[8]

In other words, the "history" with which faith has to do is that complex of meanings and relationships which constitute an individual existence.

The integrity of that existence must be respected, moreover, in any attempt to present the gospel. The approach to the individual is never head-on, therefore, but employs instead a Kierkegaardian maieutic method to draw out the felt needs of the person, the thirsts present in the desert spots of his or her life, the prior "sentiment for meaning." It is these felt needs, this sentiment, which constitute the pre-understanding (Vorverstandnis) to which the gospel must make its appeal. The gospel cannot force itself on anyone, for if it does the event which occurs cannot be genuine faith but only assent to an external and imposed authority. Here Michalson casts his lot with pietism against orthodoxy. Faith must be a free response of the individual, a free response which is possible only where inner history is actually transformed and a new configuration of meaning arises.

It is just at this point, however, that traditional revivalism all too easily errs whenever it exercises psychological oppression over the minds of hearers by attempting to convince them of a ready-made and imposed set of needs rather than eliciting from them in maieutic fashion the honest expression of their predicament. As the pastor/apologist, Michalson assiduously avoided any approach that smacked of the imposition of alien authority, and I suspect that his sensitivity in this respect was due at least in part to early experiences of the manipulative approach of evangelists. By contrast, Michalson's description of Kierkegaard's skills as an apologist typifies Michalson's own style: "His efforts to lead men to Christianity were delicate thrusts and parries, nudges and insinuations which provoke men to move, but always with their concurrence."[9] Where Michalson finds a similar approach in Wesley, he quotes it approvingly.[10] And no one would deny that Michalson was himself a consummate evangelist, "a Wesleyan of an increasingly higher order," as his brother Gordon writes,[11] whose whole effort was directed toward a moment of break-through, of enlightenment in the minds and hearts of his hearers. Yet he always operated with a sense of restraint because realized that "the Christian Gospel is a proclamation that strikes the world with the force of a hint. Some 'get it,' some do not."[12]

Now we are in a position to draw together Michalson's understanding of history, faith, and the Holy Spirit. As we have seen, he allows only the world of human meaning to be called "history" in the proper sense. This decisive methodological move he reinforces by relegating everything that cannot be described as history in this sense to the category "nature." Consistent with this methodological distinction he insists on an important difference between eschatology and apocalyptic: the latter refers to events in nature whereas the former is properly used only to describe transformations in human meaning. Genuine faith is "an acoustical affair." It is that event of communication which occurs when the story that is proclaimed casts my existence into a whole new light. The biblical text, composed as it is of the "sediment of meaning" which sustained life for past generations, is presented in such a way that "the text interprets the hearer," so that a significant change is brought about in one's self-understanding.[13] The shift in history is from pre-understanding to Christian self-understanding under the impact of the gospel story.

In this description of the birth of faith Michalson came to feel that he had in effect explained in an alternative, non-supernaturalistic way what has traditionally been referred to as the work of the Holy Spirit. The Spirit is not an independent agent added to the Word which insures that the latter takes effect but is rather the power implicit within words themselves to change human history when they open up a new way to view oneself and one's situation.[14]

What I have been describing thus far is vintage Michalson; and I am suggesting that it is no injustice to describe him as a Wesleyan evangelist of a higher order, one whose method and the passion with which he exercised it are inexplicable apart from his roots in the Wesleyan holiness understanding of the nature of saving faith.

But there is a new element which enters the picture in the early 1960's. Previously I had regarded this new element solely as the result of the influence of Friedrich Gogarten. But after a more careful study of Michalson's essay, "The Hermeneutics of Holiness in Wesley,"[15] I began to suspect that the turn to Gogarten in Michalson's case was not unrelated to a basic difference between Wesley and Reformation thought. This essay on sanctification was the first extensive treatment of Wesley which Michalson had committed to writing, and the care which he gave it was extraordinary. The footnotes disclose the range and intensity of reading Michalson had done in the Wesleyan materials. And significantly the essay concentrates on the aspect of Wesleyan theology which Michalson knew best from his own holiness background.

The decisive difference between Wesley and especially the Lutheran Reformers was that for Wesley faith was not the goal, but was rather the means to a goal which lay beyond it. Michalson rightly identifies what from the Reformation standpoint can only seem a shocking departure from Protestant doctrine, that "for Wesley faith is only instrumental. Works are given the primacy."[16] Why is this the case? Because Wesley sees the doctrine of salvation as fitting within an overall divine initiative to restore creation to its original wholeness. Therefore the reconciliation between God and his creature which occurs in justification has the intent of freeing the human being to realize the potential for which he or she was created, and thereby to assist in the restoration of the whole creation. Wesley can of course insist as strongly as did Luther that justification by faith is basic. He identifies Ephesians 2:8 as the "first principle" of Christianity, the cornerstone "upon which all else is built."[17] "For by grace ye are saved through faith; and this not of yourselves; it is the gift of God: Not of works, lest any man should boast." But as the intentionality of that Pauline passage itself shows, this reconciliation is for a purpose, as the next verse proceeds to make clear: "For we are his workmanship, created in Christ Jesus unto good works, which

God hath before ordained that we should walk in them" (v 10). Both grace and faith have as their goal the work of transformation. The reconciliation which occurs in justification equips the saints, those who are being made holy, to contribute to the cosmic renewal which the epistle to the Ephesians sees as initiated in Christ.

A perusal of Wesley's sermons shows how he returns to this theme again and again, the reconstruction by God of his whole creation, of which the reconciliation with humankind is a part. Faith is the first principle of the present age because sin has brought alienation and estrangement that can only be overcome by the active grace of God appropriated by faith. But the end of this faith is love, and the goal of justification is the reconciliation of all things. Justification has its goal in sanctification, not because justification is in any sense superseded or made irrelevant by sanctification. The new status which God has granted to those who plead the merits of Christ before him remains the gracious fundament of the relationship with him. Yet Wesley speculates that faith was not even necessary before the fall, that the "evidence of things unseen," and the "confidence in redeeming love," could not possibly have any place and were therefore utterly needless before sin forced perfect love out of the human heart.[18] Faith then is the antidote to human sin and opens the way to love. Faith was "originally designed of God to re-establish the law of love....It is the grand means of restoring that holy love wherein man was originally created."[19] Therefore, as glorious and honorable as faith is, "it is not the end of the commandment. God hath given this honor to love alone....Love is the end, the sole end, of every dispensation from God, from the beginning of the world to the consummation of all things." And faith itself, "even Christian faith, the faith of God's elect, the faith of the operation of God, still is only the handmaid of love."[20] Michalson's judgment seems legitimate, therefore, that for Wesley, in contrast to the typical Protestant position, faith is not the goal but is instrumental to creative and transforming love.

It is important to see, moreover, that for Wesley this love is not viewed as an emotion but as a quality of relationship. It endures when all else passes away. That means it has a structure, and that structure is the law in its proper sense - what in classical terms is called the tertius usus of the law. When Michalson turned his attention to Wesley, it was precisely this that caught his eye and became the focal issue of "the hermeneutics of holiness." Again, I suspect his discovery at this point is linked to his own background in holiness Methodism. Pietism in general, and evangelical revivalism in particular, never seemed to be able to get law and gospel together in a creative way. The good news of grace to the sinner led to antinomianism or quietism; the reaction against antinomianism led to new moralisms and legalism. The record of Methodism in this regard is as spotty as that of other pietists, but it must be said to the credit of the holiness wing of Methodism that it did not settle for the general revivalist concentration on conversion - the revivalist equivalent of justification by faith - but insisted instead that justification is only the beginning of the road toward perfection. And at the end of that road lies perfect love, which is understood not primarily as mystical vision but as the structure of love in action. John Fletcher's systematic theology was entitled Checks to Antinomianism. And Wesley was preoccupied with the concrete effects of love. If we participate fully in the love with which God loves us, writes Wesley, we cannot avoid loving our neighbor. Love is not content simply with not doing evil; "it continually incites us to do good...in every possible kind, and in every possible degree, to all men."[21] The eschatological goal of the Christian faith functions for Wesley, therefore, not as a transhistorical escape from this vale of tears but as a vision of the possibilities for the individual and for society when the law of love becomes the dominant structure that orders this world. In an exercise of eschatological imagination Wesley says, "Suppose now the fullness of time to be come. What a prospect is this! All is peace....Wars are ceased from the earth;...no brother rising up against brother; no country or city divided against itself, and tearing out its own bowels....Here is no oppression; no extortion to 'grind the face of the poor'." But as he describes this scene Wesley recognizes how far even Christian nations are from actualizing it. "Where, I pray, do the Christians live? Which is the country, the inhabitants whereof are all thus filled with the Holy Ghost? Are all of one heart and of one soul; cannot suffer one among them to lack anything, but continually give to every man as he hath need? Who one and all, have the love of God filling their hearts, and constraining them to love their neighbor as themselves?"[22]

Yet just at this juncture - when we feel the agony of the contrast between the promised Kingdom and the present state of humankind - there is an important difference between Wesley's reaction and that of most Protestant theology. A common theological response in Protestantism has been to despair of this world and to convert the eschatological dimension of Christianity into doomsday apocalyptic or a heavenly alternative to this world. Wesley refused to do either. To be sure, he has sermons such as "The Great Assize,"[23] that paint in lurid tones the fate of the present evil age. And his language is filled with the longing for heaven which is conventional in pietism. But he succumbs to neither apocalyptic despair nor to their present day more sophisticated equivalents which turn eschatology into a purely formal category, the "impossible possibility," which functions only to disparage any human attempts to approximate a society more consistent with the Kingdom. Instead, Wesley's logic was straightforward: If God commands it, it can be done; for he would not command that which for human beings would be impossible. He commands holiness and perfect love. Therefore, they are possible; for what he requires he also provides by the power of his Spirit. His commands are really promises. And Michalson observes that Wesley translates "Be ye therefore perfect" (Mt 5:48) in the form of a promise: "Ye shall be perfect."[24] The promise at one and the same time declares the eschatological goal and energizes the process toward that goal.

Theologians have longed quarreled over whether Wesley was a premillennialist or a postmillennialist. In truth, he was neither and he was both - which is to say that these nineteenth century categories do not really apply. He never denied the traditional picture of divine intervention which ushers in the end time. In comparison to other eighteenth century preachers, however, he downplayed it. And he excised most of the apocalyptic speculation which Bengel included in his <u>Gnomen</u>, the commentary upon which Wesley otherwise so largely relied for his own <u>Notes on the New Testament</u>. There are passages, on the other hand, that seem to identify Wesley as a blatant postmillennialist, such as: "Is your heart whole with God? Full of love and zeal to set up his Kingdom on earth?"[25] But he insists that nothing can be accomplished by humans in their own strength; the power of the Spirit is the power that makes for the Kingdom, and faithful persons can only put themselves at the disposal of that power. Nevertheless, it is also clear that the entire sanctification which lies at the end of the road of Christian perfection is the structural equivalent of the Kingdom of God attainable in this world on the level of the individual. Thus, if one insists on classifying Wesley in premillennial or postmillennialist terms, he is formally a premillennialist but materially a postmillennialist. And it is this stance which has made Methodists endemically positive regarding human responsibility both for the individual growth and for social change.

This Wesleyan eschatology appears to me to have more than accidental parallels to the direction that Michalson's own rethinking of eschatology took in the early 1960's. Up to that time he had espoused a relatively straightforward Bultmannian position, which asserts that the New Testament's eschatological language is understandable only if it is translated into the language of existential encounter. It is to be deciphered as the expression of inner history. Early Christians were grasped by the new possibilities for existence which came into the world with Christ and which mythologically could be described only in terms of the inbreaking of a new age. The terminology of an expected world transformation is to be understood as the groping of the first century imagination for images powerful enough to do justice to the breadth and depth of the change in meaning that has come about through Christ Jesus as old sources of meaning are overturned by the new understanding of our existence that Christ mediates.[26]

However, when we arrive at his late essays in <u>Worldly Theology</u>, especially chapters eight and eleven in which Michalson is hammering out his own theological position, we sense that the definition and context of the term "history" has undergone a change. The focus has shifted from the more formal existentialist category, "human meaning as such," to the implicitly more normative "holiness history," or in Wesley's terminology, the history of the increase of love toward God and man. It is no longer the individual and his or her felt needs that are the object of salvation for Michalson, but the world. And the individual's participation in the redemptive processes of God depends upon his or her new "orientation toward the world."[27]

It is not that Michalson denies his previous position. The new focus is just as surely a matter of human meaning. But existential pre-understanding has been transformed into Christian self-understanding, which is now interpreted as "holiness history," a participation in the structures of responsibility for the world which is the mark of "maturity" in faith. Thus we might say it is the meaning of the world for God which moves to the center of attention, and Christians find their own meaning within God's call to responsibility for the world. This call reconstitutes history on a different basis and with a different goal than it had in the past.

This leads to a second way to describe the same change in Michalson's theology, namely, by tracing the shift in the meaning of eschatology. Whereas previously the definition was more formal - eschatology referred to a personal crisis of meaning in which one's taken-for-granted existence is suspended in the face of new possibilities - now it is more concretely teleological. It means grasping one's responsible place in the light of the salvation of the world. Whereas previously the weight was placed on the re-ordering of one's personal existence, the weight now lies outside the self, and the self is "saved" as it is placed at the disposal of the larger enterprise of the world's destiny.

I think these changes represent something more basic in Michalson's theological enterprise than simply a shift from the first to the third use of the law. It indicates that he is seeking in a positive way to put together the two realms, nature and history, which previously were kept so antiseptically distinct from each other. True, he had earlier claimed that "nature" is transformed into "history" whenever it is drawn into the sphere of human meaning. But the force of that distinction no longer seems as cogent when the natural world, as well as the world of meaning, becomes the object of salvation.

The figure who was a prime influence in this shift was, as we have seen previously, Friedrich Gogarten. Gogarten was of course closely associated with Bultmann, and was one of the early defenders of Bultmann's existentialist method of interpretation. However, under the impact of the kinds of questions which his physicist friends at the University of Gottingen were raising during and immediately after the Second World War, Gogarten turned to the fundamental theological issues surrounding human responsibility for the world. These scientists - Max Planck, Werner Heisenberg, and Carl Friedrich von Weizsacker - were not satisfied with a personal, existential faith. They needed to know what kind of context Christian faith provides for understanding their responsibility as scientists involved in atomic research.

In response Gogarten developed his theology of "humanity between God and the world," in which he demonstrated the legitimacy of the "secularization" of the world that occurred historically through the impact of Christian faith as it vanquished paganism, but pointed to the inability of modern "secularism" to place the world in a proper context within which it can be responsibly managed by human beings as God's stewards. Secularism makes human beings subject to a world that has become their fate, with the result that the proper relativity of the world cannot be maintained. The world becomes absolute in itself; it becomes all-in-all-with demonic consequences. The basic theological resource Gogarten draws upon in order to formulate a Christian secularity as an alternative to secularism is the Lutheran doctrine of the two realms. This doctrine spells out a division of labor between faith and reason which allows for a context of responsibility within which reason can attack the practical problems of ordering the world.

The deficiency which I now see in Gogarten, however, is that reason is freed from enslavement and called to responsibility through justification by faith, but it is not given any concrete telos in terms of which to work. Gogarten refuses to define any telos, insisting that this is just the genius of the two realms doctrine: It leaves the reason free to operate according to what seems most responsible in the exigencies of the situation. From the perspective of the Marxist critique as employed especially by Latin American theologians, however, I now see that what this complete freedom for the reason in fact usually means is that the bourgeois reason is left to respond in a bourgeois angle of vision. No wonder, then, that what one person views as Christian responsibility is seen by another as class-motivated defense of the status quo. And the weak link I would identify in the otherwise extremely helpful Gogartian position is his reliance on Luther. For Luther, the end has already arrived in principle in justification by faith. Therefore the introduction of a telos that relegates faith to a penultimate position and gives explicit shape to the structures of a new order in this world would be inconsistent with the Lutheran position.

Michalson's The Rationality of Faith, published in 1963, makes moves similar to Gogarten's and therefore was determined by Gogarten's method - or so I assumed. In the final chapter, entitled "Faith as Historical Maturity," for instance, he suggests that Christian faith "is response to the word of God the content of which is reducible to very simple terms: 'Accept the world from God, make it your responsibility, and do not allow yourselves to be enslaved in it again'."[28] The formula sounds more like Gogarten than Gogarten. This is the point at which we see the decisive difference, however. Michalson's basis for rethinking the relationship of humanity to the world is not Luther's two realms but Wesley's doctrine of sanctification. The traditional understanding of Christianity which centers on sin and forgiveness - and therefore on the doctrine of justification - tends to lock humans into a position of immaturity in which they are constantly dependent upon a religious system which provides release from guilt but expects little from them other than "more of the same." Simul justus et peccator remains in that system the fundamental description of the Christian life, and as such tends to preempt the Christian telos of the Kingdom of God as the decisive hermeneutic. But other religions provide means of forgiveness, Michalson points out. "Forgiveness of sins is a phenomenon known prior to and outside the Christian movement, hence not at all unique to it."[29] If this is the case, then Wesley's question is appropriate: "What do ye more than others?"[30] The doctrine of holiness demands that human beings not remain in the position of immaturity but go on to "perfection," i.e., (negatively) toward the eradication of all that prevents creatures from realizing the potential for which they were created, and (positively) toward the expression of perfect love toward God and fellow creatures. Wesley interprets this love in concrete terms of fruits of the Spirit that minister to physical, spiritual, social, and economic needs. Where the eschatological gift of the Spirit is present Christians "cannot suffer one among them to lack anything."[31] Love is structured. "Wherever holiness and not forgiveness has been the distinctive mark of faith," says Michalson,[32] forgiveness is seen as only the first step along a way that leads to the fruits of the Spirit. These fruits are "fully historical realities," he claims "which are lived out in men. Among them are love, joy, peace, patience, kindness, goodness, faithfulness, gentleness, and self-control. These are the attributes of a life of freedom, a life of responsibility," made available to us through the proclamation of the true son and steward, Jesus of Nazareth. "Life in Christ realized in these eschatological attributes is the maturity of history."[33] This is why Michalson can claim that "holiness secularizes the world."[34] Here he shares Gogarten's intention to deny the sacredness of the world in its own right and relativize it to God while placing it in the care of human beings as the inheritance granted by a loving Father, who gives us the world precisely in order that we might begin to exercise our maturity. But this is done not via Luther but with the help of the Wesleyan concept of holiness which Michalson first encountered, albeit in quite different fashion, in Park Avenue Church in Minneapolis and at John Fletcher College.

In summary, the concrete structures of love operative in the world which Wesley sees as the fruits of sanctification and the telos toward which faith and the whole process of Christian perfection move, provide the later Michalson with the materials for his distinctively Wesleyan interpretation of a contemporary Christian faith that goes beyond the limitations of Reformation and neo-Reformation approaches. Pre-understanding, as he now interprets it, is no longer exclusively determined by existential questions of personal thirst but by world-historical questions of human responsibility. And the answer is not so much an enlightening insight into personal meaning as a new way of understanding one's role and responsibilities in the world. As a result, says Michalson, the basic question of pre-understanding asked out of the Wesleyan context would now sound like this: "How shall we assume responsibility for the world without turning it into a new object of devotion? And the Gospel answer would be, 'Ye shall be perfect!,' which is to say, 'Love the Lord thy God with all thy heart, and thy neighbor,' meaning, the new law of life which is a world of promise and permission: 'Receive the world from God!'"[35]

Would it be too bold to suggest that if the vectors which we have drawn from Michalson's existentialist period through his last developments were extended down to the present they would bear surprising resemblance to what is now emerging in Latin American liberation theology? For the Latin Americans have decried the dependence of North Atlantic theologians, both Protestant and Catholic, on Reformation views which equate salvation with personal faith. On the basis of Marxist analysis the Latin Americans are calling instead for an understanding of salvation which is world-transforming. Where in church history, we might ask, has such a transformationist theology come to the fore? It would be difficult to find a better historical precedent than Wesley's doctrine of sanctification wherever its social as well as individual implications have been spelled out.

Though it may be true that on a continuum running from Luther to Marx (which is not necessarily the same as the continuum from justification to entire sanctification!) Wesley and Michalson would be only about half way, this is no reason to consign them to pietism and existentialism respectively and assume that they have little to contribute to the current theological debate. While our evaluation of them has been sharpened by a liberationist hermeneutic, I am convinced that theologies of liberation could themselves benefit from the insights and correctives they have to offer. Indeed, this cross-fertilization ought to be high on our theological agendas during the next decade if we are to be faithful to the rich inheritance which all have received who have been touched in one way or another by the life and writings of Carl Michalson.

ENDNOTES

1.     Faith for Personal Crises; NY: Scribners, 1958, p. 11.
2.     Ibid.
3.     Cf. John Godsey, "The Maturity of Faith in Carl Michalson's Theology," The Drew Gateway, 49, No. 3 (Spr 79), pp. 1-9. This volume, p. 41.
4.     Michalson, Worldly Theology; NY: Scribners, 1967, pp. 153f.
5.     Ibid., p. 207.
6.     Cf. Barth's attack on Bultmann's Melancthonian subjectivism in Rudolf Bultmann: Ein Versuch ihn zu verstehen; Zollikon-Zurich: Evangelischer Verlag, 1953, pp. 12ff, and Bultmann's defense in Essays; London: SCM Press, 1955, pp. 259ff.
7.     Cf. Michalson, The Hinge of History; NY: Scribners, 1959, p. 30; and Worldly Theology, p. 199.
8.     John Godsey, op. cit., p 3. Michalson was, of course, always very careful to distinguish this emphasis on meaning from subjectivism. His summary of Bultmann's presupposition of "the intentional nature of consciousness" is a good description of Michalson's own method: "Every act of consciousness is always a consciousness of something. Every subjective impression 'intends' an objective correlate. However, in acts of understanding, it is the relation of the subject to the object that is investigated. It is then that the question of the existence of the object is bracketed, for it is a secondary consideration. Only the question of its meaning is raised, for the question of meaning is the juncture at which consciousness joins itself to the object contemplated. That relationship is the meaning. Meaning does not inhere either in the subject (how I feel) or in the object (what it is), but in the meeting between subject and object (what is meant)" ("Rudolf Bultmann", in Ten Makers of Modern Protestant Thought ed by George L. Hunt; NY: Association Press, 1958, p. 106).
9.     Michalson, The Witness of Kierkegaard; NY: Association Press, 1960, p. 118; italics added.
10.    Worldly Theology, p. 151.
11.    Hermeneutics and the Worldliness of Faith, A Festschrift in Memory of Carl Michalson ed by Charles Courtney, Olin M. Ivey, and Gordon Michalson (Drew Gateway, Vol. 45), p. x.
12.    Worldly Theology, p. 184.
13.    Ibid., p. 151.
14.    Michalson even proposes to correct Bultmann at this point, whom he accused of maintaining "a rather traditional understanding of the Holy Spirit which augments historical work like a deus ex machina" (Rationality of Faith, pp. 54, 150ff).
15.    This is the title Michalson gave a shortened version which appeared in the Robert Calhoun Festschrift, The Heritage of Christian Thought ed by Robert E. Cushman and Egil Grislis; NY: Harper and Row, 1965, pp. 243ff. It was printed in its original version in Worldly Theology, under the title, "Holiness and the Maturity of Faith - John Wesley's Theology," pp. 127-158.
16.    Worldly Theology, p. 131.
17.    Ibid., p. 10.
18.    Wesley, Works, Vol. V, Jackson edition, 1872; reprinted by Zondervan; Grand Rapids, pp 463f.
19.    Ibid., p. 464.
20.    Ibid., p. 462.
21.    Ibid., p. 465.
22.    Ibid., p. 47.
23.    Ibid., p. 171.

24.     Worldly Theology, p. 138.
25.     Works, V:49.
26.     Cf. The Hinge of History, Part II.
27.     Worldly Theology, p. 203.
28.     The Rationality of Faith, p. 138.
29.     Worldly Theology, p. 203.
30.     Ibid., p. 158.
31.     Works, V:47.
32.     Worldly Theology, p. 203.
33.     The Rationality of Faith, p. 139.
34.     Worldly Theology, p. 151.
35.     Ibid., p. 158.

# MYTHIC RESONANCE: LIFE STORY AS THE SEARCH FOR STORY

James P. Carse

"According to my mother, the way I was born," Gerry said, "is that she went to the A&P and when she came home I jumped out from behind the kitchen door and surprised her. I actually believed this until I took health ed in junior high."

Gerry was a college girl friend. She told me this while we were taking a break from studying in the library. We were on our way to the A&W root beer stand in my Nash Rambler. I was telling her something about Don Hutson, all time great end for the Green Bay Packers, when she broke in with this peculiar little story. Why she told me at just that moment I cannot imagine. It certainly had no connection to Don, or with anything else we had been talking about. That it was a warm fall evening, that it was the nineteen fifties, that we were seniors in a midwestern college were all completely irrelevant to it.

Gerry laughed when she told me, not because of the oddness of the story but because she expected it to amuse me. But it didn't amuse me. It had no impact at all. On the contrary, I found it so inane that I dismissed it at once, without comment. Not only did I see no point to the story, I saw no point in her telling it. I took it to be a meaningless, forgettable falsehood, senseless to repeat.

So why then have I not forgotten it?  Why do I even recall such minute details as the way she interrupted my story about Don Hutson, or that she told it just as I was turning into the root beer stand?  Although I visited the place dozens of times in my college years, I have no other specific memory of being there.  I even recall the exact intonation of her voice and the way she was sitting in the far corner of the front seat, wearing my Milwaukee Braves cap.  Gerry was capable of making unexpected and usually thoughtful remarks, the kind you think at once you should try to remember.  Curiously, those remarks are nearly all lost while this thoughtless little tale lives on.

What the story might have meant to her I have no idea.  We spent countless hours in conversation but neither of us ever referred to this story again.  For that matter, once she got the facts straight about her origin, why didn't Gerry forget it herself?

I am not even sure why I tell the story here.  It popped up in my reflection with as little connection to anything around it as when I first heard it.  It has done this before, often.  Could it be that the story is not as inane as it appears?

The very persistence of this one sentence birth narrative is itself revealing.  It is not quite correct that I suddenly remembered the story.  It is rather that I never really forgot it.  Once heard, the tale took permanent residence in some reservoir of narrative fragments from which it leaps up now and then to grab my attention.  This may seem to imply that the story has its own life, that it acts by itself.  In fact, that is the way I experience it.  It simply elbows its way into whatever I am thinking whenever it wishes.  I don't search for it; it comes after me.  In more ordinary speech I would say, "the story occurred to me."

But isn't this always the case?  Do we actually "make up" our stories?  We see them there or we find them and later we tell them.  At least, this seems to be true of really good stories, the stories which once found or once heard we never forget.

I do not mean to suggest that we find good stories everywhere or that they are constantly popping up. When children tell stories, for example, they are rarely stories in the true sense, but chronicles - one event following another without the structure of a story. Children know a story when they hear one but they have not yet learned how to "find" a story in a mere sequence of actions. Children have not yet learned to let stories occur to them.

Finding stories is a skill, or an art, difficult even for educated adults. It does not require intelligence so much as a certain kind of openness, perhaps a need, or a special appetite for narrative. If you were asked to report what happened to you yesterday, you would probably offer a chronicle like what a child might offer and do so without much hesitation. If you were asked, however, to tell the story of what happened yesterday, you would hesitate. You would immediately stumble over the fact that the events you have just reported do not already come in the form of a story. It may take considerable thought to find the story in those events, if you find a story at all. If you do find it, you are likely to have the experience that you did not invent the story but that it popped up at you as you were looking over the facts.

The skill of telling begins with the skill of listening. Great storytellers are rarely big talkers. They are too busy paying attention. But when a story comes to them they will quickly find or create an occasion to tell it.

If good stories are rare and require special attention to find them, then how much rarer are great or truly important stories, and how much more deeply attentive you must be to find them - like the story of a life or the story of a culture, not to mention stories of the origin of humankind or the origin of the universe. Many stories are offered for greatness but very few are great enough they cannot be forgotten.

Inevitably, story and fact enter into uneasy tension with each other. No matter how carefully we line up the historical data or how honestly we report the actual events through which we have lived, this will not by itself tell the story of our lives. To tell all is not to tell a tale. Getting the facts straight is not enough to find the story to which they belong. In fact, getting the facts straight is a very different activity than that of finding a story that can be "faithful" to the facts.

The faithfulness of stories to fact is often the way we evaluate them. "Is that story true?" "Did that really happen?" The assumption is that stories live and die by fact. But here, too, experience tells us something else. Stories have an energy of their own. Fed by nothing but their inner brightness, they can race on without so much as a glance at the factual.

Because of such inner brightness, stories will command a sharper attention than facts, however appropriate facts may be to the matter under discussion. The way an audience is visibly awakened by a narrative example during an otherwise precisely factual lecture shows that stories touch us closer to a listener's center than accurate descriptions of objective states of affairs. The liveliness of a story seems to arouse a corresponding liveliness in its audience. Gerry would not have grabbed my Milwaukee Braves cap and slid over to her corner of the front seat to lecture on the gynecology of her conception and delivery, nor if she had would I have remembered. The mythic story of her birth was abruptly invalidated by a few physiological details but it obviously had far too much vitality to be buried by the truth.

In fact, the relation of fact and story might be just the opposite: it is fact that lives off story. A well told story may seem oblivious to one array of facts while drawing attention to another. Gerry's story is physiologically false but perhaps it lights up truths invisible to physiology, even invisible to our most sophisticated thought. Although physiology proves the story false, the story shows that physiology does not know the truth about Gerry's birth.

Birth may be a kind of fact but not the kind that responsible scientific thought can comprehend.

In searching for the deeper meaning of the myth of Gerry's birth, or of birth myths in general, we might begin by noting that birth and story have something in common: they both point to a mystery of origin. Answers to questions about where stories come from are as notoriously inadequate as the answers to questions about where babies come from. In this story it is remarkable that while Gerry does not actually come from her mother, the story does. If it is true that the mother did tell Gerry this story, she was probably responding to the child's demands to know where she came from. Why then did her mother tell a story when a few simple facts would have done the job? She may, of course, have wanted to avoid certain facts that were unpleasant or even unknown to her. But she might also have known that Gerry was not asking for facts. Gerry did not want to know where babies come from but where she came from. Perhaps the mother understood that the facts would not address that question. Indeed, there is every likelihood that Gerry's mother had the same question herself. If the mystery of her own origin had remained untouched by fact, how could she answer her daughter with the same useless knowledge?

The mystery of origin, after all, does not wait until we are old enough and educated enough to know the limitations of scientific knowledge. It emerges as soon as we experience our disconnectedness. As young children we can already see that however well defined our context may be, we do not quite fit into it. There is an irrelevance to our presence in the world. As the Romantics and then the Existentialists put it, our experience is characterized by an Undachbarheit, a rooflessness. We find an uncanniness or Unheimlichkeit, literally a not-at-home-ness, at the heart of being. Camus referred to this as the disproportionality between oneself and the world. What is a person like me doing in a place like this with people like you?

Somewhere deep within us something essential to our existence is as irrelevant and without context in the world as the story of Gerry's birth seemed to be in the Fall of 1953. There was no reason for her to tell that story. There is no reason for us to be here.

The resulting absurdity of personal existence, Camus continues, is not a threat to our liveliness but its very source. Contrary to popular thought, it is absolute rationality, a sense of inextricable connectedness, that leads to madness and suicide. Gerry's mother, either by design or accident, was protecting the child from the despair of rationality. I can tell you where babies come from, but that's not where you came from. Reason never surprises but you are nothing but surprise. Your very origin coincides with astonishment. Nothing about you is predictable.

Whatever the woman had in mind in telling this fable, it was brilliant enough that it kept her daughter off the question until she was twelve. A story will satisfy the way facts won't because a story, like a child, has a mysterious origin and no reason for being. Good stories also jump out and surprise us.

But not any story will do. Our question for Gerry's mother is not just why she would tell a story, but why she would tell this story. If, say, she had tossed off this little tale simply to shut the kid up, the story would no doubt have shown it. If the reason shows through and overpowers a story, the story will be quickly forgotten. Like the stories the Chinese leaders tell of the model soldier, Lei Feng, the designs behind the telling are so palpable that the story will never take a life of its own and live on in generations of storytellers, or if it does it won't be for the reasons the leaders had for telling the story to begin with.

When a story takes on its own life, the reasons for its first telling are quickly lost and subsequently have nothing to do with the story. That Melville wrote <u>Moby Dick</u> for money has absolutely nothing to do with the tale's abounding energy. A powerful story will display the mystery of its own origin within itself. Just as we know that Gerry did not really come from her parents, we know that a story does not really come from its author. When we search for a story's origin, trying to look it straight in the eye, what we find is not some ancient storyteller's intention, neither is it some archetypal pattern - for if this were the case we would just take hold of the pattern and forget the story. But it is the story that remains unforgettable and not the pattern. What we find at the deepest level of a story is the haunting presence of another story or maybe even many other stories. That is to say, one great story will lead us to another. They echo in each other. Deep stories call to still deeper stories. They resound with each other - just like we resound with each other.

The myth of Gerry's birth shows its brilliance only when we listen carefully to its narrative resonance, only when we hear the deeper myths that sound in it. In spite of its extreme brevity, this is a tale of essentially unlimited resonance.

It is, at the very least, a story of childhood prowess. A newborn leaps out from behind a door, a bold and calculated gesture full of advanced skill and a grownup sense of theatre. The resonance here is intense for the myths of heroes' births are full of such amazing acts, like Heracles strangling deadly serpents in his cradle, or the Buddha dropping without warning from his mother's womb, radiantly dressed in princely armor, announcing his greatness to the universe.

The element of surprise in the tale is rich with mythic echoes. Surprise, of course, can mean either delight or menace. Sarah, astounding those around her by giving birth to Isaac when she was at an advanced age, was an occasion for laughter. Jesus' birth occasioned both joy and terror. The unexpected appearance of the child, Krishna, was an erotic delight to the milkmaids but brought only jealous grief to their husbands.

If birth can be a surprise it can also be a shock and most dangerous to those around it. Rival or prior children are displaced - like the illegitimate

Arthur overshadowing his stepbrother Sir Kay, like Jacob tricking the firstborn Esau out of his inheritance. Gerry had older sisters but they were certainly crowded out of this myth; they are of no importance in determining her deeper identity. Since I happened to know they were women of strong personalities, there is something dark in their absence from this tale. Even that resonates.

This cautions us not to see the newborn as a helpless babe in arms, dependent on those around her, for we would overlook one of the central features of birth narratives: this small being is a terror. Even her possible appearance threatens existing orders of power, causing the powerful to protect themselves by such desperate measures as locking wives and daughters away to prevent their conceiving an heir and competitor. Any number of tiny rivals have been abandoned to rivers and seas, locked into cells and caves, left for dead in wastelands. The Pharaoh, King Herod, even the legendarily gentle Arthur of Camelot went so far as to slaughter an entire generation of children to make certain no babe would undo them.

On first hearing Gerry's story, we might think the mother's reaction would be one of happiness. Maternal happiness, however, has no mythic depth whatsoever. The mother, too, is in danger. She was not prepared for this little surprise and therefore anything can happen. There wasn't a hint when Gerry's mother left for the A&P there would even be a surprise waiting for her, much less a child. Accordingly, the mythic record is not kind to mothers. Like the Babylonian urgoddess Tiamat, their offspring sneak up on them with evil design. The hero god Marduk tricked Tiamat into opening her great maw which he entered unseen; then in a fury he destroyed her bone by splintered bone.

We are still not sure here whether Gerry heard this story from her mother or "found" it somehow by herself. It is however the case that neither woman knows how to connect herself directly to the other. In spite of the facts, the mother does not seem to believe this child came from her.

Ignorant of the facts, the child knows that her origin is too mysterious to be located in anyone or anything else. In short, the mythic danger to the mother is reflected in Gerry's story in the way both of them have eliminated the mother as mother.

Without question, however, the greater danger is to the father. The mother at least appears in this story and plays a crucial role. The father is not even mentioned. His absence is far more conspicuous in this story than the absence of the sisters. This is a fatherless birth, an event that occurs only in the presence of women with no male assistance whatsoever. It is typical of the great birth myths that the father's role is either ignored altogether or forced to be played out of view like the Holy Spirit secretly entering the virgin's womb or Zeus sneaking through the bars of Danae's cell outlandishly disguised as a shower of gold. The father in Gerry's myth has been done away with as decisively as Oedipus' father, Laertes, leaving only her mother to love, hate, or fear. If there is a miracle here, it is that the event defies all rational account. The fatherlessness of the tale is the primary mark of its triumph over rationality. It is another way of saying that my origin is not outside me and obvious, but within me and hidden.

The mother, on the other hand, although in some danger and with a doubtful connection to the daughter, is far more formidable than the father. Her enormity is clearly represented in Gerry's myth. She has come back from a journey to the A&P like Demeter with the seasonal fruits to greet Persephone at her emergence from the obscurity of Tartarus. Even grander, for she has come from the A&P, the Atlantic and the Pacific Tea Company, representative of the vast oceans that embrace us all, the beginning and the end, watery birth and watery death, like the serpent Ouroboros eternally consuming and giving birth to itself. The A&P is a supermarket, a higher exchange, an inexhaustible reservoir, a place so complete it can embrace its own contradictions: it is both abbatoir and garden, sacrifice and harvest, death and life. In the mythic record providing food and consuming it often overlap. What the mother gives she can take away. The child is fed by the mother but can also be eaten by the mother. Gerry surprises an unprepared mother but she is even less prepared for the surprises her mother might have for her.

She finds Gerry, after all, in the kitchen. Children know the kitchen as the place where you can be burned and cut but also fed and mended. But myth knows the kitchen as a hags' workshop where knife and fire are the chief media, where small animals and children are chopped up and brewed into magical concoctions and potions.

And where did Gerry hide? Behind the door, the portal, the gates, an architecture of ceremony: "Lift your head, O ye gates, that the Queen of Glory may come in!" The door is also a symbol of passage, a boundary between realms, a line of no return, a threshold of irreversible loss: "Abandon hope all ye who enter." It is a barrier at which one age meets another, and a threshold across which one age becomes another. It is a site of hostility but also of hospitality. Just as it can lock away the old it can open to the new: "Knock and it shall be opened." What it opens to we can never know before we knock.

Why Gerry was behind that door we never learn, and neither did her mother. This child was an angel of surprise but what she was surprising her mother with was not yet completely revealed. In fact, her mother may have told the story this way exactly because she did not herself yet know the outcome. She knew at the time she told it that she was not telling a story about Gerry's birth but about Gerry. Even at the time she was telling the story she may not have known whether Gerry was opening or shutting that door. This is common enough in myth where birth and death merge seamlessly into one another. This is what is hidden from physiology but so obvious to her mother.

Of course, Gerry did not say any of this. Indeed, we can be certain nothing of the sort passed through her mind. Maybe nothing at all passed through her mind. By the time the carhop in her cute little uniform was looking in at me through the window of my Nash Rambler and asking for our order, the story itself had left us and returned to its dragon's lair where it would wait until it needed to be heard again. We had no such understanding at the time. But we didn't need to. The thousand threads that connect Gerry's story to the race's most unforgettable tales belong not to us but to the story. It is the story, not the listener, that resonates. We could hear the deeps sounding in this handful of words but we did not know what treasure those deeps contain, nor do we now, nor will we ever.

Gerry had no reason to tell her story at that moment. There was no point to my listening to it. The story had its own reasons for leaping out at us with so little warning. It was sounding us. But we were an easy catch. We were in a state of acute narrative need. In our last year of college, we old enough to know that our childhood was forever behind us but too young to be certain what lay ahead. We were on a journey but it was not to a root beer stand. The inner design of that journey was hidden and there is nothing about ourselves and our world that we wanted to know more than where that journey was taking us. This was more than an appetite for narrative. It was a case of mythic starvation.

While we were oblivious and uninterested in the stories that lay in the shadows of Gerry's mythic birth, we were aware that we did not know our own story. Gerry and I wanted to know each other as intimately as possible but what we wanted to know in each other is not how our inner parts looked and worked but where all this was going to end, whether we got there together or alone. We tried to tell each other our stories in the form of hopes and dreams, as though we were looking back at a life we had not yet lived. This only made the mysterious more mysterious.

Gerry's myth made its appearance that soft fall evening as a story of origin. But it might as well have been a tale of destiny, for how could our ending be any less a surprise than our beginning? There was no possibility I would forget it.

* * *

One of the more comforting illusions of growing older is the belief that we have grown into a more complete understanding of the story of our lives. It is true that there is a greater quantity of fact. The chronicle is longer and we are probably more willing to let chronicle stand for story. But, still, a chronicle has no design, no meaning, no energy of its own. It is an accidental sequence, perfectly forgettable and empty of all mythic resonance.

Decades passed and I decided I would go back to that college for a scheduled class reunion. Except for the public lecture I had delivered there shortly after I started teaching, this would be my first visit. It was clear enough why I wanted to go back. If I took a closer look at the chronicle, I thought, I might find new threads of my story. Is there something I knew then but have since forgotten? Maybe if I answered some of the boy's questions the man would have a clearer vision of his own still unfolding narrative.

Strangely, I found myself hoping my best college friends would not be there. What would I tell them about myself? What did I want to know about them? And, of course, I wanted to avoid the pain of acknowledging the way friendships can be so deeply made and just as quickly abandoned.

It was a hot clear day with just a hint of an afternoon thunderstorm. Small groups of alumni drifted onto the large lawn, looking. I found the sign for my graduating year and walked up. A young man seized my hand like I was an old friend, tossing off his name quickly as though I must already know it, but too quickly to recognize. When he did this to several others, I realized this was the college president. In the first sweep of my assembled class not a familiar face emerged. Relieved, I stepped away and studied the campus architecture. Very little had changed but it was all oddly remote.

"Hi there."

A small, round woman about my age but with a remarkably smooth face and clear happy eyes was looking up at me.

"Hi, Gerry."

We quickly exchanged facts. She had married her high school boyfriend. They have four children, two in medical school. Girls. I offered a corresponding chronicle. Her husband appeared and introduced himself. They were holding hands. He referred to her as Geraldine. We agreed it was the kind of day you can expect to end with a thunderstorm.

There was a sort of a parade with the oldest classes at the front leading us into the new sports complex for a sit down lunch. By then I knew that the person I was looking for was not in that crowd, so I decided to skip lunch and look around.

I had some good guesses as to where I could find him but I was a little worried I might not recognize him. I had only the vaguest sense of his appearance, even after looking up his photographs in the college annual. These were the photos of a dreamer, someone there and yet not there.

First I thought I'd try to find him coming down from the old fraternity houses up on the hill. Nobody there, so I looked in the library, but it had been expanded so many times that I had to ask the librarian for directions. It was quite empty. The football practice fields were so unchanged that even the grass smelled the same. But the blocking sleds had been pushed off the field and stowed away in the stadium. The stadium, too, was empty except for the swallows picking feathery insects out of the windless June air. I stopped in a few of his favorite classrooms, sitting for a while in his regular seat in the Shakespeare seminar room.

I never really found him. Something stranger happened. It was later that afternoon. I was sitting near the spring at the bottom of the campus when he walked by. I didn't recognize him even then but he recognized me. I caught him standing there, taking in the graying hair and what had been an athlete's body.

--Well, here you are, he said.

He seemed almost stunned by my appearance. I was suddenly selfconscious and, in fact, a little pained that he had to see me this way. I wasn't sure what to say to him.

--It's beautiful here, I said.

He nodded absently.

--It's as beautiful as I remember it.

I wondered for a moment if he actually saw the beauty. He seemed to be somewhere else and not noticing much around him. There was a long pause. He sat down, not close, and turned toward me.

--So what are you doing now?

I told him. He looked down at his feet in silence.

--You're disappointed.

--So you never played pro ball?

--Nope. I know the coaches encourage you but, frankly, you're not that good.

--You could have been a coach.

--I know. Maybe it was a mistake but I chose not to. In fact, other things came up and it ceased being a choice at all.

--So you're just a teacher. A professor.

--Just a teacher.

--You're obviously not rich. You famous?

Rich? Famous? This was a surprise. I found it hard to believe he could take such things seriously.

--Only with my friends, I answered.

He wasn't amused.

--I mean, any brilliant books to your name? You teach in a great university?

--No, neither of those.

--What about Gerry?

--Each of us married someone else.

--Someone else? How can that be? I've never met anyone like Gerry.

So far he had just been disappointed. But this was completely unexpected. He obviously could not take it in and just stared at me.

--I fell in love with someone else. That's all I can tell you.

--What happened to Gerry? Wasn't she upset. I mean, God, she really loves me.

--She was upset. She sent back everything you ever gave her in a big box. The first thing, right on top, was your Milwaukee Braves cap.

--She...?

--But I doubt if she was very upset. She married that guy she was dating when you met her.

--The one from her hometown that goes to Harvard?

--That one.

--She's much too good for him.

--She seems happy. She has four kids, all older than you.

--What's she like? Your wife, I mean.

--If you met her right now, I doubt if you would notice her. You sure wouldn't fall in love with her. But then, she wouldn't be too crazy about you either. You have some growing up to do before you and this woman can love each other.

This comment didn't reach him. He sat quietly for a while then pressed me again about my career. Why would I become a teacher, of all things? He never once thought of doing that. The fact that I live in New York City was alarming to him.

--New York City?

--New York City.

--How could you have a campus there?

--We don't.

--And you raised your kids there, too?

We talked a lot about my children. They are definitely not like the children that he and Gerry talk about having. They are so shockingly different from those children that he began to see for the first time how much his life would have to change, how profoundly he would have to alter his understanding of himself.

--Those dreams of yours, I said. They're lousy dreams. Not one will come true.

I began to realize that if the boy was disappointed in me, I was much more disappointed in him. I was even a little angry. What a limited vision of his future this young man had.

--And it's a good thing those dreams haven't come true, I continued. You may not want to be where I am but I can tell you that I definitely prefer being where I am to where I would have been if even your most heroic fantasies had come true.

I believe I went on like this for some time. After a while I became aware that he was no longer listening. He had turned toward me, waiting for me to finish, and smiling.

--You seem to have forgotten who I am, he said.

It was the tone of this remark that caught my attention. There was authority in it. This I had not expected.

--I don't know why you think you've come back here. To me you're just looking for a sucker you can deliver these sermons to. You talk like you've arrived, like you've gone out into the world and made it, like you got your little journey all wrapped up. And now you come back trying to straighten things up here. You say I'd better clean up my dreams or I'll never end up where you are. But, you've forgotten something, haven't you? It's these dreams that got you where you are.

This isn't bad, I thought. The kid's a better thinker than I remembered him to be. I realized for the first time how well he understood the inadequacy of dreaming. He already got the main point: it was not that he wasn't good enough to fulfill his dreams but that his dreams were not good enough to fulfill him. His dreams were not of the story he hoped he would live but simply a way of reaching out for that story.

The boy had more to say. I was a bit apprehensive at what was coming.

--You forget something else, coming back here like this. You talk like my future is all question mark and yours is all exclamation point. Look again. You really think the end of your story is whatever you tell it as? You actually believe the question mark's gone?

He's right, of course. I had been trying to show the boy a future his present had not foreseen but now he was showing me a present that's as blind as his - and as full of surprise. I was afraid of hearing something like this. I could see this wasn't all.

--You really want to tell me like I was a story, wouldn't you? You'd like me to be the myth of your childhood or something. But I'm sorry. I don't tell like that. I'm no more a story you can tell than you are. I mean, what is there to tell? You look back at me and what do you see? You see me looking ahead at you. Now, how can you tell that?

That's true. I came back, looking. I wanted to find someone I could put in my story like a character. I would give him his lines, of course, but I would do it carefully, remaining faithful to the facts of his life. I would write only the words he really said. He could play his own real part and I would just watch. More than that, I would listen. I really wanted to learn from it. I wanted to be able to see the plot lines, to catch the narrative thread that connects one generation to another - in myself. But this is what the boy already knew: he is not a character in anybody's story, he does not live by a script. No matter how honestly I try to describe and quote him, no matter how artistically I evoke him, I will miss him and miss him completely. This is why honesty and accuracy are not enough. I came back to find my story and the story I found is that of the search for a story.

In fact, it was his reaching out for a story that made his story possible. If he had been living out a script already composed, if he was really trying to be Don Hutson, there would have been no story there.

The boy did not yet have his story. And I don't have one for him now; neither do I have one for myself. At the same time, the boy knows and I know that life is not a mere chronicle, an adventitious parade of facts. There is a story, maybe a whole mythic lore, that has decided to tell itself by way of our life, but in doing so it necessarily remains hidden from us. We cannot simultaneously live it and view it from without; we cannot stand at its conclusion and also wonder at its outcome.

Therefore, each of my stories about myself is flawed. If it is truly my story, I cannot be its author. There will be something in the story to show that I am not its hero but its fool, that I am neither the master of my destiny nor its victim, but an active participant in it. Every story I find in my experience, every story I tell about myself must therefore show that it is not the story I think it is. If it is truly a story of me it will be a story about getting my story wrong.

This is what astonished the man, to see that the boy already understood this. I thought if I stepped out of my story to look at it, if I paused in my journey to get a clear grasp of what kind of a journey this is, I would finally be able to tell it. What the boy already knew is that by the time I have done that I have become a character in a scripted tale I do not and cannot live in. It is what I thought the boy himself was doing with Don Hutson.

-Don Hutson?

--Don't you remember with what perfect passion you would have changed places with Don?

--Sure, who wouldn't? So what?

The boy seemed confused that I would use this story against him. I tried again to remember that fall night.

--You were telling Gerry the story about Don when she interrupted you with her childhood birth fantasy.

--Right. I got to the part about where I went out for football in high school for the first time. That's where she cut me off.

--Would you have told her the whole story? With the ending?

--I am not sure. Maybe not.

This was a kind of admission, I suppose. But I noticed that he was smiling again.

--At least I know the ending, whether I tell it or not. That's the important thing, isn't it?

*       *       *

You didn't go to see the Chicago Bears play the Green Bay Packers when Don Hutson was the Packers' star, you went to see Don Hutson play in the game between the Bears and the Packers. The final score mattered much less to the fans than the brilliant catches they expected Don to make. They were rarely disappointed. He is arguably the greatest end ever to play the game.

I saw Don every chance I got. I had a lot of chances because he was a hero for the whole family and we bought our tickets early.

I cut a full page picture of Don from the program of one of the games and glued it to the wall above my bed. It showed Don leaping skyward and looking back over his shoulder for the ball. His left knee was raised against his chest and his right toe was pointed straight back at earth. With his hands he had formed the perfect basket that every player emulated: the left arm extended full out and the right slightly under it and bent in the classical cradle shape. There wasn't the least doubt he would sweep the ball out of the air, complete the arc of this balletic leap and head for glory. I was fourteen when Don retired from professional football. We learned of it from a headline in our local newspaper. Editorials were full of phrases like "the close of an age" and "the last of the greats."

Not two months later a much larger headline dominated the front page of the same paper: HUTSON BUYS CADILLAC AGENCY IN CITY. We had not seen print this large since VJ Day. Editorials spoke of "the beginning of an era," and "the presence of greatness."

One hot summer day, my brother and I were out tossing a football to each other across our lawn and onto the lawn of the vacant house next door. The two yards together made an acceptably large touch football field. Hot as it was, we were adding further refinements to the Don Hutson catch.

We stopped to watch as a moving truck pulled up next door. The house had been empty for months and we were wild with curiosity to see if anyone our age was moving in. By the time most of the contents of the truck had been spread out on the lawn, it was obvious there was no adolescent in this household.

A yellow Cadillac convertible turned the corner at the end of the block and came slowly in our direction. It pulled in behind the moving truck and stopped softly at the curb. The top was down. A handsome man with a deep tan and sunbleached hair sat behind the wheel. He opened the door, got out, and walked around the front of the car.

No mere mortal could step to the curb with such perfect grace.

My brother and I were standing at the edge of his yard, unable to breathe, motionless as the pieces of furniture all around us.

"Hi, boys."

That's all he said: "Hi, boys." In fact, in all the time the Hutsons lived next door to us, he never said anything but, "Hi, boys." This was, of course, no ordinary "Hi." It was said in the slow, rich drawl of Don's native Alabama, and to the ear of a Wisconsin boy it could not have been more magnetizing or more exotic if he had been speaking Aztec.

Starting the next day, our yard became the site of an endless touch football game. Boys we hardly knew would stop us on the street to tell us their best dirty joke and split a Baby Ruth bar with us, on the outside chance we would include them in a game. Sometimes whole mornings, whole afternoons, ten or twenty of us would do nothing but practice our Don Hutson catches between his house and ours. I could do killer imitations of Don opening the garage door, Don sliding into his Cadillac, Don touching his forehead and saying "Hi, boys."

That Fall I went out for high school football for the first time. I marked off the days until the first practice. An unusually large number of boys appeared for tryouts so the equipment manager had to go back deeper into the storage rooms to suit all of us. Instead of a uniform as such, you got a heap of parts, dozens of parts, in a big laundry bag. There were pads, straps, guards, shirts with numbers, shirts without numbers, things made of loosely attached pieces that had no apparent inside or outside, miscellaneous elastic bands and wraps, odd leather pieces that seemed to go nowhere. It was hard to think of Don putting on this stuff. Carefully but not too conspicuously watching others, I did manage to get most of it on. I had the most trouble with the helmet. It was a hinged sort of affair. If I put it on one way, it didn't protect my ears. The other way, I couldn't see. Finally, I found if I tightened the strap across the front of my chin I could make it serve both functions pretty well.

The coach told us to line up at our positions. Easily three-fourths of the boys were there to play end. When his lecture recommending other spots on the team didn't work, the coach said he would have last year's star quarterback throw all of us ends some passes so he could get a sense of our talent for the position.

This was my moment. I felt the thrilling whisper of destiny. When my turn came, I shot off down field, pumping my knees. I turned sharply to the right, sprang perfectly from the earth, made the classic basket, and turned back just in time to see the ball sail beyond me. Crashing to the ground, I found myself rudely stuck, pinched, and jabbed by assorted pieces of uniform. Plenty of pain but no injury so I bounced up and raced back to the line.

On my second try, I got off the ground much more effectively, but a shoulder pad that had come loose in the fall popped up, blocking my vision, so I never saw the ball. The third time, I snagged a cleat on some kind of a pad that had slipped down around my ankle and took an unexpected roll three steps from the line. I was still not discouraged, however, since there was no question that, once I got this uniform business straightened out, my innate talent for the position would be obvious.

The coach lined us up and started assigning positions, pointing recklessly from boy to boy. "You. You play tackle," he said to someone in my direction. "No, you," he said. I thought for a moment he was talking to me. I looked around.

"That's right. You. The one with the helmet on backwards."

--Is that the way you remember it? I asked the boy.

--Exactly what happened.

--And so you became a tackle, the player no one notices, always on the bottom of the pile.

I was a little surprised at the way I said this. Maybe I still thought he could do better. But the boy was smiling again. It would be too much to say that he was happy with what he was seeing. It is rather the way you smile when you realize that what you thought would happen did happen.

--You don't look much like you could play tackle now, he said. But I'll bet there's one thing that's never changed. I'll bet you still can't get your helmet on straight.

--Sometimes I'm sure I've got everything right. Then later I discover the helmet. What I discover is that although I did almost everything right, what I really did is put my helmet on wrong.

--Like now.

--What do you mean?

--You are almost getting these thoughts straight, but what you are really doing is sitting here in this thunderstorm.

*     *     *

The carhop was fidgeting at the window. I had given her my order and was still trying to coax one out of Gerry. She leaned down and looked across the front seat, reciting the list of ice cream flavors to Gerry one more time.

"How about a weenie and a pop, honey?" I asked.

Gerry had pulled my Milwaukee Braves cap down over her ears and was moaning with indecision.

Finally, she raised her face enough that I could just see her eyes under the brim of the cap, and said, "Surprise me."

I never did.

## FURTHER READING

Roy C. Amore and Larry D. Shinn, Lustful Maidens and Ascetic Kings: Buddhists and Hindu Stories of Life; NY: Oxford University Press, 1981. xii + 198 pp.

Peter L. Berger, The Sacred Canopy: Elements of a Sociological Theory of Religion; Garden City: Doubleday, 1969. vii + 229 pp.

Bruno Bettelheim, The Uses of Enchantment: The Meaning and Importance of Fairy Tales; NY: Knopf, 1976. vi + 328 pp.

Robert McAfee Brown, "Story and Theology." pp. 55-72 in Philosophy, Religion and Theology ed James W. McClendon. Missoula: Scholar's Press, 1974.

Jerome Bruner, "Life As Narrative," Social Research 54 (1987), 11-32.

Martin Buber, Tales of the Hasidim, 2 vols; NY: Schocken, 1948.

Gabriel Fackre, "Narrative Theology: An Overview," Interpretation 37 (1983), 340-352.

Michael Goldberg, Theology and Narrative: A Critical Introduction; Nashville: Abingdon, 1982. 304 pp.

Stanley Hauerwas and L. Gregory Jones, Why Narrative? Readings in Narrative Theology; Grand Rapids: Eerdmans, 1989. viii + 367 pp. Excerpts and essays drawn from publications from 1941-1988. After the editors' introduction (to the subject as well as the book) come three parts on story rediscovered (H. Richard Niebuhr, et al.), as a critical tool (Lash, et al.) and the theological significance of story (Metz, et al).

James W. McClendon, Jr., Biography as Theology: How Life Stories Can Remake Today's Theology; Nashville: Abingdon, 1974. 224 pp.

Rafe Martin, The hungry Tigress: Buddhist Legends and Jataka Tales, rev. Berkeley, CA: Parallax Press, 1990. 288 pp. (original 1984)

Kirin Narayan, Storytellers, Saints, and Scoundrels: Folk Narrative in Hindu Religious Teaching; Philadelphia: University of Pennsylvania, 1989. xi + 285 pp.

Paul Nelson, Narrative and Morality. A Theological Inquiry; University Park: Pennsylvania State University Press, 1987. 180 pp.

Wendy Doniger O'Flaherty, Other Peoples' Myths: The Cave of Echoes; NY: Macmillan, 1988. x + 225 pp.

Paul Ricoeur, Time and Narrative, 3 vols; Chicago: University of Chicago Press, 1984-.

J. Wesley Robbins, "Narrative, Morality and Religion." Journal of Religious Ethics 8 (1980), 161-176.

Terence W. Tilley, Story Theology; Wilmington, DE: Glazier, 1985.

James Wiggins, ed., Religion as Story; NY: Harper & Row, 1975. 218 pp.

# III.

# BIBLICAL INTERPRETATION

# COSMIC DIMENSIONS OF THE GENESIS
## CREATION ACCOUNT

Bernhard W. Anderson

Three recent books have focused attention sharply on the biblical doctrine of creation, and specifically the Genesis creation account.

The first carries the curious title, Is God a Creationist?[1] As indicated by the subtitle, "The Religious Case Against Creation-Science," this book was evoked by the recent controversy over the teaching of the origin of the universe in public schools. Advocates of so-called "creation science," a term coined to refer to a strictly literal interpretation of the Genesis creation account, maintained in a losing court case that this view deserves equal time with a scientific account, especially the doctrine of evolution. In this book, edited by Roland Frye, Professor of English at the University of Pennsylvania, the case against creationism is argued by Jewish, Protestant, and Roman Catholic leaders (including Pope John Paul II). The argument rests on the premise that God has two books - one the Bible which deals with God's relation to human beings, and the other the book of Nature, which displays God's work of creation. It is a mistake to confuse these two books by supposing that each gives the same kind of knowledge, although they belong side by side in the library.

The second recent book is entitled Cry of the Environment: Rebuilding the Christian Creation Tradition.[2] This book, edited by Philip Joranson and

Ken Butigan, is a project of the Center for Ethics and Social Policy in Berkeley, California. The contributors to this volume agree that Christian tradition has been so preoccupied with human salvation, that is, the relation between God and human beings, that it has failed to give adequate attention to the natural world. The essayists, however, are primarily concerned about refurbishing the doctrine of creation, so that both nature and history, the human and the nonhuman creation, are given proper theological consideration. This could be an exciting textbook for our time!

The third recent book, God and the Astronomers, is by Robert Jastrow, the NASA astrophysicist who has a flair for writing about science. A preface informs us that the core of the book was originally presented as a Phi Beta Kappa lecture to the American Association for the Advancement of Science in 1978. Subsequently it appeared in the New York Times Magazine under the flamboyant title, "Have Astronomers Found God?" The essay describes the debate between the so-called "steady state" theory which holds that the universe has no beginning and will have no ending, hence is eternal; and, on the other hand, what is popularly called "the big-bang theory," which holds that the universe was created in a fiery explosion at a sharply defined instant, some 16 billion years ago. Jastrow, a self-professed agnostic, maintains that the big-bang theory, which now commands the field, brings us close to the story of creation found at the beginning of the Bible, a story that opens by portraying the origin of the universe in a cosmic flash of light. He concludes with an oft-quoted paragraph that has brought laughter to many:

> "At this moment it seems as though science will never be able to raise the curtain on the mystery of creation. For the scientist who has lived by his faith in the power of reason, the story ends like a bad dream. He has scaled the mountains of ignorance; he is about to conquer the highest peak; as he pulls himself over the final rock, he is greeted by a band of theologians who have been sitting there for centuries."[3]

What these three books have in common, despite their divergent approaches, is the attempt to understand the cosmic dimension of the biblical creation faith. There was a time, not too long ago, when theologians and biblical interpreters were in swift retreat from "cosmology," a term which refers to the study of the universe as a whole and the interrelation of its parts. The Bible, it was said, deals with "anthropology, not cosmology. What cosmology it has belongs to the naive "three storied view of the universe" - heaven, earth, and underworld - that Israel shared with other ancient peoples. Hence the task of the interpreter is to demythologize the world view of the Bible, that is, to translate its cosmological language into terms which modern persons can appreciate existentially. Carl Michalson, to whom this lecture is dedicated, was one of the most scintillating stars in this hermeneutical constellation, generally identified with the name of Rudolph Bultmann.

That was a significant chapter in modern theological thought which sought to come to terms with the exciting new vistas of science. We have come to realize that the Bible is not a book of nature, but a book which addresses the inescapable issues of what it means to be a human being in a world of mystery, uncertainty and threat. The Bible, we have found, does not deal with the processes and interconnections of "how" but the purpose and design of the "Who." Moreover, we know that the Bible is not written in the kind of language in which words function to represent the precise sense of factual propositions (Wittgenstein). Biblical literalism, as Conrad Hyers observes in a stunning essay, is a form of "constricting the cosmic dance." Quoting the statement of the early ethnologist R. R. Marett that "religion is not so much thought out as danced out," he goes on to say:

> But even when thought out, religion is focused in the verbal equivalent of the dance: myth, symbol and metaphor. To insist on assigning to it a literal, one-dimensional meaning is to shrink and stifle and distort the significance.[4]

All of this is true as far as it goes, and many of us have been saying these things in one way or another. However, the danger of a retreat from the dimension of the cosmological into the dimension of the anthropological, the existential, or the aesthetic is that the realm of the nonhuman, what we call "nature," is regarded as theologically out of bounds. This in turn may result in an abdication of responsibility for the environment in which we live and move and have our being, and it may foster a sharp dichotomy between religion and science. Theologians today find themselves in a time of startling new horizons of science - in astronomy, physics, biology, medicine, and more - and that calls for a theology with cosmological interests.

So, in this new situation in which we find ourselves I would like to take a new step - maybe "a giant step" comparable to that human step on the moon - and to consider with you the <u>cosmic</u> implications of the Genesis creation story. I am intrigued by Robert Jastrow's suggestion that scientists have ventured into an area which theologians have occupied for centuries! However, I am not altogether satisfied with his illustration. For one thing, many theologians in recent years have left the mountain in order to concentrate on more pressing issues of liberation down in the valley. Moreover, one wonders about the encounter itself. Can these two, the agnostic scientist and the believing theologian, who speak different languages and espouse different modes of knowing, actually shake hands on meeting and talk together, realizing that they share - if not common meanings - common interests at least? Modestly realizing that, as a biblical theologian, I am going out beyond my depth, I invite you to turn again to the Genesis creation story, and specifically to consider three matters of common interest: the mystery of origination, the mystery of cosmic order, and the mystery of the emergence of life.

I.  <u>The Mystery of Origination</u>  The Genesis creation story opens with words that unfold before us the far horizon of the ultimate beginning of all things in a cosmic perspective: "In the beginning God created the heaven and the earth." This lapidary sentence, according to the usual translation, carries us imaginatively into the Time known only to God, before there were any witnesses to the mystery of creation, before there were any instruments to measure or calculate. Nothing survives as evidence for human examination, and even the boldest scientists can fall back only on imaginative inference. It is the beginning, therefore, which exceeds human comprehension and which can only be spoken about in poetic or mythopoeic language. This is the mystery which finally overwhelmed Job, after all his expostulations with God and his attempt to penetrate the secret of cosmos. The Voice out of the Whirlwind ignored his questioning and, instead, put the question to him:

> Where were you when I laid earth's foundations?
>     Tell me if you have gained discernment!
> Who fixed its dimensions? Surely you know!
>     Or who stretched out the measuring line over it?
> On what were its pillars sunk?
>     Or who set is cornerstone,
> When the morning stars sang together
>     and all the [heavenly beings] shouted for joy?[5]

Admittedly, there is some grammatical uncertainty about the first word of the Bible (bereshith, "In beginning"). Some translators argue that this word does not refer to an absolute beginning but initiates a circumstantial clause that leads up to verse 3: "In the beginning of God's creating the heavens and the earth....then God said, 'Let there be light.'" So for instance the American Jewish translation: "When God created the heaven and the earth - earth being unformed and void, with darkness over the surface of the deep and a wind from God sweeping over the water - God said, 'Let there be light.' and there was light." (So also NEB and NAB). This interpretation goes back especially to the medieval scholar Rashi (Rabbi Shlomo son of Yitzhaq), who said that "the plain sense" of this passage is not to teach the order of creation, i.e. heaven and earth first in the sequence, but rather say that in the creative process the first significant divine event was the creation of light.

Translation, of course, is an act of interpretation. The Italians have a proverb to the effect that "translators are betrayers" (traduttori sono traditori), and perhaps the first verses of Genesis illustrate this hermeneutical boldness. Some years ago my colleague at Princeton Theological Seminary, George Hendry, gave a presidential address to the American Theological Society on "The Eclipse of Creation," in which he chided theologians, and especially biblical theologians (myself included), for reducing creation to a relationship between God and creation (creaturely dependence) or a dimension of history (salvation) and for failing to deal with the biblical witness to creation as origination.[6] The influential biblical theologian, Gerhard von Rad, insisted that in Israel's faith, creation was ancillary to election, that is, the story of God's involvement with Israel.[7] Another theologian, Claus Westermann, goes so far as to say that "the stories of origins are concerned with the subsistence of the world and mankind, not with the intellectual question of the origin."[8] It may be that the time cometh and now is when biblical theologians, like Job, should "repent in dust and ashes" in the face of the cosmological mysteries of creation.

Even if one follows Rashi and construes the first two verses of Genesis as a circumstantial clause leading up to the main sentence in verse 3, the creation of light is to be understood as a cosmological event. But there are, in my judgment, compelling reasons to follow translations (e.g. RSV, JB, NIV) which take the first Hebrew word of the Bible (bereshith, Greek en arche) to refer to an absolute beginning. For one thing, the creation verbs used ("created" [bara'], "made" ['asa]) indicate something more than "the subsistence of the world and mankind;" they connote origination. Furthermore, if the formula "these are the generations of" actually introduces the story of the Garden of Eden (Gen 2:4a), as redaction criticism would show, then the creation story in Genesis 1 is placed before the genealogical sequences of the book of Genesis and deals with what is prehistorical and even suprahistorical. Add to this the testimony of the Greek translation of the Old Testament (Septuagint) which renders the first verse as an independent sentence and we reach the plausible conclusion that the first word of the Hebrew Bible refers to an absolute beginning of the cosmos.

It is not accidental, then, that the Bible opens with the story of creation, or that this story opens with a sentence that deals with the very beginning. The Biblical Story starts at the beginning, as does any good story; but this is the beginning for which there was no other beginning, no other story.

In short, the biblical creation story deals with a cosmic matter: the origination of all things, and it is in this sense that theologians have understood creation down through the centuries. Creation means that the cosmos is finite: it had a beginning and it will have an end. This belief seems to be, at least superficially, in agreement with the scientific view that the universe came into being in a cosmic flash, like the flash of a cosmic hydrogen explosion, at a sharply defined instant, some sixteen billion years ago. That explosion, says the poet Robinson Jeffers, exceeds the powers of human expression:

.....All that exists
Roars into flame, the tortured fragments rush away from each other
    into all the sky, new universes
Jewel the black breast of night; and far off the outer nebulae like
    charging spearmen again
Invade emptiness.[9]

That is the way the biblical story begins: with a cosmic flash of light, "God said, let there be light, and light came." Furthermore, in the biblical story this primeval light (Urlicht) is not associated with the light from the sun and the stars, heavenly bodies that came later in the drama of creation (Gen 1:14-15). It seems that the scientist and the theologians share a common cosmological interest, though they see things from different angles and with different modes of knowing.

Here we face a problem in the philosophy of language. Scientific language, as we know, aims for mathematical exactitude and objectivity, even though its symbolism presses reason into the realm of imagination. It is based on human observation, experimentation, and control, and is - above all - neutral about questions of meaning. That is the language that has enabled us to bend nature to human control, to achieve marvels in the field of medicine, to revolutionize transportation and communication, and to launch explorations into space. But the biblical story is written in a different kind of language - language that provides a different approach to reality via the faculty of poetic intuition and artistic imagination. And this language, akin to expressions in art, poetry, and music, functions metaphorically to reveal the God who is beyond the human world yet involved in it. Biblical language does not aim for accuracy of description, but uses language inaccurately, as does a poet, to allude to God who is beyond description and explanation.

These two languages should not be confused. Religious (mythopoeic) language cannot be converted into scientific language any more than poetry can be reduced to prose. And, on the other hand, scientific language, which methodologically is godless, can hardly be equated with religious language which deals with who the Creator is and the Creator's design. Nevertheless, these languages intersect at points of common cosmological interest. Therefore, when the scientist and the theologian meet, neither should claim to be "king of the mountain," to recall a childhood game some of us used to play. They should be able to enter into dialogue as friends who stand humbly before the mysteries of creation.

II.    The Mystery of Order Turn now to a second dimension of the biblical creation story: cosmic order. It is not just that the cosmos originated in the creative will of God, but God is the one who gives order to the vast cosmic whole in which everything, from the least particle to the largest star, has its proper place and function.

If the Genesis creation account comes to us from the hand of Priestly theologians, according to the judgment of critical scholarship, we can understand the concern for order that is manifest in the structure of the story itself. The story displays an aesthetic order. It begins with an announcement of God's creation in the beginning (1:1), and the story is rounded off at the end with the announcement that the Creator's purpose was accomplished (2:1-3). Each creative act is stated in a formulaic style that emphasizes order: The Creator (the Executive) speaks, and the command is executed. Moreover, in between the opening and the closing of the literary unit, the creation drama unfolds in two major movements, each of which occupies three "days" with two acts of creation on each of the triads of days. And in each of these two major sections, the reader's attention is directed from heaven to earth: in the first instance, the greening of the earth with vegetation, and in the second the population of the green earth with creatures that live and move and breathe.

It is possible to study this story only as a work of literary art, and to observe its stylistic symmetry and ordered wholeness. What strikes me theologically, however, is the narrator's emphasis upon cosmic order, which was not only a matter of observation but of theological wonder.

This is true also in the case of Psalm 104, which follows essentially the same sequences as the Genesis creation story. In this psalm we find the motif of Wisdom: "In Wisdom God made all the creatures" (Ps 104:24). The sages of the ancient world produced lists of observed phenomena and catalogued them in categories based on observation. The Genesis creation story reflects wisdom thinking to the degree that it displays a studied reflection on things observed in the earth and the universe. Let me mention only one small detail: we read that "the earth brought forth vegetation:

(1) plants yielding seed according to their kind [min], and (2) trees bearing fruit in which is their own seed, each according to its kind" (verse 12). This one sentence discloses a great deal of botanical information: not only the distinction between plants and trees, but the recognition that these reproduce according to their own species or min. This empirical observation, found here and elsewhere in the Genesis creation story, is surely akin to the scientific approach, even though science has refined its methods of observation and the categories of classification.

The narrator's sense of cosmic order, however, is manifest above all in the view of the whole in which each of the creatures has its proper place and function. Nothing is out of place; nothing is unnecessary; nothing is without meaning. Rather, the narrator invites us to be amazed that we, observers from an earthly vantage point of the vast creation, are - as Samuel Taylor Coleridge once put it, "parts and proportions of one wondrous whole." This poetic sense of the mystery and wonder of the cosmos that finds expression in the Genesis creation story is an invitation to praise the Creator.

In this doxological perspective, God's creation is a wonderful cosmic order, which is without blemish and is harmonious in all its parts. The verdict of the divine Artist, upon perceiving the whole, was tob meod, "very good," (1:31). This, however, was not an ethical judgment, but an aesthetic one, in the sense that everything belongs where it should be and functions according to the divine design. [Maybe this is something like the judgment we make of our new car: "beautiful" in the sense that it functions perfectly according to the purpose for which it was designed.]

This sense of marvelous order surely is akin to the modern scientific worldview; but there is something else about this cosmic order which may be consonant with the scientist's perception. This marvelous order is "contingent," that it is constantly threatened by disorder or "chaos." The power of the Creator is not only evident in origination, but in maintaining and sustaining the order of creation.

In the Genesis creation story the contingency of the cosmos is expressed in poetic language derived ultimately from the ancient myth of the conflict of the creator-god with the powers of chaos. One of the best examples of this ancient myth is the Babylonian creation epic, <u>Enuma elish</u>, which portrays the creator-god, Marduk, defeating the powers of chaos, represented by a monster (dragon), and splitting her carcass in two, part of which becomes the watery realm above the firmament and the other the abyss upon which the earth rests. Faint allusions to this ancient myth are found in the biblical story, which begins with a portrayal of chaos: a watery abyss, inky black darkness, and a wind sweeping over the waters. As in the preface, so in the rest of the story creation is seen in relation to chaos. By the command of God, light is separated from the primeval darkness, a firmament is placed in the midst of the waters to separate the waters (above) from the waters (below), and the waters under the heaven are gathered into one place so that the dry land appears. In this view the watery chaos is not destroyed; rather, the primeval Sea surrounds the habitable earth on every hand. Were it not for the Creator's power, by which the firmament was created and the Sea assigned its boundaries, the earth would be engulfed by the flowing together of the waters and would return to primeval chaos - as almost happened in the Flood Story (Gen 6-9).

No language could express more forcefully the contingency of the creation. Contrary to the ancient Greek way of thinking, the cosmos is not a self-existent, self-operating realm, without beginning and end. The cosmos is finite: in scientific perspective, it began with a "big bang" and it will end with "a big burn-out." In agreement with this, the biblical language of faith assumes the contingency of the earth, as in the covenantal pledge at the end of the great flood, according to old Epic tradition:

> So long as the earth endures,
> Seedtime and harvest,
> Cold and heat,

> Summer and winter,
> Day and night,
> Shall not cease.　　　　(Gen 8:22, AJT)

Meanwhile, the Creator holds the world in being, so to speak, in the face of the potentialities of chaos.

Ecologists have taught us how delicate is the "Web of Life"-the title of a book by John H. Storer.[10] For all living beings, from bacteria to human beings, "fit into a pattern of life and depend upon each other and the world around them for existence." And we know, too, how our human lifestyle can upset this delicate balance and threaten to release the powers of chaos.

Indeed, the original creation was only part of the Creator's activity: there is also a continuing creation, which is not only a work of sustaining the order of the cosmos but, more than that, doing the "new thing" which surprises all expectations (see Is 42:9, 43:18-19).

One of the most eloquent statements about creatio continua is found at the climax of Psalm 104, where the poet uses verbs that express action that is incomplete, frequentive - a meaning that can be translated into our English idiom only by using the present tense. The psalmist's prayer to the Creator expresses the confidence that creation is not just an event that occurred in the beginning, but God's continuing activity of sustaining creatures and holding everything in being. Says the psalmist:

> All of them [animals and humans] look to you
> 　　to give them their food in its season.
> When you give to them, they gather up;
> 　　When you open your hand, they are satisfied to the full.
> When you hid your face, they are disturbed,
> 　　when you take away their breath, they expire and return to
> 　　their dust.
> When you send forth your spirit, they are [re] created,
> 　　and you renew the surface of the soil.　　(Ps 104:27-30).

III.    The Mystery of the Emergence of Life  There is one more interest that the theologian shares with the scientist - and this one has become highly controversial in the twentieth century: namely the emergence of life on this planet.

A while ago I observed that the creation drama is divided into two main movements: the first reaching its climax in the greening of the earth with vegetation: plants and trees according to their various kinds, and the second reaching its climax with the creation of life, especially human life. All of this is conceived as a dramatic totality. We must be on guard against imposing upon the story philosophical views derived from our Western tradition, such as the philosophical separation between nature and history, mind and matter, cosmic and existential.

Biblical theologians have noticed that nature provides God's "peculiar language" for praising the Creator. For in the Bible nature is not regarded as the sphere of mechanical operations, as in the Newtonian world view, but as a sphere that is somehow "alive" and which therefore joins with human beings in praise of the Creator. Years ago (in fact, in 1946), in a projected work on Old Testament Theology (which was never fully realized), H. Wheeler Robinson called our attention to this divine aspect of nature. "Nature," he wrote, "is alive through and through, and therefore the more capable of sympathy with man, and of direct response to the rule of its Creator and Upholder, on whom it directly depends."[11]

This view of the responsiveness of "nature" to the Creator has been picked up with poetic passion and insight by Virginia Stem Owens in her book, And the Trees Clap their Hands: Faith, Perception, and the New Physics. She maintains that nature should not be regarded mechanistically but dynamically, and that the biblical language about the participation of nature in our human creatureliness should not be regarded as "mere metaphor" but as metaphor which corresponds with reality. She writes: "And still the mute mountains, the dumb desert, the dying stars wait for us to provide a throat for their thanksgiving."[12] This, I believe, is consonant with the biblical creation story, and we can be thankful that women are helping us to understand the text with poetic sensitivity.

However, we must turn our attention to a special matter in the creation drama that moves from the greening of the earth to the climactic creation of life, preeminently human life. In Hebrew there is a special word for "living being": nefesh hayya. This expression is not applied to the vegetation that greens the earth on the third day of the drama. Today we make a distinction between animate things (trees, plants) and inanimate things (rocks, water, soil); but the biblical narrator does not make this distinction. Rather, the expression "living being" is reserved for the new forms that appear in the second movement, and strikingly these new creatures (living beings) first appear in connection with the waters, the remnant of the waters of chaos.

It would be unwise, in my judgment, to make too much of this association of emerging life with the waters, as though the Bible anticipated modern views of evolution. The connection of emerging life with the waters is undoubtedly a coincidence. Nevertheless the reader sees that something radically new appears in the case of water-beings (fish, sea monsters) and the flying creatures that soar over the waters (birds, winged creatures). For the first time in the story, creatures are called "living beings" (nefesh hayya, Gen 1:20). At the executive command of the Creator, the waters generate marine creatures (and, if we follow the LXX, birds too: "Let the waters bring forth reptiles having life, and winged creatures flying above the earth in the heavenly firmament"). Moreover, this momentous development is marked by a dramatic pause, during which the Creator gives these creatures a special blessing which grants dominion to them in their medium of water or air (1:22).

The narrator's climactic interest, however, is reserved for the nefesh hayya (living beings) created on the last day of the drama: the animals according to their species ("kind") and the supreme earthling known as 'adam (humanity, human being, 1:26-27).

It is evident, first of all, that the story intends to show that there is affinity between these earthlings: animals and humans. They were created on the same day (a subtle literary indication of affinity), and later on we are told that they share the same table in a peaceable kingdom, for they eat the vegetation that was prepared at the climax of the first movement of the creation drama.

What are the characteristics of this kind of nefesh hayya? Let me mention several:

| | |
|---|---|
| mobility: | they creep upon the face of the earth |
| sexuality: | they are capable of reproducing their species |
| breath: | they are animated by [divine] breath |
| blood: | they all share the mysterious potency of vitality, for "the blood is the life." |

Clearly the narrator wants to say that these earth creatures, created on the same day, belong together. In a sense they are relatives, if that means that they are related as God's creatures who live in the same oikos ("house"), the Greek term from which we get our word "ecology." But if all these animals are equal, to recall a line from George Orwell's Animal Farm, then some are "more equal than others."[13] The climax of the story is the creation of 'adam (human being), consisting of "male and female" equally. In various ways the narrator stresses that the human being, though related to the animal, has a special role in God's creation.

The event is preceded by a solemn announcement: a resolution that the Creator announces in the Heavenly Council.

Then God said:
"Let us make human beings ['adam] in our image, after our likeness, and let them have dominion over the fish of the sea, the birds of the sky, the cattle and all wild beasts, and everything that moves upon the earth."

> So God created humanity ['adam] in his own image, in the
> image of God he created it; male and female he created them."
> (Gen 1:26-27)

Moreover, there is another dramatic pause, during which the Creator confers a special blessing on human beings (not on the land animals!) to reproduce and to have dominion over the earth as those who are made in the "image of God."

The expression "image of God" is applied only to human beings, never to animals, and thus is crucial for understanding what makes humans different from animals. This subject alone deserves at least a full lecture, and I can only allude to some of its dimensions. The image refers to something distinctive in human being which makes possible a sense of awe and wonder, which could lead to prayer and relationship with God. The image refers to those special dimensions of human nature which lift us above the animal plane: imagination, freedom to be and to become, responsibility and guilt, intellectual inquiry, artistic appreciation. And the image refers, above all, to the God-given commission to "image" God on earth, that is, to be the agents who represent and realize God's benevolent and peaceful sway on earth.

This would be an appropriate point to launch into a discussion of our human responsibility and ethical obligations. But our major interest is in the concerns that scientists and theologians have in common, and clearly one of these is the novelty of life, especially human life, on this planet. We come inevitably, then, to the evolutionary hypothesis and its relation to the biblical creation-faith. Remember the premise of our discussion: the language of science and the poetic language of the Bible should not be confused, for they are based on different modes of perception and yield different kinds of knowledge; nevertheless, those who speak these languages (and sometimes it is the same person!) share common interests.

In this case, the common interest is the sheer novelty of life - <u>nefesh</u> <u>hayya</u>, to use the biblical terminology. Nothing that has been said about the Genesis creation story necessarily militates against an evolutionary hypothesis, provided it stays within the limitations of the language of science. Indeed, there are striking points of contact: the emergence of biological life (<u>nefesh hayya</u>) in the waters; the appearance of life on the land (earth) with its special characteristics of mobility, breathing, sentience, etc. And, further, the appearance of "the human" (<u>'adam</u>) is a novelty, even though the human and the animal are interrelated.

It may be helpful in this connection to quote in part a portion of Judge Overton's decision in the recent Arkansas case:

> Although the subject of origins of life is within the province of biology, the scientific community does not consider origins of life a part of evolutionary theory. The theory of evolution assumes the existence of life and is directed to an explanation of <u>how</u> life evolved. Evolution does not presuppose the absence of a creator or God.[14]

To sum up: In this lecture I have tried to show that religion and science, while they use different languages and give different kinds of knowledge, should not be put in opposition to one another. Moreover, I have suggested that religion, in order to find a secure haven from modern thought, should not retreat into an area of "experience" which is unrelated to the cosmos in which we live and move and have our being. The time has come for theologians and scientists to dialogue with one another, realizing that they share common interests.

Three of these interests have been treated: the mystery of the origination of the cosmos; the mystery of order that is sustained in the face of the threat of chaos; the mystery of the emergence of life, especially human life, on this planet.

In the first and last analysis, the view expressed in the first chapter of Genesis presupposes a commitment of faith - identification with a believing and worshipping community. The Genesis story speaks to and for people who have made such a commitment and who, like Luther before the Diet of Worms, say: <u>Hier stehe Ich, Ich kann nicht anders</u> ("Here I stand, I cannot do otherwise"). This stand of faith, however, does not call for a sacrifice of the intellect, a blind faith in something irrational and absurd. On the contrary, it welcomes the exciting vistas of modern science and the opportunity to dialogue with scientists who also stand humbly before these mysteries.

ENDNOTES

1.      Roland Mushat Frye, ed., Is God a Creationist?: The Religious Case Against Creation-Science; NY: Scribner's, 1983.

2.      Philip Joranson and Ken Butigan, eds., Cry of the Environment: Rebuilding the Christian Creation Tradition; Santa Fe, NM: Bear & Co., 1984.

3.      Robert Jastrow, God and the Astronomers; NY: Norton, 1978, p. 105.

4.      Conrad Hyers, "Biblical Literalism: Constricting the Cosmic Dance," pp. 95-104 in Frye, op. cit. Cf. pp. 96-97.

5.      Job 38:4-7. Tr. Norman Hebel, Job: A Commentary [Old Testament Library]; Philadelphia: Westminster,

6.      George Hendry, "The Eclipse of Creation," Theology Today 28 (1972), 406-425.

7.      Gerhard von Rad, "The Theological Problem of the Old Testament Doctrine of Creation," pp. 53-64 in Creation in the Old Testament ed Bernard W. Anderson; Philadelphia: Fortress, 1984. [von Rad original, 1936]

8.      Claus Westermann, "Biblical Reflection on Creator-Creation," pp. 90-101 in Anderson, op. cit., quotation p. 120. [Westermann original, 1971]

9.      Quoted by Owen Gingrich, "Let There Be Light: Modern Cosmogony and Biblical Creation," pp. 119-137, in Frye, op. cit. Cf. p. 121.

10.     J.H. Storer, The Web of Life; NY: New American Library, 1956.

11.     H. Wheeler Robinson, Inspiration and Revelation in the Old Testament; Oxford: Clarendon Press, 1946, p. 16.

12.     Virginia Stem Owens, And the Trees Clap Their Hands: Faith, Perception, and the New Physics; Grand Rapids: Eerdmans, 1983, p. 132.

13.     George Orwell, Animal Farm; San Diego: Harcourt Brace Jovanovich, 1954.

14.     Quoted by Bruce Vawter, "Creationism: Creative Misuse of the Bible," pp. 71-82 in Frye, op. cit. Cf. p. 77.

# A SOCIOLOGICAL APPROACH TO NEW TESTAMENT INTERPRETATION

## Howard Clark Kee

During my first years of teaching at Drew University in the early 1950's, I was in constant dialogue and debate with one of my colleagues in the Theological School, Carl Michalson, who was an early and effective champion of the existentialist interpretation of the New Testament developed by the late Rudolf Bultmann. The major emphasis in this way of understanding Jesus and the gospel was on the call to decision: Jesus called his hearers to respond in faithful obedience to his message, and in so doing they died to the present world, its values and claims, and entered a new life and a new relationship with God. Jesus himself had experienced this radical obedience, which resulted in his crucifixion. In the faith of his followers, he was raised to new life, into which they also now had the possibility of entering.

This way of interpreting the Christian message provided - in my opinion - a sophisticated but misguided equivalent for the traditional American Protestant understanding of Christian faith as basically the way individuals may find personal relationship with God. The one-to-one relationship expressed in such a range of hymns and songs as "I come to the garden alone... and he walks with me and he talks with me" or "Just a little talk with Jesus makes it right" or "My God and I, we walk the fields together" now found through scholars like Bultmann and Michalson an intellectual substitute in the existential encounter: the isolated "I" addressed by and responding to the transcendent "Thou."

Among the many distinguished visitors to the Drew Campus in those years was the Jewish philosopher-theologian, Martin Buber, whose book, Two Types of Faith, had just appeared in its English version.[1] The thesis of the book was that Judaism was the religion of the community, while Christianity was the religion of the individual. I was dissatisfied by this distinction of Buber's and its implication for Christianity as I was with the theological position of my colleague, Michalson, and I asked Dr. Buber in the question period following his address what the source was for his estimate of Christianity as individualistic. He replied, "The writings of Rudolf Bultmann." I was mildly surprised, greatly amused, and deeply relieved to find that Buber was not attributing his theory about Christianity to the New Testament.

It is ironic that Bultmann should have adopted this individualistic understanding of Jesus and the gospel, since one of his major contributions to New Testament scholarship was in the development of so-called form criticism, according to which the stories about Jesus and sayings attributed to him were classified in terms of formal patterns, such as parables and prophetic pronouncements, miracle stories and legends. These forms, as they were called, were then analyzed to see what their original setting in early Christianity had been. The German phrase, Sitz-im-Leben, which might be translated literally as "situation of life," was supposed to bring into focus for the interpreter the specific circumstance in early Christianity in which these traditions about Jesus' words and works took shape.

Unfortunately, Bultmann and other form-critics were content to offer such broad categories for the classification of these forms (teaching or preaching; Jewish or hellenistic) as to be valueless in the analysis of a text. These very general labels were useless for determining the context out of which the form may have come that is now preserved in the gospels. There was, in fact, a nearly total split between the technical, formal analysis of the Jesus tradition and the theological importance that was seen in that tradition. The distinction between proclamation and instruction paid lip service to the community setting, since both teaching and preaching would take place in the context of the church. But the terms, Jewish and hellenistic, were merely intellectual, conceptual distinctions at best, and they did not take into account that the Jewish and hellenistic cultures of this epoch were varied and undergoing constant change. And of course such simplistic classifications left out of consideration the corporate nature of Christian existence. The so-called "situation in life," therefore, was a mere scholarly abstraction.

The tragic, premature death of Carl Michalson obviously precluded any change in his theological outlook. But although Bultmann lived on for decades, he never shifted from the existentialist, individualistic position he had outlined in the early decades of this century. Yet precisely during these decades of the 50's, 60's and 70's, several factors contributed to basic shifts in New Testament interpretation, in terms of both historical and theological understanding. These include both new discoveries and new insights concerning ancient documents. In addition, there arose new methods of historical and theological interpretation.

The newly discovered documents which have had the greatest impact on our understanding of the New Testament were the Dead Sea Scrolls from Palestine and the Gnostic library from upper Egypt. In both cases these writings not only provided writings which had never before been known and more ancient copies of known documents, but they also gave scholars insights concerning the nature of the religious groups by whom the writings had been written and preserved. This latter factor was especially clear and important for the Dead Sea Scrolls, which included two writings which gave specific information about the circumstances for the founding of the community which had its headquarters at the site overlooking the northern end of the Dead Sea, as well as detailed rules for guiding the common life of the group. The Manual of Discipline, or Scroll of the Rule, was the rule book for the community. The Damascus Document, a copy of which had been found earlier in this century in Egypt, but with no clear indications of the place of its origins, was now seen to include a description of the circumstances which led the founder of the group to launch this people of the New Covenant. The commentaries on scripture, as well as the copies of various books of the Bible, show what their canon of scripture was and how they interpreted it in relation to their own past, present and future. The War Scroll and the Temple Scroll found there give detailed evidence of how they expected God to act in the future in their behalf, vindicating them and establishing them fully as his chosen people. The corporate acts of worship of the community are reflected in the collections of hymns, the expositions of scripture, and in the evidence for such shared sacred acts as a meal of bread and wine, looking forward to the time of their divine vindication. The significance of these documents, therefore, extends far beyond the religious ideas that they contain and the possible links of their theological concepts with those of the early Christians, important as those factors are. Still more significant is the way that these writings alert the student of Christian origins as to what were the issues that were important for a new, dissenting movement within the context of first century Judaism, how the members of the group understood and experienced their new mode of common life, and what prospects for their corporate future they discerned as they read the scripture and contemplated God's purpose for them.

The social nature of renewal movements within Judaism at this time has been further clarified by the work of Jacob Neusner, of Brown University, whose analysis of the documents of rabbinic Judaism has resulted in a revolution in the understanding of Judaism in general and of the Pharisees in particular during this epoch. He has shown that the Pharisees shifted from their role in the last century before the birth of Jesus from one of political involvement in the struggle for power among the descendants of the Maccabees to the attempt to develop within Judaism voluntary circles of the pious, bound together by devotion to the Law of Moses, to the maintenance of personal purity under that law, and to the celebration of their new-found communality in the group study of the law and in table fellowship. Building on Neusner's insights about the Pharisees, we may see that for Paul, the ex-Pharisee, to have become the preeminent apostle to the Gentiles must have required him to redefine completely the basis of purification, or to use the term that Paul prefers, of sanctification of God's people. What Paul and his fellow Pharisees had sought through human conformity to legal prescriptions is now effective through Christ and the power of the Spirit. Yet the new covenant community continues to find its identity and its purpose through the fresh interpretation of Scripture and through table fellowship. What Neusner has perceived concerning the Pharisees has important implications for our analysis of the gospels, not merely in relation to the rules for individual piety, but for the overall understanding of who are the people of God and how they come to share in the new covenant.

Concurrent with the availability of new sources and consequently of new insights concerning familiar first-century evidence in the 1960's was a surge of creative activity in the identification of patterns in religious movements, ancient and modern - patterns which are apparent with respect to origins, leadership, ritual, as well as social and cultural factors among the members of these various groups. The writings of Emile Durkheim and especially of Max Weber were brought to the center of discussion and made available in English translations. The dynamics of religious movements were studied with the aim of discerning typical features, such as Weber's insight into the way new movements begin under the impact of a charismatic leader and are no more than launched until they have begun to develop certain institutional forms. After such a movement has had its start with someone who lacked any sort of official sanction or authorization, and whose authority derives from his own claims of relationship to or knowledge of the divine, there begin to appear certain lines of control and delineation of proper procedures.

Significantly, the impetus for this line of inquiry lay, not with professional religion scholars, but with social scientists, or to be more precise, with anthropologists. Two prime examples of this phenomenon are Clifford Geertz and Mary Douglas. Clifford Geertz, in his The Interpretation of Culture, distinguishes between a culture and a social system.[2] The former is an ordered system of meaning and symbols, in terms of which social interaction occurs. Included in this system are a framework of beliefs, of expressive symbols and values, in terms of which individuals define their world, express their feelings and make judgments. The social system, on the other hand, is the pattern of social interaction, and the process of interactive behavior, which manifests itself in forms of action and a network of social relationships. Truth is not some set of objective factors which varies with social, psychological and cultural contexts, but the symbols that a group constructs in its effort to grasp truth. Central to this symbol-constructing enterprise is the question asked implicitly or explicitly by a group as to "Who we are?", by which is implied, What is the system of meaningful symbols that are employed to give value and significance to the activities of the group and to the life of its members? The aim is to provide a meaningful framework in which, through a shared symbol-system, a group of human beings can develop a meaningful framework for orienting themselves to their natural and social context, to the world around them, and to themselves. The task of the interpreter of a culture, ancient or modern, primitive or sophisticated, is the intellectual reconstruction of the conceptual systems that have animated that culture and given it form. In relation to all of culture, but especially significant in relation to religion and religious identity within groups or movements, a culture - including a religious culture - is, as Geertz phrases it, "an historically transmitted pattern of meanings embodied in symbols, a system of inherited conceptions expressed in symbolic forms by means of which human beings communicate, perpetuate and develop their knowledge about, and their attitudes toward life.[3] It is my conviction that all that Geertz has said about culture in general is equally appropriate when it comes to assessing and interpreting the traditions of ancient religions, such as Judaism in the time of Jesus and the origins of Christianity.

Mary Douglas' writings, Purity and Danger and Natural Symbols build on evidence from religions as varied as those of tribal groups in the Third World and the Levitical Code of ancient Israel to show that social groups maintain identity by drawing the boundaries between themselves and the rest of the world.[4] Purity is not, therefore, an arbitrary feature of a religious group, but an essential factor in preserving social identity. Often, she notes, aspects of the human body are essential features of this process, so that anything given off by the body - such as spittle, feces, or body fluids - is seen as a threat to the purity of the social group. She has proposed a scheme in terms of which any group can be characterized, based on two factors which she calls group and grid. By group she means how strong or weak is the sense of cohesion and distinctive identity within a group; by grid she means how sharply are delineated the criteria for acceptance within the group and for maintenance of status. Some social groups have weak group and strong grid, and some have the reverse. The Dead Sea community, on the other hand, had both strong group (a powerful sense of cohesion) and strong grid (demanding requirements of its members, including a process for expulsion of violators). The factor of community definition must now be raised in a precise and nuanced way by anyone interested in the various forms of group identity that emerged among the early Christians - and there was by no means a single uniform model, as the conflicts between Paul and the Jerusalem apostles over the criteria for admission of Gentiles in Galatians and Acts attests. With regard to purity considerations, it is no accident that this issue assumes such an important place in the gospel accounts of Jesus, beginning with Q and Mark, and developing to the more intensive levels of conflict between Jesus and the Pharisees as depicted in Matthew's gospel.

Simultaneously with the emergence of these features of the social sciences that offer such a potential for shedding fresh light on questions of Christian origins, there arose in the field of sociology a way of analyzing how human knowledge develops as a process within a community of shared assumptions and values, rather than as an inevitable development from the availability of new data. The leading figures in the development of this approach to human understanding, which is called sociology-of-knowledge, are Alfred Schutz, Thomas Luckmann, and especially Peter L. Berger. The latter scholar brought this new approach to the attention of scholars in this country through his The Sacred Canopy, and with Thomas Luckmann, in The Social Construction of Reality.[5] In this approach to human understanding, the central factor is the shared view of the world, in its social and cultural, as well as its physical dimensions. To describe this encompassing view of reality that is shared by a social group, the sociologists of knowledge coined the term "life-world." What this consists of has been effectively epitomized by Alfred Schutz as follows:

> The social world into which one is born and within which one has to find his or her bearings is experienced as a tight-knit web of social relationships, of systems and symbols with their particular structure of meaning, of institutional forms of social organizations, of systems, of status and prestige, etc. The meaning of all these elements of the social world in all its diversity and stratification, as well as the pattern of the texture itself, is, by those living within it, "taken for granted." They consider it to be the socially accepted way of life for the members and the appropriate means for coming to terms with things. This social world is perpetuated by ancestors, teachers and authorities, and is deemed adequate for action and understanding, and as a guide for problem-solving and other forms of action. It is assumed that the traditions should be transmitted whether we understand their origins or not. Through the tradition one learns to

define the environment, what is taken for granted, what are the typical constructions and solutions.[6]

Schutz observed at one point that the most revealing statement anyone makes is when he or she says, "And so forth." He meant by that the speaker assumes - correctly - that once a part of the point of view under consideration has been verbalized, the hearers will automatically extrapolate on the basis of shared views and convictions. "Etc." and "and so forth," as well as the (to me) maddening current cliche, "you know what I mean," are familiar reminders of the life-world shared by speaker and hearer.

Closely akin to this development within the social sciences is the increasing attention paid by philosophers to the social nature of human language. Ludwig Wittgenstein's perception that human speech is possible through, and gives expression to shared views of reality, rather than a neutral, objective instrument of transmitting information has had an enduring impact on subsequent philosophy. Similarly, the important study by Suzanne Langer, Philosophy in a New Key,[7] shows that philosophy is a mode of communication in terms of shared symbols rather than of objective linguistic terms. And in the field of Bible translation, the approach to this task has been revolutionized through the insights of scholars like Eugene Nida, who have drawn attention to the factor of "dynamic equivalence" - that is, of discovering and utilizing for translation purposes the dynamic equivalent for the socio-linguistic context of the biblical writers in the language of the social and cultural setting for which the translation is being made. The result has been the phenomenally effective new translations in current popular language such as the Good News Bible in the English-speaking world, the Version Populaire in Latin America, and the Gute Nachricht in Germany.

Jesus, as he is portrayed in the gospel tradition, is one who both literally and symbolically talks the language of his contemporaries. He is seen as one who shares many of the basic features of the "life-world" with his Jewish contemporaries. These would include the belief that Yahweh, the God of Abraham, Isaac and Jacob, is the sole Lord of the universe; that he has disclosed his purpose to the patriarchs, to Moses, to David and Solomon and others in the royal line, as well as through the psalmists and the prophets of Israel; that God has not given up on his disobedient people nor been thwarted in his purposes by hostile powers at work in the world; that he will move through chosen agents in the future to achieve his sovereign control over his creation. Jews in the time of Jesus would have disagreed on important details as to how his purpose was to be accomplished - whether through priestly, royal, or scribal agents - but they were by and large united on what God's agenda was and the conviction that the renewal of the covenant people was essential to the attainment of this divine goal. Clearly these are social goals, significant not only for Israel as a group but for the whole of the human race.

Had Jesus done no more than share the life-world of his Jewish contemporaries, we should not likely have ever heard of him. But, as the New Testament evidence shows, he challenged the common assumptions at a number of crucial points with his way of perceiving the Good News of God's Rule and his redefinition of who and how one might participate in the New Covenant people. As we might expect, his message was heard by various groups, both within Syria-Palestine and in other parts of the Greco-Roman territory, in a variety of ways and from within a range of life-worlds. The diversity of ways in which Jesus and God's purpose through him are perceived among the New Testament writers bears testimony to this, and is precisely what we should expect on the basis of an approach which takes as its starting point the social context of communication. In a variety of forms and modes, and in various parts of the world, this social dimension of the New Testament has moved to the center of attention in recent biblical scholarship. The methods deriving from the social sciences and from sociology-of-knowledge have altered much of the work being done in the field. In the 1920's at the University of Chicago, there was a relatively brief surge of interest in a sociological approach to the study of early Christianity, but the motivation seems to have been the attempt to explain away the rise of Christian orthodoxy by appeal to the dynamics of certain social factors. There was lacking any nuanced use of social theory in the interest of tracing the dynamics of Christianity's origin within and break with Judaism, and the variety of forms which the Christian movement took from the moment of its origins. The results of the impact of these recent documentary and methodological discoveries, by contrast, have been widespread and, I think, of enduring significance.

Among the first to draw on the social sciences for New Testament interpretation was Gerd Theissen, of the University of Heidelberg.[8] For example, his essays include the study of the gospel reports of Jesus sending out his disciples to carry forward his work of proclamation of the kingdom of God and the manifestations of its powers and renewal of human life through the exorcisms and healings which he and they performed. Theissen noted the similarities (as well as some differences) between this kind of activity and the Cynic-Stoic itinerant teacher-preachers who wandered about the cities and villages of those parts of the Middle East strongly influenced by hellenistic culture from the time of Alexander the Great forward. The message proclaimed by the Jesus group was utterly different from the appeal of the Cynics to divest oneself of the values of this world and live in detached freedom. Jesus, of course, called attention to the evil forces and false values of the present age, but summoned his hearers to accept the grace of God, to enter the community of love, and to share in the coming victory of God's purpose over powers of evil when the Kingdom of God had fully come. Nevertheless, the similarity of strategy between Jesus and the itinerant philosophical radicals is striking and shows how Jesus and his followers were able to adapt to their own special purposes features of the culture of their time.

Wayne Meeks has also made a major contribution to a social basis for interpreting the New Testament in his analysis of the social context of the urban centers in which Paul and the other apostles launched the Christian movement in the eastern Mediterranean world. His studies of Antioch, Ephesus and Corinth show what the power structure of these cities was, what the rights of persons at various levels of the social and economic stratification were, and the kinds of groups within which Christianity first made its inroads in these centers. The result is an awareness for the reader of The First Urban Christians of the challenges and opportunities presented by these cities for those, like Paul, who set out to preach the gospel there and to found communities built upon and promoting this new understanding of God's purpose and the qualifications for participation in his New Covenant people.[9] The problems that the social context created and aggravated are especially evident in Paul's Letter to the Corinthians. Further insight into these features of nascent Christianity have been offered by Gerd Theissen in his essays on the social setting of the church in Corinth.[10]

My own work on the Gospel of Mark has sought to deal with these dimensions of this writing.[11] A basic question to be raised is, How did Mark and his readers understand God's purpose for Jesus and the divine plan for them as his followers? What attitudes are evident toward the various forms of Judaism that were operative in this period? How did they interpret the biblical tradition, not merely conceptually, but in relation to themselves, as those who claimed to be God's new people? What prospect did they have for the future, in terms of the possibility of their suffering, the role God had called them to fulfill, and their future divine purpose? What responsibilities did they see devolving upon themselves in the interim between God's having raised Jesus from the dead and the full establishment of God's Rule in the world? What was the nature of the ethical demand that God had placed upon them as his people, and how did these norms relate to the Law of Moses as understood by their Jewish contemporaries?

When these kinds of questions are addressed to the text of Mark, that gospel becomes luminous in a way that scrutiny of the individual passages or conceptual comparisons with texts from other parts of the New Testament simply does not make possible. In the light of a sociological analysis, Mark may be seen as what anthropologists call a "foundation document" for a Christian group with certain distinctive features: (1) the members believe that, through his disciples, Jesus has charged them to bear witness to him as God's agent in overcoming the powers of evil and in effecting their acceptance with God through his vicarious death. (2) They are persuaded that the end of the age is soon to come, that they will suffer rejection and maltreatment by the religious leadership and by the agents of the powers of evil, but that God will soon intervene, vindicating them and establishing his Rule in the world. (3) They see themselves, therefore as a humanly powerless group, to whom, however, God had revealed his purpose for the creation and to whom he has given responsibility for preparing the human race for the establishment of the community of the New Age, which we would call the church. (4) Neither Jesus nor the disciples has any earthly human authorization for the work to which they are dedicated; instead, they represent what Max Weber has called charismatic leadership, which regards itself as empowered by God for its special work, and which stands over against the religious establishment -- in this case the Jewish authorities. Meanwhile, however, there are issues for which they have received guidance through Jesus, on such subjects as marriage and divorce, attitudes toward the state, and the necessity for their being open toward Gentiles and those who do not conform to the purity laws of contemporary Judaism. The Gospel of Mark is the document which tells the members how the movement began, what the significant features of the career of their founder were, what their privileges and priorities are, what the norms are by which their behavior is to be guided, both within the group and in their relationships with the wider world. And above all, they learn what future trials and deliverance they are to await.

The advantage of this approach to the New Testament is that it removes the faith of the church from the merely conceptual or doctrinal arena in which so much scholarly interpretation has been carried on, and puts the texts instead in the midst of the wide range of experiences, needs, anxieties and misunderstandings such as characterize human life in every age and setting. Further, by careful analysis of individual writings within the New Testament, we may see how this approach illuminates some of the opaque parts of those writings, and at the same time helps us to understand clear differences between parts of the New Testament, including some important differences of detail among the gospels.

We may begin with a comparison of Mark and Matthew in terms of the social context and symbolic universes which each of them seems to presuppose or embody. In Mark, Jesus appears on the scene without advance notice, and with no indications of his origins or prior experience. The story is told with a pervasive element of haste, as indicated by the oft-repeated "immediately," which Mark has used to tie together the various narrative accounts of Jesus' public activity. Further, there are the frequent occasions in Mark in which Jesus, having made public statements, offers private explanations to the inner circle of his followers. There are constant references to the coming of the end of the age, which will bring punishment to those who reject Jesus and destruction to the powers of evil, as represented by the demons which Jesus expels. The longest discourse in the gospel is a series of predictions about the destruction of the temple and the coming of the end of the age (Mk 13). Jesus faces his death with a prediction of his coming in triumph as the Son of Man. The gospel ends abruptly with the promise that his followers will see him, risen from the dead, and that he will meet them in Galilee. Earlier, the issue of the authority of Jesus and his followers is raised, but brushed aside, when Jesus refuses to perform a miracle on request in order to prove that his authority derives from God (Mk 8:11-13). Throughout, the authority of Jesus and his followers is portrayed in a purely charismatic fashion.

Matthew has not merely supplemented Mark by the addition of the infancy stories and some sayings material. Both the basic structure and the overall intent of the gospel have been transformed by Matthew. The stories of Jesus' birth and childhood place him within the wider context of Jewish history, as the genealogy and the various events - all of them noted to be in fulfillment of a scripture - attest: his birth in Bethlehem; his flight to and return from Egypt, on the model of the experience of ancient Israel; the holy family's move to Galilee. The contrast of Jesus, as founder of the new covenant people, with Moses, the founder of the Old Covenant people, is explicit: through the setting of Jesus's understanding of God's will for his people over against that of Moses (in the Sermon on the Mount); in the location of Jesus as authoritative interpreter of God's will on a mountain, as Moses was in Sinai; and in the division of this gospel - like the Law of Moses - into five parts, marked off by the telltale phrase, "When Jesus had finished ..." (Mt 7:28; 11:1; 13:53; 19:1; 26:1).

Also indicative of the movement of the Matthean community from the charismatic stages to increasingly formal, institutional style are the evidences of set patterns for worship and for the way of life of the members. Comparison of the Lord's Prayer in Mt 6:9-13 with the earlier version from the Q source in Lk 11:2-4, for example, shows the development of elaborated liturgical modes: Not simply the direct address of God as "Father," but the more elegant, "Our Father, who art in heaven." Other phrases are similarly elaborated in the familiar Matthean version. Peter's confession in Mark is simply, "You are the Messiah" (Mk 8:29), but in Mt 16:16, there is the familiar expansion, "You are the Messiah, the Son of the living God," which is then followed by an assurance of the enduring nature of the movement that was launched through Jesus (16:17-18). It is called "the church"; it will endure in spite of the powers arrayed against it. But even more significantly, the leaders of the church are given the responsibility of determining who is to be admitted or excluded from membership (16:19). That authority is confirmed and expanded - only in Matthew - in Mt 18, where the procedures are laid out for dealing with disputes within the community and for expulsion of members. The commissioning of the disciples by Jesus in Mt 28 confirms this picture of movement toward institutionalization: the leaders of the church are explicitly given authority; their role is not evangelization, but instruction, and the ritual acts they are to perform are accompanied by a liturgical formula, the Trinitarian designation of God. Clearly, Matthew's gospel represents a major move on the part of early Christianity from its charismatic origins in the direction of institutionalization. It is fully understandable why Matthew was placed at the head of the Christian canon, why its form of the gospel tradition is by far the most frequently quoted by the fathers of the church in the second and subsequent centuries. Instead of a sketchy set of information and instructions for the interim period before the End of the Age (which is how Mark might be described), we have in Matthew a structured, formal document which draws ever sharper lines between the Christian community and the mounting Jewish opposition, and which prepares the leaders of the church for the ongoing tasks that are theirs, both within the church and in its wider relationships.

Similar patterns of sociological development are evident in the move from the authentic letters of Paul to later writings in his name, or from the Gospel of John to the Johannine epistles. From Paul's indisputably authentic letters two major themes are evident: (1) that the people of God have been redefined by God through Jesus; and (2) that the fulfillment of God's purpose for and through his people is to take place soon, probably within Paul's own lifetime. The issue of the new covenant includes who may enter, on what terms, and with what responsibilities. These concerns are addressed in Galatians and Romans, especially. There Paul seeks to show that, from as early as the time of Abraham, membership in God's people was dependent on trust in God's promise, rather than on conformity to regulations, moral or ritual. We are set right with God by faith, not by our accomplishments, Paul states repeatedly. When he declares that "all Israel" will be saved (Rom 11:26), the people of God will include "the full number of the Gentiles," so that the traditional distinction between Jew and Gentile no longer has validity in new people of God.

The life of the community of faith he depicts in organic terms, especially as a body with many members and diverse functions. Rather than lay down set rules for the leadership and for the assignment of roles, he tends to work on a situational basis, adapting his guidelines in light of the varying social circumstances in which the different Christian communities exist. This strategy is set out in his familiar utterance in I Cor 9, where he describes his adaptability to Jews and Gentiles, to weak and strong, to those under the law and those outside it, "I have become all things to all people, that I might by all means save some" (9:22). He enumerates the various gifts ("charismata"!) that are essential for the ongoing life of the Christian community, including wisdom, healing, prophecy, ecstatic speech and its interpretation (I Cor 12:4-12). These functions are granted by the Spirit; they are not assigned through the authority of Paul or of anyone else within the church. And all are necessary for the welfare of the community as a whole.

Paul is content to live and work in this unstructured approach to the new covenant people because he is persuaded that in a short time, God's purpose will be accomplished, and the end of the age will come. This expectation is explicit in such passages as I Thess 4:17 and I Cor 15:23, where he assumes that he and others will be alive when this climatic event occurs. There is no need for long-range strategies: what is required, as in Mark, is effective means of preaching the gospel in order to prepare as many as possible for participation in God's new people. Similarly, Paul's depiction of Jesus as Lord is based on his role as God's agent in reconciling the world to himself and in overcoming the powers of evil in preparation for God's ultimate rule over the creation, as in II Cor 5:18-19. Paul's work, and that of all Christians, is to share in that ongoing ministry of reconciliation (II Cor 5:20-21).

Already in Colossians and Ephesians, however, Christ is pictured in timeless terms, drawing on earlier Jewish speculation about Wisdom as God's eternal agent. Faith has become, not so much trust in God's promise, as belief in correct doctrine of a unified sort (Eph 4:4-6; Col 1:23). The image of the church is architectural rather than organic, with a hierarchical representation of the leadership roles. Among the members of the community, there is an assignment of tasks and specific rules for how those various levels of society are to behave (Col 3-4). These dimensions of the developing ecclesiastical institution are expanded in the Pastorals, where there is clear differentiation and ranking of the several offices within the church: bishops, deacons, elders, and possibly "widows," which may have become a technical term for what we might call nuns or deaconesses (I Tim 3-5). In Titus there is an emphasis on sound doctrine (Ti 2), and warnings about the care that must be exercised in selecting persons for leadership roles (Ti 1). Institutionalization is well developed by the time these letters are being written in Paul's name. For our purposes, it is essential to observe that the differences between Paul and the Deutero-Pauline letters are not merely conceptual or theological, but rest on fundamental shifts in the sociological structure and strategy of their respective communities.

A similar shift is evident when we move from the Gospel of John, with its theory of complete mutuality to the Epistles of John, where submission to the elder is demanded, on penalty of expulsion (II Jn 9). This contrasts sharply with the absence of hints of structure in John's gospel, and with the insistence that the only merit to be found within the community is that of outdoing others in humility, as shown by the washing of the feet of the other members (Jn 13). Raymond Brown has traced these changes effectively in his Community of the Beloved Disciple.[12] The attention to the changing social structures within the church and its changing role within the wider society of the Roman world is essential to responsible New Testament interpretation. And it has the potential for enabling the student of the New Testament to identify in fresh and deep ways with the situations of the early Christians as they heard and responded to the challenge of the gospel.

There are, however, at least two ways in which insights from the social sciences are being employed in biblical interpretation which seem to me to be irresponsible or illegitimate, or both. One is the so-called Christian Marxist approach, which imposes on the biblical evidence the categories and values of nineteenth century Marxist theory, ignoring the fact that there was no middle class in this period of history, and that the vast majority of the population was hopelessly locked into a role of economic deprivation and political powerlessness. To speak of a revolt of the proletariat in these circumstances is nonsense. The Jewish nationalist revolts, for example, from the time of the Maccabees on, were conflicts within the structures of power at the upper levels of society, with segments of the populace joining the effort. The other inappropriate approach to analysis of Christian origins in the name of the social sciences is represented by those scholarly efforts to take over from cultural anthropologists various systems of classification of features of primitive culture, and use them to categorize the phenomena that come to us from the New Testament. There are a number of points at which this approach can shed light on specific details of the rise of Christianity, but the classificatory method tends to ignore the dynamics of social change which characterize every historical movement, including the early Christian movement. Full attention must be paid to the specifics of the cultural context and the world-view shared by the members of each particular early Christian group, and at each stage of its evolutionary development.

When these factors just mentioned - as well as the methods that derive from the sociology of knowledge and the analysis of primitive cultures - are taken fully into account, we have the possibility of an illuminating view of the common as well as the distinctive features that characterized nascent Christianity. We have fresh questions to address to the New Testament texts, which are concerned with the dynamics of human, social, cultural situations, instead of the arbitrary, conceptual analyses that have characterized so much biblical interpretation in the past. By this means we can see what the range of ways was in which the gospel was heard and responded to, the variety of contexts in which early Christian communities sprang up, and the differences among them in their respective responses to the culture that surrounded them.

By this approach it is possible to determine what was unique about early Christianity, especially in contrast to the various modes of covenantal definition that had arisen in Judaism by the turn of the eras, and to the modes of religious aspiration that were found throughout the richly diverse lands under the Roman empire. In the latter connection, this approach helps us to sense why Christianity spread so rapidly, since its concern was not merely with religious insights for the individual, but with the presentation of a new social context in which personal meaning and social reinforcement of identity could be attained. As Rome's power shattered one after another of the ancient traditional cultures and modes of life in the area which the empire had come to dominate, there was a widespread longing for precisely the fresh kind of social identity offered by Christianity that transcended the older ethnic or regional boundaries.

This sociologically-informed way of coming at the New Testament can also provide the churches today a range of models for fresh assessment of what the role of the church in society might be, and for precluding the attempt of many Christians in modern times to impose their own particular paradigm for Christian community on all other Christians. The diversity and adaptability that is represented within the New Testament should also serve as a counterbalance to the imposition of new orthodoxies which dismiss all non-conformists to the realm of heretical outsiders. Above all, this approach reminds us that at the heart of the Christian faith is the claim that in Jesus of Nazareth the Word of God became fully human, and therefore a factor which shares in the social, cultural context which characterizes in diverse ways all human existence. A sociological approach, therefore, takes with fresh seriousness the mystery of the incarnation.

142

ENDNOTES

1.    Martin Buber, Two Types of Faith; London: Routledge & Kegan Paul, 1951.
2.    Clifford Geertz, The Interpretation of Cultures: Explorations in Cosmology; NY: Basic Books, 1973.
3.    Ibid., p. 89.
4.    Mary Douglas, Purity and Danger: An Analysis of Concepts of Pollution and Taboo; London: Routledge & Kegan Paul, 1966, and, Natural Symbols: Explorations in Cosmology; NY: Pantheon, 1982 (original 1970).
5.    Peter L. Berger, The Sacred Canopy; Garden City: Doubleday, 1969. Thomas Luckman, The Social Construction of Reality; Garden City: Doublday, 1966.
6.    A. Schutz, On Phenomenology and Social Relations; Chicago: University of Chicago, 1970, pp. 82, 96.
7.    Suzanne Langer, Philosophy in a New Key: A Study in the Symbolism of Reason, Rite & Art, 3rd ed.; Cambridge, MA: Harvard University Press, 1951.
8.    Gerd Thiessen, The Miracle Stories of the Early Christian Tradition (1983), The Shadow of the Galilean: The Quest of the Historical Jesus in Narrative Form (1987), Sociology of Early Palestinian Christianity (1978), all Philadelphia: Fortress Press.
9.    Wayne Meeks, The First Urban Christians: The Social World of the Apostle Paul; New Haven: Yale University Press, 1983.
10.    Thiessen, The Social Setting of Pauline Christianity: Essays on Corinth; Philadelphia: Fortress, 1982.
11.    Howard Clark Kee, Christian Origins in Sociological Perspective: Methods and Researches; Philadelphia: Westminster, 1980, and, Jesus in History; NY: Harcourt, Brace & World, 1970, and, Medicine, Miracle and Magic in New Testament Times; NY: Cambridge University Press, 1986, and, Miracle in the Early Christian World: A Study in Sociohistorical Method; New Haven: Yale University Press, 1983.
12.    Raymond E. Brown, Community of the Beloved Disciple; NY: Paulist, 1979.

# PAUL THE THEOLOGIAN?

## Karlfried Froehlich

Who is a theologian? Obviously the one who does theology. Carl Michalson was one, and he was not shy to confess it: "I am vocationally neither an historian nor a philosopher. I am a 'theologian'."[1]

In the ancient world, theology meant the mythical talk about the gods in cult and poetry. In this sense, Homer was a theologian, in fact the theologian of the Greek world. For Eusebius of Caesarea, at the threshold of the new Christian world of the 4th century, it was confessional talk about the Christian God, one in three, the "theology of the Fathers." For Thomas Aquinas, it was the analogical talk about God whom both reason and faith must approach in ascending order, theology as "science." For Karl Barth, it was the responsible talk of the Church - the Church which always must rethink its contemporary proclamation of God in confrontation with the biblical witness of the God revealed in Christ. For Carl Michalson, theology was a "method of thinking about the Christian faith," an existential, historical and eschatological method - theology in the light of the experience of human existence, historicity and ultimacy.[2]

Theology has come a long way since antiquity. But it has always been connected with talk, speech, thought. And as such it has always implied explanation, interpretation, "hermeneutics." Hermes was the god of commerce and communication, the bringer of intelligent speech and poetry, who with these wonderful gifts taught humans the ambiguity of language, the ability to speak the truth but also to deceive, to lie. Carl Michalson was a hermeneutical theologian. As I remember him, he was fascinated by the ambivalence of language and of languages. In his own passion for communication as a speaker, preacher and teacher, he was a master of the rhetorical arts, of the power of plain words, but also of images, of the intentional ambiguity of the message which calls for an existential commitment to truth rather than the docile and thoughtless acceptance of truth as factual information.

In the framework of the Christian tradition, existentialist theologians have always found a warrant for their method of thinking in the writings of the Apostle Paul, especially the Epistle to the Romans. Rom 10:4, "Christ is the end of the law," was behind their affirmation of Christ as the end of history, which Carl Michalson reinterpreted with the paradigm of the Christ event as the "hinge of history." Rom 10:17, "Faith comes from hearing," provided the basis for Barth's insistence that faith, in the first instance, is an "acoustical affair" - a dictum to which Michalson often referred. I remember Carl quoting to us in class Luther's famous pronouncement on the true theologian: "The real theologian is the one who can rightly distinguish between Gospel and Law; this is the most difficult art of all; I myself have not mastered it." Carl Michalson was lecturing on Bultmann and thus proceeded to explain the law/gospel dialectic in terms of "Historie" and "Geschichte," regretting all the while that the English language, unfortunately, had only one single word for this monumental duality!

Luther, of course, took his clue from Paul, and more specifically from Romans. His Romans commentary of 1515/16 marked the emergence of the unmistakable vocabulary and the revolutionary conceptuality of his new theology. One hardly claims too much if one suggests that Paul more than anyone else provided the language for the central affirmation of Protestant theology ever since. Many of the battles over the nature and structure of theology have been fought out, in biblical terms, in the exegesis of Romans commentaries.

Karl Barth did not write his "Roemerbrief" as a piece of technical scholarship, but as a theological statement, a scathing indictment of the prevalent values of the culture Protestantism of his day. Barth has been rightly criticized that his commentary is all krisis and offers very little exegesis. But even one of the most recent commentaries by a professional "exegete," Ernst Kaesemann, displays this Christian daring.[3] Kaesemann's commentary engages one's full attention precisely at the points where its author turns "theological," fighting the dangers of wrong-headed theologies which claim to rest on Paul, or at least to be in line with the Pauline gospel. Behind the critical discussion of the text, the reader senses the author's passion for a theology of Christian freedom which must be defended against the straight-jackets of a supposed Pauline mysticism, sacramentalism and institutionalism as much as a Pauline enthusiasm, moralism and pietism. The blows fall to the right and to the left, one after another.

One is reminded of Jude 9: The Archangel Michael disputing with the devil over the body of Moses - a war of truly cosmic dimensions. Kaesemann wages his battle in the name of the true Paul of Romans. But this Paul is not a dead body, a corpse of the past. He is the voice of God in the living word of the ancient writer. No student should be allowed to avoid the challenge of Kaesemann's Paul in this commentary. Kaesemann's Paul? Kaesemann has been criticized as presenting no more than that: at best, a "typically Lutheran" Paul, at worst an idiosyncratic maverick who reflects more directly the personality of the author of the commentary than the author of the Epistle.

Which Paul? The "true" Paul? Is there a true Paul anywhere, at least in Romans? The question is not new. It goes back to the earliest centuries when the Pauline epistles were canonized. In fact, the process of Paul's canonical reception itself reflects a struggle over the very definition of what was Christian theology and what was not.

Marcion seems to have been the first to "canonize" a collection of Pauline epistles with the purpose of verifying his own understanding of the true gospel by proper authority. His Paul was the only true apostle of Christ and of the God whom Christ proclaimed, the norm by which all other Christian proclamation must be measured. While we do not have the actual text of his Apostolos, the very arrangement of this part of his canon reveals the polemic thrust: Galatians, not Romans, is first, the letter in which Paul is arguing most vividly against "Judaizers," the advocates of the Old Testament God and his law.

Marcion probably did not trigger the development of our New Testament canon. A normative collection of four gospels was already forming elsewhere. Pauline letter collections in some form probably existed prior to his initiative. Irenaeus accused Marcion of a biased selection not only with regard to the gospels but also with regard to the Apostolos. He was the first to use clearly a Pauline corpus enlarged by the Pastoral Epistles. That does not mean that the Pastorals existed before Marcion's canon as part of a larger orthodox canon as Irenaeus implies. It is no wonder that some modern scholars have suggested an anti-Marcionite origin for the Pastorals, attributing them to a Lucan circle in Asia Minor, or to Polycarp.

Of even more interest is the Paul whom Tertullian defended. Here we see some of the consequences of having to promote a canonical Paul who included the Pastorals and was clearly opposed to the Marcionite "distortion." Tertullian honored Paul as an apostle, even as a special vessel of God's election. But Paul for him was an apostle only along with the Twelve to whom he was "posterior" by his own admission. At one point, Tertullian calls him "haereticorum apostolus," the apostle of the heretics. The term does not disqualify Paul as an apostle but certainly does not qualify him as the Apostle either. Tertullian's interpretation of Gal 1-2 simply ignored the thrust of 1:11ff, and emphasized that Paul needed and received approval for his mission from the other apostles. Thus, Paul's criticism of Peter at Antioch (Gal 2:11-14) was the typical overreaction of a new convert, to put it mildly. Against Marcion, Tertullian also tried to minimize Paul's apparent criticism of the Law, especially in Romans. Law and Gospel, he held, were not antithetical. It is the <u>onera legis</u>, the ceremonial laws, which are abolished, not the Decalogue and the moral law of God.

A second front where rival understandings of Paul clashed, was the controversy over Christian Gnosticism in the second and third centuries. Elaine Pagels has shown that the Valentinians developed their hermeneutical grid from terminology they found in Paul: outer and inner man; flesh, soul and spirit; letter and spirit; gnosis and wisdom. Obviously, they regarded Paul as a pre-eminent gnostic. Irenaeus did not challenge the Valentinian use of Christian writings in general and of the Pauline epistles in particular. He <u>did</u> fight their claim of a <u>deeper</u> understanding which he criticized as their taking apart the beautiful mosaic of a king and re-assembling the pieces into the shape of a dog. The anti-Gnostic front still dominated the Pauline interpretation of Greek theologians in the 3rd century as far as we can judge from the scant evidence. It is even possible that the first running commentaries by Clement and Origen, of which only Origen's Romans is known to us in a heavily revised Latin translation, were written in order to refute the Gnostic interpretation by carefully retracing the Apostle's own argument sentence by sentence.

This apologetic purpose of writing a detailed commentary in order to prove a particular use of Paul wrong is even more likely in the case of the commentaries of the astonishing "rediscovery of Paul" among Western theologians of the late 4th century. The term refers to the strange phenomenon that six major Latin commentaries on the Pauline corpus were written or begun during the 50 years between 360-410 A.D.: Marius Victorinus, the Ambrosiaster, Jerome, Augustine, Pelagius, and an anonymous work recently edited by Frede.

These commentaries have nothing to do with the Pelagian controversy; even Pelagius' own commentary antedates the beginning of the struggle in 411. Some of them reveal no obvious polemical or apologetic purpose. The situation is different for Augustine. We have only three odd pieces from his pen, all dating to the first years of his tenure at Hippo: a brief exposition of Galatians, a miscellany of 84 <u>propositiones</u> on Romans, and a long fragment on the opening lines of Romans. The latter text suggests that Augustine planned a major commentary on Romans but never took up the task. Paula Fredriksen Landes, its most recent editor and translator, has demonstrated that, in all these texts, Augustine developed his own Paulinism in antithesis to the Manichean Paul he had encountered during his years as an auditor of that religious movement.

Following the lead of Marcion, the Manicheans in North Africa rejected the Old Testament and used the Pauline Epistles to argue against "the Law" in all its unspiritual forms. Polemic against the Manichean Paul can also be discerned behind the first of the new commentaries, that by Marius Victorinus. Recent close inspection of this work has revealed an additional polemical background. The professional philosopher not only wanted to refute pagan polemicists such as Porphyry and the Emperor Julian who poured out their contempt for Paul, but he also tried to establish Nicene orthodoxy against the use of Paul by the Arians. His argument was basically philosophical but employed quite deliberately the genre of the detailed commentary of an authoritative text. In this climate, the example of this highly respected commentator may have triggered the attempts of other would-be "philosophers" to develop their true Christian philosophy by producing commentaries on Paul in the wake of the Western acceptance of Anti-Arianism as orthodoxy in the 350s.

Our survey of three clashes between rival interpretations of Paul in the early church does not suggest the smooth linear reception of Paul into Christian theology which many scholars have assumed. From the beginning of Christian theology, the Roman Catholic exegete Otto Kuss maintains, Paul was a dominant factor. His letters were collected early on and enriched by pieces issued from a Pauline school which tried to protect the master against unwarranted consequences drawn from his teaching.

I think we must reckon with a far more confusing interplay of assertions and reactions, affirmations and denials; in short, with a much more colorful palette of normative images of Paul. Which Paul influenced the beginnings of Christian theology? Which Pauline school upheld the "true" Paul against distortions? In terms of the Epistles, we should not forget that there is early evidence for more reticent, if not outright negative reaction coming from various quarters.

One might mention the caution expressed in II Peter 3:16, a document sympathetic to Paul. It speaks of Paul's Epistles "in which there are some things hard to understand which the ignorant and unstable twist to their own destruction." Or one could note James 2:14-16, the famous passage about faith and works. The author of James may not polemicize against Paul's letters themselves but certainly argues against some kind of Paulinists. More obvious is the strong Anti-Paulinism of the Pseudo-Clementine "Grundschrift" which attacks passages of Paul under the name of Simon the Magician.

I for one am still wondering about the assumed universal impact of the Pauline Epistles among Christians in the early 2nd century. Were there no churches that did not know them or had no use for them? It seems clear that the late 2nd century epistolary canon of the New Testament with its two parts, Paul or Pseudo-Paul, and the Catholic Epistles, had its Sitz im Leben in anti-Marcionite and anti-Gnostic circles which valued Paul highly. But what was the situation before 140/145? Recently, Ernst Dassmann has surveyed the material once more and concluded that "a large number of writings of all kinds and genres of early Christian literature betray a knowledge of the person and work of Paul."[4] Dassmann's discussion is balanced and allows for considerable variety in the reception of Paul. With regard to Paul's letters, however, I am still impressed by the large numbers of authors before 140 who show no knowledge or interest at all: Acts, Didache, Barnabas, II Clement, Hermas, but also Papias, Hegesippus, Aristides. One can cite good reasons for their silence. But reliance on the Pauline Epistles and their theology apparently did not belong to the sine qua non of Christian theologizing.

With Dassmann and others, we may even have to distinguish between knowledge of Paul's work and of his person, the Paul of the Epistles and the Paul of story and legend. The latter could exist without the former. Hans Martin Schenke has argued that the tradition of a Pauline legend extolling the exemplary missionary and wonderworker, antedates the epistolary collection by a considerable margin. Small collections may have developed locally after Paul's death, but the legendary Paul had a life quite independent from such material. The apocryphal literature of the late second and early third centuries such as the Acts of Peter, the Acts of Andrew and Paul, the Epistola Apostolorum, and especially the Acts of Paul, witness to a popular veneration which was nourished by traditions whose origin is hard to trace.

In a study published in 1983, Dennis MacDonald tried to link the development of the legend to two startling hypotheses.[5] First, assuming that the Acts of Paul were based on older oral tradition, and taking his clue from the prominence in the stories of Paul's convert Thecla, he claimed a Pauline circle of ascetic women as the likely matrix for the legendary Paul of the "Acts." For the second, he rests his case on I Tim 4:7 which, he claims, should be translated, "Avoid the profane tales told by old women (muthoi graodeis, from graus, 'old woman')." The RSV has, "Have nothing to do with godless and silly myths." He suggests that the Pastoral Epistles were written to counteract this sectarian image of Paul, presenting the Apostle as a social conservative who would silence the tale-telling women.

While the basis of this bold theory is slim, there are some implications worth pondering. Dassmann has shown that apart from his pairing with Peter in Rome, the archaeological and liturgical evidence for a veneration of Paul is astonishingly meagre, even in places such as Ephesus, Thessalonica, Philippi or Corinth. In Asia Minor, the Thecla cult [of Seleucia] vastly outdistanced any veneration for Paul. In the known iconography of Paul and Thecla, the Apostle is almost exclusively a companion figure of the female saint, not the main subject. Was Thecla more important to certain groups of women in Asia Minor than Paul?

A second implication which commends itself quite apart from MacDonald's hypothesis is this: We can not simply assume that the Pastoral Epistles were "the rightful second century heirs of the Pauline legacy." For the 2nd century, we have to reckon with a plurality of "Pauls," all of whom had their supporters in smaller or larger circles of Christians who regarded themselves as disciples, pupils and adherents of Paul. The theory of a single "Pauline school" is insufficient. Pauline pluralism was fed, on the one hand, by varied appropriations of the legendary image of the great missionary by groups of his converts and admirers. On the other hand even more importantly, it was fed by the versatility if not ambiguity, of Paul's own theological language in the surviving remnants of his correspondence. In a very real sense, it was the Paul of the Epistles who could become "all things to all people."

This holds true even for the time of the fully canonized Paul of later centuries. In a little known essay, Ernst Benz made this point 40 years ago in relation to the differences between Eastern and Western Christianity.[6] In a general sense, Benz said Western theology was always concerned with the juridical aspect of the relationship between humanity and God, with law and gospel, covenant and human obligation. The East, on the other hand, stressed soteriological themes such as deification, rebirth, new creation, resurrection, and the glorification of human nature. Consequently, the Eastern churches remained deaf to the theme of justification as Paul laid it out in Romans, and they never developed a doctrine of justification. Instead, the East took up and deepened the mystical impulses of Pauline theology, the themes of christology, sacraments, Spirit and spiritual gifts, which the West never knew except in a partial, muted and ecclesiastically modified form. As proof for his observation, Benz pointed to the history of Pauline exegesis: The great interest in Romans in the West from the 4th century onward simply was not shared in the East. None of the great fathers of the 4th century produced a commentary on Romans; in fact, Didymus the Blind wrote on I-II Corinthians, Galatians and Ephesians, but not on Romans. When later writers such as some Antiochian exegetes and Cyril of Alexandria included Romans, it was more for the sake of completeness; the great themes of the Epistle found no echo here. Benz concluded that, roughly speaking, "the East could be described as having accepted the Paul of Corinthians, the West the Paul of Romans."[7]

One might want to question Benz' proof from the distribution of sources. The catenae fragments reveal that, just as in the West, there were Arianizing and Anti-Arian Romans commentaries written by Greek theologians of the later 4th century and the sustained interest in Romans among the Antiochian school theologians demands explanation. But Benz' basic point remains intriguing. Compared with the East, the interest in Romans and its theological themes was infinitely greater in the West. A recent author counted over 50 Romans commentaries in the Latin Middle Ages before the Reformation.

## II.

Working with medieval commentaries on Romans is not easy. One faces first of all the problem of availability. The 12th century, for example, saw a tremendous upsurge in commentary production; no less than 20 unedited Romans commentaries are known from this period. Even among those that are available in print, the question of interdependence remains unclear. We have learned only recently that an anonymous commentary of the latter half of the 12th century, which was used as a standard text in the High Middle Ages, served as an agent for spreading Peter Abelard's daring and innovative Romans interpretation to a much wider readership than had been assumed.

Incidentally, this standard commentary from the School of St. Victor in Paris, bears the title, "Allegories of the New Testament." For Romans and other Pauline Epistles, this title itself is a total misnomer. There is no allegorization in it whatsoever. In fact, a reader who expects medieval exegesis of Paul to proceed by the fourfold sense of literal, allegorical, moral and anagogical interpretation, or at least by the twofold method of literal and spiritual, will find that allegorical interpretations are almost totally absent. All pursue one sense only, the literal.

What is the reason for this startling fact? The answer has to do with the role assigned to Paul in the context of the medieval canon. The medieval understanding of "allegory" was no longer synonymous with "spiritual interpretation" as it had been in the early centuries. In a very technical sense, "allegory" meant the interpretation of the Old Testament in New Testament terms or the interpretation of all of Scripture in terms of Christian doctrine. This doctrine, the "Gospel," was hidden in the text of the Old Testament and the stories and parables of the Evangelists. The older biblical authors proclaimed the mysteries of Christ under a veil: the apostles, especially Paul, declared the full truth without allegorical cover.

As the "latest" among the apostles, Paul was the last of the inspired canonical writers; in this sense, he stood at the end of a line. At the same time, he was the first doctor evangelii, opening the long succession of biblical interpreters after him. The text of the Pauline Epistles was therefore manifesta expositio. Understood in its own literal sense, it contained the full spiritual truth about the Old Testament and the things of Christ with no cover in need of being lifted and no allegory to be supplied. In the East, the Apostle John was called ho theologos. In the West, the theologian was Paul.

He was the steward at the wedding feast of Cana, the first to serve the wine into which the Lord had changed the old water. If Peter was given the keys of the kingdom, Paul received the key to open the words of the Law. It is well known that the development of "systematic theology" as a separate discipline in the Middle Ages started with exegetical questions (<u>quaestiones</u>) being added to the exposition of biblical texts in the schools. We probably need to be even more specific: being added to the exposition of the Pauline Epistles, primarily Romans, in the work of Peter Abelard and his school. Paul was the exemplary teacher of theology; his theological language was the norm, the purest expression of that which any formulation of doctrine could only hope to achieve.

With this emphasis on the literal understanding of Paul, it is no wonder that medieval exegetes were interested in the rhetorical analysis of Romans. To take an example, Rom 8:1-11 is a central passage in the Epistle. Its most impressive rhetorical analysis was offered by Aquinas. His summary of the argument in the same passage reads as follows: After demonstrating in ch 7 that we are freed from sin and the law, Paul adds in ch 8 that we are freed from condemnation. First, he establishes our freedom from guilt (1-9), secondly, from the punishment of death (10-11). Concerning the first, he states the theme (vs 1), then proves his proposition (vs 2). The proposition itself has two parts: first, it establishes the benefits of grace in terms of a conclusion from prior premises ("there is <u>therefore</u> now no condemnation"); second, it names the beneficiaries noting two conditions, (1) that they must be "in Christ Jesus," (2) that they must not walk according to the flesh. In vss 5-6, Aquinas discovers two formal syllogisms, one concerning the flesh, the other the Spirit: (A) The wisdom of the flesh leads to death, (B) Those who live according to the flesh follow its wisdom, (C) Therefore, those who live according to the flesh are on the way to death. Thomas identifies major, minor, and conclusion, and explains with obvious admiration how skillfully the Apostle has interwoven the various elements; no classical rhetorician could have done better!

In a delightful essay, Otto Hermann Pesch has described Aquinas' Paul as "The Professor Among the Apostles."[8] Indeed, for Thomas Aquinas the Paul of Romans is not only the teacher of the <u>content</u> of Christian doctrine but also the master of its scholastic <u>presentation</u>, the professional role model for Thomas' own aspirations. Paul handled the art of rhetorical division with such subtlety and applied formal logic with such skill that the interpreter can never hope to do more than retrace the steps of this "vessel of God's election."

For the medieval exegete, interpreting Paul's Epistles was the sublime training ground for proper theological argumentation and systematization. What Maurice Wiles observed with regard to the early commentators applies even more to the medieval theologians: they present Paul's thought as uniform throughout and reduce his various affirmations to a wholly self-consistent system. Since God is a God of "sweetly disposed orderliness" (Wisdom 8:1), Paul's text must be shown to reflect everywhere the "fittingness" and "necessity" of God's actions under the Old Covenant and under the New. Paul was a teacher, not a prophet.

One cannot fault medieval exegetes for inattentiveness to the Pauline text or for simply reading their own ideas into it. They were careful, meticulous readers precisely because they looked to Paul as <u>the</u> teacher both of the content and language of Christian theology. To a large extent, medieval theology itself was based on a Pauline vocabulary which gave it its main concepts. But their reading of Paul labored under some serious drawbacks. There was first of all, the Latin Vulgate. This text could influence the interpretation as in the subject of justification. The word <u>iustificatio</u> in its very etymology as a Latin compound suggests a specific model of reading our salvation in Christ: <u>iusti-ficare</u> means to <u>make</u> righteous, to <u>transform</u> the impious into a pious one, the sinner into a righteous person. The entire Augustinian tradition reads justification in this way. There was also the Paul of the commentary tradition. It included almost no Greek Fathers. Augustine, on the other hand, was omnipresent. From Carolingian times on, Augustinian chain commentaries were available, glossing the Pauline Epistles by excerpts from all of Augustine's writings. But it is also a fact that, along with Augustine, Pelagius' commentary on the Pauline Epistles remained a standard tool throughout the Middle Ages. Three differently revised versions circulated under orthodox names and were used without any suspicion. If one adds that from the 9th century through the 16th, the pro-Augustinian decisions of the Synod of Orange in 529 had simply fallen into oblivion, one realizes that the Pelagian reading of Paul with its strong ascetic imperatives was alive and well.

What then happened in the Reformation? Certainly, the rediscovery of the Greek Paul in humanistic circles was opening new horizons. There was indeed another "Paulusrenaissance" in the 15th century. Humanists admired Paul's Greek and continued to extol him as a master of rhetorical form. Another factor may be more important. In his letters, the humanists discovered Paul as an individual and thus as an ideal figure with whom to identify. Many humanists wrote commentaries on Romans reflecting this trend. Marsilio Ficino understood Paul in the light of II Cor 12:2f as the great mystic whose ascent into the third heaven gave him the vision of the same eternal truth to which Plato had access and which Marsilio himself felt called to proclaim in a great synthesis of classical and Christian thought. Erasmus' "Paraphrases" on Romans and Galatians promoted an anti-clerical Paul whose teaching of Christ's philosophy was really aimed at a simple piety of the heart. This Paul was for everyone; all true theology is for everyone, not just for schoolmen.

Luther's theological conversion was inextricably linked to his exegesis of Romans. He was aware of the parallel to Augustine. For him as a late medieval theologian, Paul was still primarily the normative systematic theologian whose teaching must open the meaning of all scripture. His discovery was a new form of the Pauline key to this meaning which he too worked out in a language nourished by Paul, and for that matter, by the Paul of the Latin Vulgate: iustificatio impii, simul iustus et peccator, the dialectic of lex and evangelium, the theology of the Cross and the theology of Glory. Why then does the Paul of Luther's reading sound so different from the Paul who taught medieval theology?

I think, the strength of Luther's reading, just as that of the Romans commentaries of the Early Church, was its anti-heretical, polemical bias. In Luther's eyes, the church and theology of his time had succumbed to the Pelagian error. The Paul he discovered was the anti-Pelagian Paul whose picture Augustine had never fully drawn out exegetically. The task had been left unfinished and had become ever more difficult in the wake of the development of the exegetical tradition. Measured by the standards of his day, Luther's reading of Paul revealed to him a startling truth: "Here you have Paul, the most heretical of all heretics; his heresy is unheard of: dead to the law to live for God!" (Gal 2:19).

Was Luther's "heretical" Paul the real one? Luther still had no sense for the historical situation of the Epistles. Romans, he claimed, "was written to Christian believers of a congregation which was to have a witness of its faith and doctrine from the pen of this great Apostle in their fight against Jews and Gentiles in Rome." In the same vein, Melanchthon's commentary on Romans called the Epistle "a compend of Christian theology" and proceeded to subject it in good Ciceronian fashion to a rhetorical analysis by loci which systematized its content into a schoolbook of Lutheran orthodoxy.

Today we will always remain uncomfortable with this blatant disregard for the historical Paul. If one thing is clear, it is that the real Paul was not a professor of systematic theology, as medieval exegetes firmly believed and Luther and Melanchthon still assumed. Well, then - what was he? In trying to answer this question our way we should keep in mind for which Paul we are looking in our exegesis: The legendary author of the 1st century, whose historical personality will probably remain as elusive as ever to our grasp? The great system builder whose interpretation of the Christ event established the true form of Christian philosophy once and for all? Or the ever challenging and militant apostle who has helped the church of all ages to fight the good fight of the faith, then as much as now? I still would settle for the third. I know Carl Michalson would have. What did he say? "I am vocationally neither an historian nor a philosopher. I am a theologian."

## ENDNOTES

1.    Michalson, The Rationality of Faith; NY: Scribner's, 1963, p. 18.
2.    Michalson, The Hinge of History; NY: Scribner's, 1959, p. 9.
3.    Kaesemann, Commentary on Romans; Grand Rapids: Eerdmans, 1980.
4.    Dassmann, Paulus in fruh-christlicher Frommigkeit und Kunst; Opladen: Westdeutscher, 1982, p. 316.
5.    Macdonald, The Legend and the Apostle: The Battle for Paul in Story and Canon; Philadelphia: Westminster, 1983.
6.    Benz, "Das Paulusverstaendnis der morgenlaendischen und abendlaendischen Kirche," Zeitschrift fur Religions- und Geistesgeschichte 3 (1951), 289-309.
7.    Ibid., p. 291.
8.    Pesch, "Paul as Professor of Theology. The Image of the Apostle in St. Thomas's Theology," The Thomist 38 (1974), 584-605.

IV.

PRACTICAL INTERPRETATION

# THE FOOLISHNESS OF PREACHING

Lawrence E. Toombs

To address the subject of preaching in the context of the theology of Carl Michalson, for whom kerygma was a concept of almost overwhelming importance, is to confront at the outset a basic dilemma. Will the discussion be an attempt to draw from his published writings and from personal memories of his "table talk," Michalson's insights into the nature and function of preaching? Or will it be an analysis of his sermons in an effort to recover the source of their dynamic and power?[1] Fortunately, it is not necessary to settle for one or other of these alternatives, or to navigate the narrow strait between Scylla and Charybdis. A fourth choice is to follow the advice received by Peer Gynt when he confronted the Great Boeg, and to "go round about."[2]

The point of departure for this exploratory essay, one out of many possible choices, is Michalson's distinctive understanding of the nature of myth. In The Hinge of History, he points out that the ancient myths "referred to their gods as if they were actors in world history,"[3] that is, the mythographers incorporated their understanding of the divine in a time-space framework, freezing it into an extended, chronological sequence of events. In an analogous manner, the Apocalyptists mythologized their view of salvation by hardening it into a pattern of occurrences which extended the time-space framework into the future and even beyond history:  the deterioration of the present age; the appearance of the Messiah; the final conquest of evil; resurrection; judgment and the establishment of a new Kingdom of Righteousness. The Apocalyptists thus did to the concept of salvation what the ancient mythographers had done to the divine. They gave it the rigidity and objectivity of a sequence of actions or happenings following one another in chronological order. When cast in this form, the past, the future, and the "hidden" can readily be studied and discussed. However, the nagging question remains whether what is being examined is a dead thing, the corpse of something once alive, but killed by the process of turning it into a mythology or a history, which in the end amounts to much the same thing.

This understanding of myth makes it clear that a historical-mythological trap lies in the path of the Christian preacher. He or she may identify the kerygma with the historic Jesus, equating it with a fixed sequence of events which constitute "the life of Our Lord," or with sayings and doctrines recorded in the Gospels as the earliest form of Christian teaching. Alternately, one may identify the kerygma with a series of events yet to come: immortality in some blessed realm after death; the Second Coming of Christ; or the achievement of social justice in a transformed society. Emphases of these kinds will, of course, result in preaching, but it will be historical or mythological, not kerygmatic.

## Preaching as Eschatology

Kerygmatic preaching is eschatological, and not historical or apocalyptic. The moment with which the preacher is primarily concerned is not extracted from a sequence of past events nor from a series of happenings yet to come. It is a perpetual "here and now." In the moment of preaching the old is coming to an end and the new age is about to begin. The act of preaching is the proclamation of the eschatological "now."

The fundamental conviction which underlies eschatological preaching is, "When anyone is united to Christ there is a new world; the old order has gone and the new order has already begun" (I Cor 5:17). The link between the hearer and Christ is not forged by the preacher. The Messianic agent who ushers in the new order is Christ. The preacher is a voice announcing the end of the old and the beginning of the new, a herald proclaiming that by the power of God in Christ a new order is even now breaking in upon the old. He or she is witness that the moment of preaching, or indeed any moment in the experience of the hearers, may be for them both an end and a beginning.

The historical-mythological scenario, however, is extremely difficult to avoid. The eschatological now can be, and frequently is, seen as a single and unique turning point between two contrasting ways of life. The old order is Satan's dominion, evil and corrupt; the new is the realm of light, peace, and godliness. Conversion is the "eschatological" moment which whisks the believer totally out of one and into the other. That moment has only to be experienced once for the transformation to be complete. Such a view captures and pins down the eschatological moment between two mythologies, and in so doing makes it a part of the very mythology from which it sought to escape.

The sin-conversion-righteousness pattern assumes the existence of two discrete and definable "orders" of human existence, in one or the other of which the human being in the totality of his or her personality must stand. It deals with human beings as if they were actors in a predetermined drama, and neglects altogether the autonomy, complexity, and ambiguity of the human personality. To be a person is to be an intricately interwoven web of contrasting and often conflicting emotions and motives, aspirations and doubts. It is to experience needs and powers, strengths and weaknesses at many different levels simultaneously. It is to stand, not in a single definable order of existence, but in many at the same time. To be human is to be inescapably ambivalent. For this reason, the human being may experience a death to the old and a birth to the new repeatedly, or even continuously. The necessity of using terms with a chronological connotation tends to obscure and falsify the reality being referred to, but the genuineness of the experience is readily recognizable.

Seen in this perspective, the eschatological moment cannot be dispensed with, outgrown, or superseded. The new is perpetually breaking in on the old through different points on the perimeter of the stockade by which life seeks to protect the familiar and the comfortable from change.

It is possible for the preacher to be deflected from eschatological preaching by the surface tranquility of the congregation, and its apparent complete acceptance of things as they are. The preacher may react to this presumed condition of the congregation by allowing the sermon to degenerate into a teaching session in which the "basic facts" about Christianity are expounded, or into eulogies of the minor virtues such as generosity or neighborliness, which the hearers are assumed to possess but in the practice of which they may make some improvement. Or the sermon may degenerate into homilies on the advantages - personal, social, and financial - to be obtained from Christian faith, considered as synonymous with Church membership. The existence of the "comfortable pew" is an illusion used to justify preaching of these kinds. The apparent self-satisfaction, expressing itself as total approbation of one's own nature and circumstances, is more often than not a mask that hides the face of discontent. The people know, none better, the places where their lives have decayed like a worn-out garment. They require no preacher to tell them where their humanity has become stagnant and tired. What they need a preacher for is to assure them that the moment of change is now, the place of change is here, and the power of change is the power of God in Jesus Christ.

Preaching as Humanistic

If preaching is the proclamation of the eschatological moment in which the old ceases and the new begins, it follows that preaching is a humanistic enterprise, in the sense that its motivation arises from the human condition, its direction is toward persons, and its focus is upon human beings. The preacher, then, is not primarily a lecturer about God, or an instructor in abstract Christian principles, although in the act of preaching both functions may incidentally be discharged. The preacher first and always speaks to the human condition and to human needs.

In Faith for Personal Crises Carl Michalson wrote two provocative sentences, one directed to the minister and the other to the theologian. "Is not the ministry of the church responsible to its craft only when it addresses the needs of the people from the deepest resources of the Christian faith?" "A theologian who does not think of the Christian faith in relation to the needs of the people has defaulted in his responsibility to the practicing church. Moreover, he has missed the joy of theology and to miss the joy is to miss all."[4] The common denominator of these sentences is the words "the needs of the people." The preacher is both minister and theologian and, therefore, has a double share in the joy and the responsibility of which Michalson speaks.

In referring to preaching as humanistic, there is no intention of robbing it of its theological dimension by denying its intrinsic relationship to the will and power of God. It is the resources of the Christian faith which make the preacher's task possible, or even bearable. But those very resources show clearly that God himself is a humanist, in the sense in which that word is being used here. God's primary concern, as both the Old and the New Testaments indicate, is not to impart information about himself, but to lead his human creation into a realization of its humanity, or in other words to create a people of God. God calls his servants by their human names. He sees the affliction of his people and comes to deliver them. He brings light to the nations. He loves the world.

God-centered preaching and human-centered preaching appear on the face of the language to stand in contrast and opposition to one another. Yet, in the framework of biblical thought, an intimate, though paradoxical, relationship exists between them. They are polarities, not logical opposites. The poles are the two ends of the same axis. Revolving and functioning together, they constitute the limits of the same reality. The humanistic preaching of the eschatological moment may thus be more truly God-centered than a sermon which pretends to lift the veil and allow a voyeuristic look into the privacy of the divine.

## Preaching as Individualistic

Biblical religion is obviously concerned with the transformation of society. However, the creation of a people of God requires more than a change in the lives of a few individuals at crises points in their personal existence. It implies alterations in social structures, a reordering of the use of power - military, political, and legal. In such a transformation, complex questions are involved, such as the nature of human sexuality; the limits of individual freedom under a rule of law; the responsibility of society for its natural environment; the status and rights of minorities, gradualism as opposed to revolution as an instrument of social change.

The tension between the social and individual dimensions of Christianity has resulted in a periodic oscillation within the church between a social and an individual Gospel, popular stress falling now on one side and now on the other. Bitter accusations of distorting the Gospel have been interchanged between the two camps. How does the enterprise of preaching stand in relation to this perennial division of interest and emphasis?

The understanding of preaching which has been presented thus far would seem to place preaching in a firmly individualistic posture. To be sure, the congregation hears the sermon in the context of the Christian community, and that fact bears upon what is said and how it is heard. Moreover, the members of the congregation live in a wider society than the church, and bring with them problems and needs that are generated by that wider society. What happens to them in the preaching will be reflected in the way they act in response to social problems. These observations, however, do not go to the heart of the matter.

The encounter with Christ in the eschatological moment, of which the preacher is the herald and messenger, is a point of decision, the ultimate exercise of human freedom. The fundamental question then becomes, "What or who is the unit of freedom and decision?" Societies make their decisions in different and complex ways, but allowing for all the ambiguities inherent in that statement, societal decisions are in the end amalgamations or conflations of the choices of individuals. The chicken-and-egg argument about "which comes first" - the decision of the individual or that of society - is a futile debate. Given an operative society into which an individual is born and from which he or she learns the ABCs of life, each kind of decision becomes an ingredient in the other. When, however, change within an operative society is contemplated, two routes are open. The change may come by the imposition of the will of a few upon the many, or by agreement based on a consensus. In either case, individual decisions lie at the root of the change.

In terms of the preaching situation, the problem is less involved. By its very nature, the message must reach and touch the individual in the private citadel of his or her personality. It is there, if it takes place at all, that the eschatological moment occurs, and something new comes to birth. This is not to say that the preacher must be without political convictions or social goals, nor is it to argue that the moment of renewal has no social consequences. It is to recognize that the response which the sermon seeks is personal in the most intense and intimate way.

To those who see the pulpit as an instrument for direct social change, and feel that the function of the preacher is to chart the direction of that change and to persuade the congregation to follow the path set before them in the sermon, this may be a disappointingly pallid conclusion, a mere whisper of promise where a battle cry was called for. In the apologia for Faith for Personal Crises, Michalson wrote, "Though it does not speak with the stentorian accents of a theology of more regal days, possibly its whispers may be heard."[5]

## Preaching as Proclamation and Invitation

In no small measure, the difficulty of the preacher's task resides in what should be excluded from the act of preaching. A temptation, continuously present and never quite overcome, is to confuse the preacher's office with something which it is not: that of leader, or judge, or arbiter of morals, or former of opinions, or champion of an establishment, or educator, or purveyor of novelties, or entertainer. An understanding of what preaching is helps to exclude from the pulpit these roles, which to some degree the practicing minister may adopt in other aspects of his work.

The eschatological moment of death and rebirth, which lies at the heart of the Gospel, is not brought about by the sermon or the preacher. That moment is an encounter with Christ, and he alone is the agent and catalyst of the transformation. The preacher is, to use the biblical language, his herald or messenger. In Pauline terms, "We are ambassadors of Christ" (II Cor 5:20). The offices of herald, messenger, and ambassador are all representative, but representative in a highly restricted way. None of these functionaries bring with them the power of the authority which they represent, nor can they claim it in any sense as their own. They are witnesses that such a power exists, that it calls for recognition, and that if recognized, it may alter dramatically the situation in which the hearers of the message find themselves. The crucial feature of all three offices is that they herald or proclaim a reality outside and beyond themselves.

Heralds or ambassadors among world powers reinforce proclamation by threats and promises, veiled or open, as circumstances seem to require. The ambassadorial approach which seeks to compel concurrence with the club or the carrot is closed to the preacher. Attempts to coerce or cajole are in fact betrayals of the nature of preaching. The eschatological moment cannot be commanded, forced, or bought. If a person enters that moment, he or she must do so in full freedom, neither led nor driven to Christ, but encountered by Him. Deprived of whip, candy, or money-bags with which to influence the hearer, the preacher becomes purely a proclaimer. The experience in the cause of which he or she preaches is a Jobian encounter in which the human being, with freedom untrammeled and will unforced, declares, "I have heard of thee with the hearing of the ear, but now mine eye seeth thee" (Job 42:5). In such a moment, the preacher and his or her eloquence vanish from the scene and all that remains is the reality of the encounter.

The herald's proclamation of the Gospel does not present itself in the form of a series of directives, backed by divine authority, a statement of the laws of God with appropriate rewards and punishments attached. The imperative mood is, indeed, present in preaching, but it is there in its mildest and least coercive form - invitation. It is the echo of the prophet's "Come ye to the waters" (Is 55:1) and of Matthew's "Come unto me all ye that labour and are heavy-laden and I will give you rest" (Matt 11:28), where the "me" and "the waters" are not the preacher and his or her doctrines, but the living Christ, and the invitation is not for some future date but now.

Preaching as Foolishness

Looking back over the discussion of preaching given in these pages produces the impression that it is an extended illustration of what Paul called "the foolishness of preaching" (moria tou kerygmatos), or "the foolishness of what we preach," or "the foolishness of the proclamation," or "the foolishness of

Gospel," by whichever translation one prefers to render the apostle's words. The evaluation of preaching as foolishness contains more than a grain of truth. In both form and content, preaching seems a puny weapon with which to conquer the world, or if a less military metaphor is more appropriate, a thin gruel with which to feed the spiritually hungry. This perception of preaching has caused it to fall somewhat into disrepute within the church. (It always was something of a joke to those outside.) Many ministers and their parishioners tolerate preaching as a traditional activity of the church, preserved nowadays for its archaeological value and its sentimental associations, while the business of the church goes on in other and more effective ways.

It is the word "effective" that most surely consigns preaching to the category of foolishness. Since the dawn of the scientific age, society has been possessed by a veritable passion for quantification, and effectiveness has come to mean measurable results. What we preach is the coming together of the needs of people and the power of God in Christ, the transformation of the old into the new. No device has been invented to detect when an eschatological event has occurred. No stethoscope exists which can hear a renewed heartbeat in the human spirit. The outcome for the individual or for society of an encounter with Christ cannot be evaluated on a scale of one to ten. Even if such measurements were possible, the connection between them and the act of preaching would remain dubious, since the sermon does not produce the outcome, but only witnesses to its possibility. In a world which places a high value on quantifying results, preaching must remain a puzzling piece of foolishness.

Science has taught us to value reliability and consistency almost as highly as measurability. Reliability issues in predictability, and predictability in its turn, in controllability. Judged by this sequence, preaching fails all along the line. The preacher has no more control over the results of his or her preaching than he or she has the capacity to measure them, nor can he or she predict what outcome, if any, will follow on preaching. In fact since any outcome is the work not of the preaching but of God, preaching may be said to have no results. An unreliable, unpredictable, and uncontrollable activity that has no measurable outcome unquestionably qualifies as foolishness.

It may be argued in defense of preaching that it at least creates a context in which the saving act of God can take place, or that it produces a readiness and an expectancy which prepare the way for the activity of God. Who, one might ask, would come to the party unless he or she received an invitation? Who would know about the king's presence unless the herald announced it? "How shall they hear without a preacher?" (Rom 10:14).

This line of thought may go some way toward mitigating the charge of foolishness, but it is only a short distance. The apostle Paul qualifies on all counts as a kerygmatic preacher, but Luke tells an informative story about his preaching in Ephesus. "A youth named Eutychus, who was sitting on the window ledge, grew more and more sleepy as Paul went on talking. At last he was completely overcome by sleep, fell from the third story to the ground and was picked up for dead" (Acts 20:9). If the preacher is a herald, he or she may draw attention to themselves rather than to the master. If the preacher is one who invites, he or she may inadvertently issue the invitation for the wrong party.

Since it seems impossible to escape the foolishness of preaching, it is best to accept it, and even to look upon it as a source of strength. In a discussion of the conflict between religion and science, Carl Michalson made a distinction between living in order to know, which is the basis of science, and knowing in order to live, which is the religious way of knowing.[6] Perhaps a similar distinction can profitably be applied to preaching. When the church thinks of itself as living in order to preach, it faces sharply the foolishness of what it does. If it understands that it preaches in order to live, that its act of witnessing, of heralding the Gospel, is its life's blood pumping in its veins, the foolishness remains, but is transformed into a vital, life-renewing folly.

As to the results, we cannot go much further than the statement of Paul, who in spite of the unfortunate affair of Eutychus, was able to say, "God chose to save those who have faith by the power of the kerygma" (I Cor 1:22). If that point is secure, the heralds of the kerygma may rest content to be "fools for Christ's sake" (I Cor 4:10).

## ENDNOTES

1.     For examples of Michalson's preaching, see "Three Sermons on Prayer" in this volume. See also Edward J. Wynne, Jr. and Henry O. Thompson, eds., Prayers for Today's People; Latham, MD: University Press of America, 1982. Wynne is currently working on a volume of Michalson sermons, as yet untitled. [ed.]

2.     Scylla [a reef?] and Charybdis [a whirlpool?], the irresistible monsters on the two sides of narrow waters [?Straits of Messina?] in the story of Odyseus, have been proverbial for the danger of straying from the straight and narrow, e.g., "correct," path, since Augustine. The Norwegian dramatist, Henrik Johan Ibsen's verse drama, Peer Gynt (1867), has been published in many editions, translated into a number of languages and set to music several times. The Penguin Books (1966) publication is a convenient edition. Gynt has been described as unprincipled, buoyant, lovable, reprehensible, living by the theme, "To thine own Self be - enough." [ed.]

3.     Michalson, The Hinge of History; NY: Scribners, 1959, p. 191.

4.     Michalson, Faith for Personal Crises; NY: Scribners, 1958, p. 3.

5.     Ibid.

6.     Hinge, op. cit., pp. 56ff.

# ON ADOPTING THE ORPHAN NAMED JUSTICE

## David M. Graybeal

I am pleased to have been invited to deliver the Carl Michalson Lecture this year. The Carl Michalson Society plays an important part in the life to Drew Theological School.[1]

When I came to Drew in 1956, Mike was already a very significant pillar in the faculty. He was much beloved by his colleagues and by the students, but many members of the faculty never tired of contesting basic theological issues with him. I was one of several colleagues who audited his basic theology course, and I remember those lectures as breathtaking in their simplicity and profundity. One day he lectured on the commandment to love, and the lecture consisted of setting two theses in opposition to each other. The first was, "How can I really love my neighbor when I have been commanded to love?" He expanded on that by pointing to our experience that profound love must arise spontaneously from the heart, so that it cannot be true love if it is obedience to an order.

His second point was, "How can I truly love my neighbor unless I have been commanded to love?" And here he pointed out that the freedom and spontaneity of love, left to itself, can tire and fade, for love is never easy. If love of neighbor is to be the kind of resource the neighbor can rely upon, then I need a commandment to love when the going gets hard. That was

Mike's way of wrestling with theological issues:  dialectical, poetic, and unforgettable.

One night after a meeting he invited me to get in his car and go out to the hill in Morristown where the Michalson's were building a house. We walked around the half-finished house and talked. I said, "Mike, people say it is hard to find out where you stand in your theological work. What would you say about yourself?" He laughed with some exasperation and said, "I just don't understand that. Doesn't everyone see that I am a conservative?" Thanks, Mike.

Today I want to talk about the relation between freedom and justice, and as I do so I remember that Mike cared about justice. Our faculty was invited to send representatives to the Selma march in Alabama in the early 60's.[2] We all chipped in to pay expenses, and Dean Anderson, David Randolph, Gordon Harland, and Carl Michalson volunteered to go. We were proud of our delegation and of our representation in that historic event.

Freedom and justice are two central themes in the Biblical narratives. When the Hebrew people were in captivity in Egypt, God called Moses to go down and lead the people out of their bondage. When Pharaoh resisted the idea, the Bible reports that God acted in many ways to bring about the liberation of Israel. Moses was the leader, but he was not the liberator: liberation was God's action. Of course the people had to respond by packing up and leaving, but it was God who led them out and across the Red Sea and through the desert and finally into Canaan.

When the Hebrew people had been in Canaan for a while and had begun to settle into a social order, the prophets began to point out that God demanded that justice be central in the life of the community. They said in effect, "God did not liberate you and bring you up here just to flaunt your freedom and live irresponsibly. The God who set you free requires that you pay attention to the widow and the fatherless, to the poor and the elderly." Justice was primarily the responsibility of human beings, and it was always to be worked at under God's surveillance and God's judgement. The prophets knew that, given the nature of human beings, the establishment of justice was never easy or automatic. They knew, in effect, that eternal vigilance was the price of justice. They warned that if justice among the people was ignored, freedom would be lost. And so it was to be, and later their children would weep by the rivers of Babylon.

Last week I heard Bruce Birch, a biblical scholar at Wesley Seminary, say some very interesting things about this period of Israel's history. He said that it was not accidental that kings and prophets appear simultaneously in Israel. The establishment of the kingship moved Israel's life from an economics of justice to a politics of oppression. He suggested that Solomon's temple and Solomon's kingly house were built by slave labor, in effect. It was this movement from royal privilege into oppressive power over the people that set the stage for the prophets to confront the kings about their misuse of freedom and to speak up for justice.

Birch went on to re-tell the story of Ahab the king and the vineyard of Naboth. Ahab wanted the vineyard, but Naboth did not want to sell it. Ahab got so sick over it that he had to go to bed. But a person close to him said, "Are you not the governor of Israel? You shall have the vineyard." And so people close to the king, who knew what he wanted, had Naboth murdered without the king ordering it or having to know about it. But then the word of the Lord came to Elijah, telling him to go down and confront the king. And when Elijah came into the court, Ahab's first words were, "Have you found me, O my enemy?" Right. He had.

The New Testament events take these two themes of Israel's history and universalize them to apply to all human beings. Jesus says at the beginning of his ministry, "The Spirit of the Lord is upon me: to preach deliverance to the captives (freedom) and to preach the acceptable year of the Lord (justice)." And Paul later thunders that there is no longer any Jew or Greek, male or female. God's liberating action is for all people, and God's demand that human beings work for justice applies equally to all.

Now I want to do a fast forward to the history of our own nation. When the founders of the United States of America sat down to write the consensus on which the nation would be formed, they wrote: "We hold these truths to be self-evident; that all men [people] are created equal; that they are endowed by their Creator with certain inalienable rights; that among these rights are life, liberty, and the pursuit of happiness." And when the pledge of allegiance to the flag of the United States of America was formulated, it contained these words, "one nation, under God indivisible, with liberty and justice for all." Where did we get those ideas, if not from the Bible story? In young America, Scriptural declarations had come to be self-evident truths, and commitment to liberty and justice for all was to be central.

Liberty and justice each require the other, for its own vitality. They are like those combinations of drugs which physicians call synergistic, and must be prescribed as conjunctive medications. Either by itself is useless, perhaps dangerous, but when taken with another can become therapeutic. Liberty unrestricted and unchecked by justice can become license, filled with mischief; justice which cares little for freedom becomes rigid uniformity which crushes the human spirit. The phrase which now comes so easily to our tongues, "with liberty and justice for all" conceals a dynamo of polarized forces.

Throughout our national history, both church and state have claimed to be loyal to both these values, and American Christians until recently have had little difficulty in affirming their loyalty to God and country simultaneously. I grew up in the 1920's and 1930's with no thought as to whether there could be any conflict between church and state, or between freedom and justice. The communion table in the sanctuary of Grove Avenue Methodist was flanked by two flags, the church flag and the U.S.

flag. On Friday nights in the Boy Scout room in the basement we pledged our allegiance to one of them, and settled down to work on our God and Country awards.

During the hard years of the Depression in the 1930's, it seemed to me that church and state were cooperating, doing all they could to deal with the situation. My church distributed food and held rummage sales, and the government in the New Deal worked on the issues of justice and security. The TVA was established to develop a whole region; Social Security was begun to protect the elderly and retired; and the Civilian Conservation Corps was put to work across the nation. Many of those young people, working in their green uniforms to build the trails and the roads in the national forest that we still use, were heroes to those of us too young to join. The CCC, with its guarantee of a clean bed, three square meals a day, and $21 a month, got all the volunteers it could use. So, although the press and the wealthy screamed, and the Supreme Court declared parts of the New Deal unconstitutional, many of us were convinced that the government was committed to justice and service to the people.

John Steinbeck's novel, The Grapes of Wrath, was made into a film starring the young Henry Fonda.[3] We watched the story of these dust-bowl Oklahomans having to leave their wrecked farms and make their painful and frightening way across America to California, hungry, tired, and exploited at every stopping place. But then, as they came into California, they found a clean, decent, well-organized camp ready for them, with a sign that said "United States Department of Agriculture" on it and the American flag flying above the gate. It was sanctuary, it was caring, and it was justice in action. We wept, and we thanked God for being part of such a nation.

In retrospect, it seemed that church and state were allies in the struggle for justice; sometimes the church led the way, and sometimes the state. In the 1930's it was against the law for interracial groups to meet, but Methodist women frequently called their members from white and Black congregations to meet together. So here the church led in the struggle for justice. But in the 1950's, Emory and Henry College, a Methodist school in Virginia, was prevented by its trustees from admitting Black students until 1954, when the Supreme Court ruled in effect that the college had to admit Blacks. So here the state led in the struggle for justice.

World War II only heightened the sense that, not only church and state, but the other institutions of the establishment were joined in a common enterprise. The establishment included five major institutions; the state, the business community, the press (the media), the universities, and the church. It was a hierarchical and patriarchal organization of the society, but that did not occur to us then. My father, lay leader of Grove Avenue Church, encouraged me in my impulse to join the Navy. During the war, my home church prayed for me and the women's society knitted gloves and mufflers for my comfort. The church prayed for the nation and for the war effort. Methodism sent chaplains to war to encourage our spiritual life.

At the same time, the Navy affirmed the practice of religion. The Navy paid the chaplains. It printed our shipboard hymnbooks with taxpayers' money. It ordered that time be set aside on Sundays for "divine services" on board except when in battle, and the boatswain's call every Sunday went like this: "Now hear this: Divine Services on the forecastle at 0900. The smoking lamp is out throughout the ship." That meant that the Navy ruled no smoking on board while services were in progress, out of respect. Church and state had gone to war together, and we in the service felt fully endorsed by both. I did not meet a conscientious objector until 1946, and until that time I had hardly heard that there was such a thing.

I became the engineering officer on a destroyer escort operating mainly in the North Atlantic escorting convoys to Africa and Europe and involved in hunting for German submarines. Wartime propaganda emphasized the unity of the national effort, and the corporations which built and equipped our ships were presented as good shipmates. Westinghouse and General Electric and General Motors and Fairbanks Morse had built the machinery for our engine room. The equipment was indeed superb, and I came to love and trust those names the way I loved and trusted my other shipmates, Purvis and Murphy and Coleman and Masterton. It was not until long after the war that I discovered that you couldn't be sure if it was Westinghouse, and that someone at General Motors had assumed all along that what was good for General Motors was good for the country.

The press and the other media supported the war effort of the nation and interpreted it as a struggle for liberty and justice. No Pentagon papers were published. Few scandals were uncovered. On the one hand, it allowed Ernie Pyle and Bill Mauldin to tell some of the truth about the experience of the soldier; on the other hand, it withheld speculation about the date of D-Day and in general honored the government's desire to keep military actions secret.

The universities went to war as well. Columbia pushed its students out and took 3000 of us midshipmen into John Jay and Furnald halls, and from there, on Sunday afternoons, we marched in formation over to Riverside Church for vespers and to sing the navy hymn: "Eternal Father, strong to save, whose arm doth rule the restless wave." The University of Chicago had a team developing the atomic bomb underneath its stadium grandstand, and church colleges across the nation welcomed officer training units.

And so the Establishment closed ranks, and the nation became a community, or so it felt. The unemployment of the 30's was now replaced by the 24-hour day operations of factories, shipyards and mines. Rosie, who had been unemployed, became Rosie the Riveter to build ships and become a national heroine. Unemployed Blacks signed up or were drafted, and four came on board my ship. It seemed only natural that they were assigned to be cooks and stewards for the officers, who were of course all white. I never thought about it: they seemed content, and so were we.

So, in many ways, I experienced the war years as a great national jubilee of sharing and trust and common service of the common good. The rationing and price controls were accepted by the public in good spirit; they were assumed to be necessary to the public good. When the Snowden was to be in Norfolk for three days, and I could go ashore for 36 hours, I would ride a crowded train 12 hours to get to Radford for twelve hours, to walk down the main street of my hometown in my dress blues. I was a hero of the battle for the North Atlantic, and I was shaking hands with the heroes of the home front. It was a time of high drama and of community solidarity.

And one final note about my service to nation: when after the war I entered Yale to become a minister, the Veterans Administration did not blink an eye while paying for my theological education there on the GI bill. Church and state were still colleagues in one great enterprise.

What has happened since then? In general, these forty years have been an era of rising income, and growing wealth in private hands. It has been a time of rising individualism and of growing skepticism about service of the common good. It has been, in short, a time of rising rhetoric about the importance of freedom, and a time of growing amnesia about the importance of justice. It is not hard to see why it has happened; for the rich and powerful, freedom like that of Ahab is what we want. For the poor and the disadvantaged, justice is what is longed for. But the rich and the powerful were able to seize the microphone, to teach us all to sing the praise of freedom. We are steadily becoming a nation which espouses one value, which pledges allegiance to the idea of "with liberty for all." The devotion to freedom alone has become the national idolatry.

The effect of that focus on liberty to the neglect of justice can be seen across the board. For the state it has meant keeping taxes low while the infrastructure of bridges, highways, schools and public services decay and crumble. For the corporation, it has meant the freedom to invade and exploit our communities and the third world, while keeping the old establishment ties strong enough to bail out the banks and the Chryslers who got in trouble. And it has meant golden parachutes for corporation executives who failed, but canceled pension funds for blue-collar workers who were ejected. It has meant freedom for family farmers to be sabotaged by the Farmer's Home Administration set up to be their advocate.

It has meant freedom for the gap between the rich and poor to grow. As recently as 1973 the ratio between the average incomes of the richest fifth of the population to the poorest fifth was about six to one. By 1985 that ratio had become ten to one. In 1987 the Congressional Budget Office reported that the taxes paid by the poorest one-tenth of the population would rise by 20 percent in 1988, and that the taxes paid by the richest one-tenth of the population would be cut by 20 percent.

It can only be seen in this way: we have turned the biblical perspectives on freedom and justice upside down. Freedom is no longer the prerogative of God: it has now become the province of the American nation. So in the name of liberation we have invaded Vietnam and bombed Laos, and we have attempted to subvert the government of Nicaragua. Freedom, coupled with our enormous power and wealth, and reinforced by regular assurances from Presidents that our hearts are good, has meant that we have felt entitled to do whatever in the world we have wanted to do. El Salvador, Grenada, Libya, Lebanon, the Persian Gulf, Afghanistan. And justice, we think, is no longer our responsibility. Equity, fairness, equality, security, these are matters that are in the lap of the gods. Are you poor, homeless, disabled, unemployed? Tough luck. Or, it may be your own fault. But it is certainly not the fault of the system, and it is surely not my responsibility.

Freedom and liberation are now our American thing; and justice is left to the whim of God.

During the celebration of the rededication of the Statue of Liberty recently, with its hymns and odes to freedom and to our own achievements, it occurred to me to wonder what might have happened had the French offered in 1986 to build a second statue for us, perhaps on Governor's Island, a Statue of Justice equal to the Statue of Liberty. I confess that I concluded that we might regard that as a profanation of the sacred space that radiates out from Our Lady of the Harbor.

The emphasis on freedom without the antidote of justice has contributed to an erosion of the trust and confidence in the national community and in its institutions. Think about what happened when the Vietnam veterans walked down the streets of their hometown. The national shame of that war was heaped on their shoulders, unjustly. Not everyone would shake their hands. And recently in the nation's capital we have learned that the executive branch was so free to do what it chose and has so mistrusted the Congress that it has lied to it and withheld vital information from it. The White House crew mistrusts its own State Department, and launches ignorant overseas adventures on its own initiatives. The FBI and the CIA have played so fast and loose in their unrestricted freedom that they have lost the respect and the confidence of the public at large.

A growing cynicism affects the life of every major institution. Employees who once proudly proclaimed their identification with their companies ("I am an Eastern Airlines pilot. I am a chemist with Dow Chemical") now hide their identities. The public increasingly assumes that the media are for hire to the highest bidders. In the universities, the community of purpose that once bound the trustees, the administration, the faculty, students and staff together is harder to locate on many campuses. And even in the mainline churches, the laity's distrust of the way boards, agencies, and institutions of the church use their freedom is on the rise. And at the root of it all is the fact that a secular notion of freedom, as the right to follow one's own self-interest and self-definitions, unrestrained by accountability to the demands of justice, has now won the field.

What has enabled this secular notion of freedom to come to power? It is the trickle-down residue of a patriarchal ethos; it is a rationalization for the selfish use of the personal power and privilege now made accessible to the many by rising wealth. Everyone is assumed to be his own King Ahab. It is, in language Catherine Keller has taught us, the thrust toward separation from other selves, whereas justice has a connective intention toward other selves.

So secular, personal freedom has come to be the macho virtue in this nation. It sings, "Don't fence me in." It is assertive, individualistic, wary of cloying relationships, and competitive. It says, "When the going gets tough, the tough get going." This freedom is secretive, stoical, and unwhimpering. It is controlling, withholding, and emotionally well-defended against feeling the suffering of others. It denies that socio-historical factors have helped to divide the haves from the have-nots. It growls from the screen, "We did it the old-fashioned way: we earned it."

And what has happened to the virtue of justice, in this secular popular culture? Justice is portrayed as the wimpy, whiney sentimentality that keeps cropping up. Justice, with its questions of equity, fairness, and accountability, is pictured as suspicious, complaining, envious, vengeful, eager to take the toys away from the strong and hand them to the weak. Justice is thought to be backward-looking, unwilling to accept reality, and hung-up on a bleeding-heart concern for losers. Justice seems never willing to close the books, or run some risks, or have some fun, or raise some hell. Justice is the spoilsport footdragging cousin from out of town your parents said you had to take along on the hayride.

What can deliver us as a nation and as a people from this addiction to the drug of secular freedom? I have two suggestions, one of them institutional and one theological. First, the institutional. Of the five institutions of the Establishment, the state, the business community, and the media have been the loudest in their devotion to freedom. A word count on the pronouncements from Washington, Wall Street and the media centers shows a steady use of terms like free enterprise, free nations, freedom fighters, free trade, and the like. Justice rarely is mentioned. The universities and the mainline denominations, perhaps in an attempt to maintain a balance in the public debate, have continued to do the studies and issue the publications and the pronouncements that question the excesses of freedom and call for a doing of justice.

The state and the business community have the power and the money to underwrite their interests; the universities and the mainline churches have neither power nor money, but they do have influence and some continuing respect among the people. In the advocacy of justice we can point to the U.S. Catholic Bishops' letters on nuclear war and on the economy, and to the United Methodist Bishops' letter on the non-acceptability of nuclear weapons. These are clearly pronouncements that focus on the questions of justice in the nation and in the world. The mainline denominations, when they gather in council to debate the issues of concern and to attempt to find responsible perspectives, have generally taken stands that are responsive to the demands of justice. Their stands on the Middle East, Central America, South Africa, immigration, poverty, homelessness, substance abuse, human rights, and many other issues have generally been devoted to fairness, equity, humaneness, and care.

Nevertheless, a continuing limitation in the church's concern for justice, in its adoption of this orphan, is that local congregations rarely know much about what their own denominational governing body has said on these issues, except when they get from the public media some inflammatory snippets from the reports. A related problem is that the American Enterprise Institute, funded primarily by business, has consistently used its tribe of false prophets and its access to the media, to distort, betray, and discredit the sober work of the mainline denominations on social issues. The Heritage Foundation has been equally wicked in its consistent praise of freedom and its scorn for the concerns of justice.

One consequence of all this is that the gap between church and state is wider today than at any time in this century. It has been pushed wide by the state's advocacy of freedom and the church's advocacy of justice. The suspicions run deep in both directions. The government's suspicions of churches and universities began to rise during the Vietnam war, when questions about our pursuit of freedom for the Vietnamese began to be raised on campuses and in congregations. Recently, some congregations have declared themselves to be sanctuaries for refugees from Central America. Government spies carrying hidden tape recorders have joined their Sunday School classes and their tapes have been introduced as evidence in trials of clergy and laity. U.S. Christians have jointed Witness for Peace and gone to Nicaragua to stand along the border of Honduras, knowing that they were probably being filmed by the CIA. Clergy engaged in justice actions increasingly assume that the FBI is keeping a file on them.

It has not been all one way. The government has felt the sting of church scrutiny from time to time. Church representatives, who had been subjected to Oliver North's efforts to impress them, helped to blow the whistle before and during the Iran-Contra hearings. Congregational delegations in some places are monitoring the procedures of the Immigration and Naturalization Service during this amnesty period.

I do not long for the old days of hierarchical community, and for the hermeneutics of blind trust. The tension between church and state is to be celebrated because it is one evidence of the breakup of the old Establishment and the old patriarchal order. The churches know that justice cannot be established or made effective by church action alone. The state must be the chief instrument in the redistribution of income, in the health and education areas, and in the redevelopment of the national infrastructure without which we cannot live. So the church needs to be at a healthy distance from the state in order to press the state to do its proper work in providing justice for all, so that liberty for all may flourish. Ever since the prophets confronted the kings, the Judeo-Christian tradition has been clear on this point: governments are required to do the work of justice under God's judgment, just as much as the religious communities are required to do so. Or, to put it another way, we citizens are being held as accountable for what we do through the state as for what we do through our religious affiliations.

My theological suggestion is this: let's seek once again a biblical perspective on freedom and justice, and rid ourselves of the shallow and secular images of freedom and justice. The Bible is clear: freedom is God's gift; justice is our task. We can learn some things from our experience, if we will pay attention to it. It works like this: when I am honest about it, I know that wherever I am free, I have had help to get there. The prisoner hears the key in the lock and a voice saying, "Your pardon came through. Bring your clothes." The slave by the Nile making bricks without straw hears someone call and say, "Drop that mud and wash your hands and get over here. We are leaving this place and heading out."

The patient hears the doctor say, "Well, it's all cleared up now. You can do anything you want to." You wake up in the morning and you know you have slept well; the sun is shining and nothing hurts and you know you are free to make some choices this day. If you've got any sense at all, your first words are going to be "Wow! Thanks." And you are going to hold onto that feeling of gratitude all day, because you know you were given something better than you deserve. Your life has been placed into your own hands. That's freedom.

And then you read the Times and drink your coffee and go to your work, and all day long you are thinking about the people around you and the world around you. And wherever oppression or violence or exploitation or unfairness or inhumanity comes to your attention (and you watch yourself for these foul traits first), you fan your sense of shame or your spark of outrage into a flame of determination to do something effective about it; you use your God-given freedom just as far as you can go. Because, the Bible says, justice is our responsibility, and if we want to stay free, we are going to have to struggle for justice. And because you are determined to be effective, you mobilize your church and you stir up your community and you ask, "What are we going to do about this?"

Whenever you are tempted to think of yourself as a liberator, some kind of a spiritual Rambo running around, you tell yourself, "Stick with the human work of justice. That can set the stage for the liberating transformation of selves that is always a spiritual event." And you quote Micah to yourself, "What doth the Lord require of thee but to do justice, and to love mercy, and to walk humbly."

That is a big enough enterprise to keep us occupied. I am proud to be a part of one of the mainline churches in this era because the mainline churches are involved in the process of adopting and nurturing the orphan named justice, which has been abused and neglected and abandoned by a nation and a government become cruel, irresponsible, and selfish in its idolatrous worship of a secular freedom.

192

## EDITORIAL NOTES

1.  See the preface to this volume, "Michalson: Man and Society."
2.  See Michalson's report on this trip in this volume, "Focus on a Revolution."
3.  Steinbeck (1902-1968), <u>Grapes of Wrath</u>; NY: Viking, 1939 (473 pp), has been reprinted several times. The 1989 Viking edition (xx + 6191 pp) has an introduction (pp. v-xx) by Studs Terkel, comparing the dispossessed Okies with dispossessed Iowa farmers. The story is still relevant but lacks the governmental concern cited above.

# CHRISTIAN THEOLOGY AND THE CHALLENGES OF OUR TIMES

John J. Vincent

## I. HISTORY, FREEDOM AND CHRIST

The prospect of opening the life of the Carl Michalson Society fills me with awe and terror. So may I confess that, and apologize that I feel unworthy to do it, though deeply proud and humbled, too.

It is not the purpose of this Society to be either a perpetual remembrance service to a great man, or an old cronies club of his former admirers. Its purpose is to try to set forth and even add to that astonishment, privilege, and joy in which he lived, at being people who can name the Name and enter with fearfulness, abandon, and courage into discerning its meaning at our own moment of time.

My subject is not Carl Michalson's Theology. Able minds have written a <u>Festschrift</u> on that.[1] Nor indeed is it "the promise" of Carl Michalson's Theology, though I think that is a theme worth someone's pursuing, following the directions of his thoughts at the end, and seeing where they lead today.[2] Yet I believe and hope that what I wish to try to do will not be out of accord with his concerns.

Three things seem to dominate the latter chapters in <u>Worldly Theology</u>, and they dominate what I shall try to do. First, the centrality of history as the place where faith is initially set forth and recurringly realized. Secondly, the centrality of freedom, as the obligation, permission, and privilege of Christian existence, which has radical personal and societal implications. Thirdly, the centrality of Jesus Christ, as the beginning and the end of Christian faith.

Beyond history, freedom and Jesus, I think Carl Michalson is still right that "we live between the time of the theology which no longer makes sense to us and the time of theology which has not yet clearly dawned." Certainly, he was right that theology now "will not only decline to be systematic, it will be fragmentary, rash, and even chaotic," "stabbing from out of all our vast endowment of theological information for the word or words which will illuminate our way into the time beyond this time between."[3]

Process Theology, Hermeneutical Theology, Secularizing Theology, and Death of God Theology were in Michalson's view "the most promising fruit of the last fifty years of theological work."[4] But he also saw ahead:

> The major achievement of theology in our epoch will be in the way in which, through its concern for the reality of God as expressed in the history stemming from Jesus of Nazareth, faith will arise. Why that should be regarded as an achievement in our time will depend on whether one observes that faith emerges now as a wholly worldly reality.[5] (emphasis added)

Faith emerges in our time as calls to new freedom in our history. The "hermeneutical focus of an historical faith," in Carl Michalson's terms, must therefore be in the area between action and inspiration to action. Just as "the real genius of the New Testament faith" is "its particularism,"[6] so we must look for the particularism of action and inspiration to action as the starting-point for Christian reformation. "Neither systematic theology nor Biblical exegesis has been dramatically effective in the development of Christian history," says Michalson. But then, neither has preaching, which he calls "the church's interpretation of its faith."[7] Hence, while Michalson could say, "one studies theology not to learn theology, but to learn to preach," I would have to say "one studies theology to learn to act," "one studies theology to learn to be a disciple." If he never formulated it that way in his head, he did so in his life. And that is the way we shall pursue, a way which I hinted at the end of Secular Christ when, again in response to Michalson, I spoke of "historicising the existential,"[8] and felt that we needed to push beyond Michalson's "word-event" to speak of "incarnation-event."[9]

The clue is in Jesus. "God has chosen Jesus of Nazareth as the one in whom he calls the world to obedience."[10] On the one hand, "Jesus chose to obey God's call to act on God's behalf," and "surrendered certainty in the world for the uncertain pearl of obedience to God's call," so that "the Christ event is God's call to adopt obedience to him as the form of one's existence."[11] The issue now is: can our obedience be other than such as follows from Christ's obedience?[12] As his obedience is historically defined - eating with publicans and sinners, washing disciples' feet, exposing those opposed to him, being tempted in the wilderness, going to the cross - so also is ours. Yet between ours and his there must be the "leap of action." By this, I do not mean the "leap of faith" as some existential movement or conviction, but rather the leap into creative action and embodiment which would mirror and be held by Christ's creative actions and embodiments. Thus, in faith-action, I am both the publican and sinner with whom Jesus eats, and also the one who eats with them. In faith-action, I am both the temptations of world, flesh and devil, and also the one tempted by them. In faith-action, I am both exposed as an opposer and one who exposes the opposers. In faith-action, I have my feet washed, and wash others' feet. In faith-action, I am both the one for whom he goes to the cross, and also the one who goes to the cross.

My existence, then, is tied to the Christ-existence, not in the way of "nature" or "being," but in the way of history.[13] But history is not only happenedness, but happenings. And my obedience to the Christ is tied to the happenings which are that obedience in faith for me. My obedience is the things I get into, just as Jesus' obedience was the things he got into. The great question is, how can I discern which of his happenings are crucially for me now? How can I decide from the multiplicity of stories, images, parables and teachings which ones are to be specially determinative for my obedience now? In what way, precisely, is this or that in his total-existence peculiarly for me now?

This, it seems to me, is the question with which Christian theology as history, freedom, and Christcenteredness confronts us today. History is history of happening, history of actions, deeds, movements, events. Freedom is freedom to be "totally committed yet totally uncommitted" in the happenings of history. Christcenteredness is the way, the mode, the methodology by which disciples perform their faith-response.

I want now to pursue the question of how this is to be done in Christian theology, and then to say something about "the challenges of our times," before bringing the two together in three experimental ways.

## II.  HAPPENING AND DESCRIPTION

Christian theology is basically the Jesus story, and what disciples have done and do with it. Christian theology is the result of taking one piece of history - that of Jesus of Nazareth - as the dominant image for the creation of intermediate, temporary, and culture-determined "mid-images," which can be life-giving and immediately formative for people's lives.

The central task of Christian theology is, therefore, not so much to explain the faith to cultured or other despisers or acclaimers. The actual task is tied to a continual search at two locations for what can seem to be dominant and pregnant aspects. The first location is the New Testament, and especially the multitude of pluralistic images, metaphors, and stories used from history or from surrounding cultures to describe or convey the Jesus story of the Christ reality. The second location is the contemporary life of disciples, and especially the way in which, within their own lives, certain aspects of their surrounding culture are taken as influential and even determinative, positively and negatively, in the creation of significant expectations, patterns and faith-acts.[14]

Let me elaborate this in a six-point argument.

1. The primacy of history at least means that there is nothing to say until something has happened. Beginning with the historical cannot mean less than that much thought and much speech are superfluous except on the basis of action, of happening, of praxis. The image of the incarnation radically historicises history. God's presence and his very self are available in Christianity through a specific history, and through existence linked in some way with that history.

2. People only perceive different things, have different convictions, entertain different values, express different world-views, when they have first been exposed to different realities. If the heart of Christianity is history, this means that, as Ortega y Gasset says, "man has no nature - what he has is history."[15] So to change people, you must change their history. To alter humanity, you must alter where human beings are, who they are with, what they do with their time, their money, their work, their neighbors, their homes.

3. People will use all kinds of language, will entertain all kinds of ideas, once they have been in on some experience, situation, or happening which demands alternative language or ideas. But to give them alternative language or ideas before they have been given experiences which demand those alternative expressions, is to give them voices before they have anything to say.

This has been the problem with Christian language and contemporary people. We have been trying to deal with the "labels" of Christianity in the absence of any happenings demanding such labels. To interpret the present crisis of Christian theology as the need to find new images, or to discover fresh imagination, or to re-discover myth, or story, or parable, or a new language is to put the cart before the horse.[16] People into new things find new images out of desperation to describe what they are into. People have imagination when it is expected that they will be able to embody what they envisage. Myths arise when stories about things or people or happenings are seen to be lifegiving and significant. Stories are told when happenings have taken place which are worth telling stories about. Parables are told when happenings have taken place whose obscurity and scandal can be taken to point to the obscurity and scandal of all things. New languages are coined when people are so depressed with the impossibility of describing the reality they experience that they have to coin new words to describe it.

4. Therefore, the strategy for Christian theology must be to divert its attention from the fruits, and go for the tree, to bypass the words and go for the actions. Instead of concentrating on imagination, myth, story, parable, and language, theology must venture into the deep waters themselves - the waters of new things, new embodiments, new happenings, new obscurities, and scandals, new realities, new faith-acts, new failures, new exposures.

5. By this I do not mean another "journey inward." It is the crushing criticism of contemporary theology that "if in doubt, blame the psychologist." We assume that the reason we are ill at ease or confused is because we are not sorted out. So we delve into yet more interior sophistications - I'm OK, You're OK - transactional analysis, transcendental meditation, group dynamics, personality discovery games. We desperately search to create "learning situations" of an internal or interpersonal kind. If love, acceptance, reconciliation, suffering, hope, and brother-sister love are Christian "labels" - and they obviously are - then we conclude that we must invent for ourselves personal and community exposures which will make us have experiences demanding those labels. Hence, the constant demand for personal trips and interpersonal "enrichments" which can be "learning experiences."[17]

But the attempt is futile, as more and more people returning from T-groups, or marriage enrichment weekends, or personality discovery sessions know. It is futile because it is artificial, contrived, manipulated. It is futile because it has tried to change one by giving one an artificial, temporary, imposed history. I remain essentially what I was before, with the added complication that I have been on this "trip" which was supposed to have cured me.

6. The task of Christian theology may therefore be more specifically defined as the task of (1) discovering those situations in which the total real-life commitment of disciples is being peculiarly exposed or being felt to be peculiarly significant, (2) using a variety of gospel stories and paradigms to assist disciples to discovering where precisely the affirmation, judgment or expectation of the Gospel is being encountered, (3) awaiting, projecting and facilitating faith-action responses to both situation and gospel within the peculiar limitations and possibilities of each person and group of persons within their own times. This I understand to be essentially the task of "Doing Theology."[18]

Let us now say a little about the question so far only indirectly referred to - the challenges of our times.

## III. THE CHALLENGES OF OUR TIMES

The problem with talking about the challenges of our times is that we think that they are all things somewhere "out there," over against us, whereas they are really all things we have aided and abetted. What are the challenges of our times? Materialism? It is the product of our own Christian centuries. Technology? We who have so long worshipped humanity as steward of creation can hardly now object that humanity now all but controls nature. Communism? We know the New Testament too well to call it our enemy. Fascism? It has always been the friend of the churches. Ecology? We have provided prayers and sanctuary for nature's despoilers for two centuries. Energy Resources? Our churches will close when the oil pipes dry up. Living Standards? We have prayed indiscriminately with rich and poor, and preached that poverty of the soul is more important than poverty of the body.

What, then, are the challenges of our times which we can do something about? They are, I venture to think, the challenges not from outside, where we can combat them. They are the challenges from within, that give us a sense of growing boredom, superficiality, artificiality, and a mood of non-genuineness, inauthenticity, and non-engagedness. This mood is not the result of the modern consciousness or the youth culture or the sociology of knowledge or the self-doubt of Christianity - though all of them have helped put us down. Rather it is the cumulative result of piling more and more things and possessions and expectations and techniques and innovations and gadgets and insights and exposures on us, that we know not either who we are or what we are for. If God has died the death of a thousand qualifications, we have died the death of a thousand accretions. And, in the midst of it, as W. H. Auden says,

> We would rather be ruined than changed,
> We would rather die in our dread
> Than climb the cross of the moment
> And let our illusions die.[19]

In a word, the challenges of our times are challenges to our understanding of who we are supposed to be, what is open for us to do, where we can move to, whether we are entirely determined by our accretions, whether there is anything left of us when our education, our affluence or technology or profession are taken from us. The challenges of our times are the classic challenges of humanity in all times: ours feel more threatening - and perhaps are so!

But what to do? We can accept old death more easily if we are discovering new life. And most of us, despite all the psychology and management and human enrichment and expanding horizons and intercultural explorations and educational expansions and spiritual growth experiences are <u>not</u> discovering new life. We are merely adding a few more bits, a few more accretions, a few more sophistications, a few more places of death.

Can theology help? I believe it can, if we will let it be liberated from being the bland chaplaincy to our dead accretions, and allow it to be the generator of alternative myths, the projector of alternative futures, the inspirer of alternative native expectations, presuppositions, and lifestyles. For one task of theology is to function as a liberating myth-maker, whereby humanity is kept at its task. Theology, like philosophy, or love, or patriotism, or race, or class, or society, is one more way in which human beings are kept, as in wars, marching into point-blank fire, on the assumption, as Freud observed, that always one's neighbor will be shot, never oneself. We need what Ernest Becker calls "hero systems."

> It doesn't matter whether the cultural hero-system is frankly magical, religious, and primitive, or secular, scientific, and civilized. It is still a mythical hero-system in which people serve in order to earn a feeling of primary value, of cosmic specialness, of ultimate usefulness to creation, of unshakable meaning..... "civilized" society is hopeful belief and protest that science, money and goods <u>make men count</u> for more than any other animal. In this sense everything that man does is religious and heroic, and yet in danger of being fictitious and fallible.[20]

Becker observes that

> religion is no longer valid as a hero system, and so the youth scorn it. If traditional culture is discredited as heroics, then the church that supports that culture automatically discredits itself. If the church, on the other hand, chooses to insist on its own special heroics, it might find that in crucial ways it must work against the culture, recruit youth to be anti-heroes to the ways of life of the society they live in. This is the dilemma of religion in our time.[21]

We have generally opted for culture, and not had heroics and not had many young people. It might be worth opting for heroics rather than culture. We might get some committed young people. We might, even more, be into what Christianity is about.

So the challenges of our times are basically challenges to produce hero-systems, to produce signs, models, paradigms which can begin to produce and expect alternative responses. In Christian terms, this is the demand to make some decisions about what signs, models, and paradigms are "for us." Choosing biblical paradigms, or making "snaps" and "identifications" with bits of the scriptural sagas, may seem to be a fun game, even Sunday School stuff. But we should warn ourselves that many lives have been lost in the process. Many people were never the same again, once they had seen themselves in the light of some obscure Near-Eastern tale that leapt at them with an urgency and contemporaneity greater than the latest world-news catastrophe. It was enough for Francis Bernadone, a rich young man of Assisi, to hear Christ's call to his disciples to cure the sick, raise the dead, cleanse the lepers, cast out demons, in Matthew 10:8 - that was the end of him - or the beginning.[22] So we must approach the fire with caution.

What biblical paradigms are appropriate for us?[23] Is it Abraham, or Exodus, or Promised Land, or Two Kingdoms, or Exile, or Return, or Apocalypse? Take Abraham. Though he gave up a good living in Ur of the Chaldees, he had a promise of something, being called to do it (Heb 11:8), and at least according to Hebrews, "looked forward to a city which has foundations, whose builder and maker is God" (Heb 11:10). But our problem is that we are running away from a city built for two or three hundred years by people who worshipped that God.[24] And Exodus assumes God is delivering us. Promised Land assumes we are moving to something better. Two Kingdoms argue we can divide up our lives. Exile is attractive, for then we can weep. Return would be great, but we haven't yet been away. Apocalypse is tempting, for then we only have to wait.

So, what biblical bits are for us?

Before we go to it, let us add more hesitation. Surely, we might think, all we want is a belief in God who will do what is needed. But is that enough? The theology of the "God who acts," one is compelled to conclude, was all very well in the post-1939-45-war mixture of utopian hopes, relieved self-aggrandizement, and return of the heroes. Perhaps God had acted, after all, in the denouncement of Hitler and of Imperial Japan. Perhaps it was possible still or again to think of history with a "mid-point," from which time God built ever again his Kingdom amidst the vicissitudes and glories of history. But soon the full horror of the murder of six million Jews emerged, and Richard Rubenstein and others declared that the God of both Christians and Jews did nothing.[25] And then the revolution of black power occurred, with its black God (Albert Cleage) proclaiming liberation for the captive blacks (Cone) as he had for the ancient Israelites; yet liberation did not come, and William R. Jones concluded that the only proof of a black-liberating God would be that he liberated blacks today - which he palpably did not.[26] Certain other divine non-performances in Viet Nam, or ecology, or South Africa, could be added. The theology of the God who acts died the death of a thousand divine inactions. Whatever the biblical paradigms were about, they were not about a God who acted in history to get his will done for all mankind, through the medium of contemporary events.

The biblical paradigms were signs, dynamics, expectations, patterns, which gave permission and obligation for people to act, because they were acting in response to the perceived God-reality in their situation. They indicate the history created by stories of actions which are "ultimately significant" - which Christian faith calls the actions of God. They are not norms or authorities, they are "frames of reference,"[27] they are paradigms and models, and we simply have to choose, in faith, between them and then live by them.

Is not to do so already to put the cart of conceptuality before the horse of action? I do not think so, provided the horse and the cart can be got going simultaneously. Part of the task of discovering relevant and prophetic images and paradigms has to be performed by looking at those aspects of the contemporary situation within which people already, here and there, perhaps on the frontier, are forging ahead with new actions, deeds, and happenings. So that we are not simply talking of new paradigms but also of new deeds. The reformulation of theology does not come yet. The deeds may be misjudged, the paradigms may be the wrong ones.

But faith is about living a bit of the action that seems both impossible and possible. Prior proof is not allowed.

Let us try three paradigms from scripture and from the tenuous fringes of happening.

### IV. A JOURNEY BACKWARDS

The first biblical paradigm I want to suggest for our use today is that of the Journey Backwards. The Journey Backwards is the proclamation of Jesus in the putting right of things that never ought to have been wrong. It is the "restitution to the original state" which is proclaimed in the Jubilee of Leviticus 25[28] and the proclamation of Jesus of Nazareth in Luke 4:18-19.[29]

> "The spirit of the Lord has been given to me,
>         for he has anointed me.
> He has sent me
>         to bring good news (of prosperity?) to the poor
>         to proclaim liberty to people who have been made captives,
>         to give new sight to those who are blinded,
>         to free those who are downtrodden by others,
>         to proclaim the Lord's year of favor!"

The synagogue congregation, according to Luke, was astonished, but soon got enraged when the local lad (Joseph's son, v.23) was unable to do any mighty work there, and explained to them that God always by-passes those who expect his blessings, and selects foreigners - a widow at Zarepath or a Syrian leper (vv.25-27) - at which point they tried to lynch him (vv.28-30).

So from the beginning of his ministry Jesus sets about restoring things to what and where they should be. People into whom demons have come have them cast out, people who have lost their health receive it back again, the son of the widow of Nair is brought back to life - and so on. Thus the first sign of the inbreaking Kingdom is the restoral of things and people to what they should have been. The same applies to Luke's teaching on poverty and riches. There is a reversal of everything, so that people are restored to what they should be. In Leviticus 25, the Jubilee means a restoration to people of their personhood (release from slavery), their financial solvency (cancellation of debts), and their land (termination of leases). In Luke, it means the same - personhood (release from demons), finance (return of money to people swindled), and land (common ownership among disciples).

Paradigms of return are never very attractive. Going back to visit places long lost in the memory is not always wise. The moving finger writes, and, having writ, moves on. Only a fool tries to retread old paths and relive old memories. We must keep up with the times. Progress is inevitable. You can't put the clock back.

Yet the past is where we come from. Christianly, we are not the originators of faith. Biographically, we all came into Christianity with a radically different faith than the one we now hold.

But a journey backwards is not the same as a journey into the past. A journey backwards takes place when we, in the moment before us, take as our future a realization of what the past has been. The journey backwards is a journey we have to take, not in the memory, but in the actual living future.

The Journey Backwards means a journey into the sources, foundation, myths, and archetypes which formed our present. It is a journey which begins exactly where we are. It is a journey everyone has to do for oneself. Saul Alinsky says to people like us:

> It is useless self-indulgence for an activist to put his past behind him. Instead, he should realise the priceless value of the middle-class experience. His middle-class identity, his familiarity with the values and problems, are invaluable for organisation of his "own people." He has the background to go back, examine, and try to understand the middle-class way.[30]

But we go back in order to comprehend and become responsible for the past. We do not go back historically to rediscover the rock from which we were hewn - or the pit from which we were dug. We go back in order to discover where, along the way, certain life-and ethos-determining shifts and new directions took place which can show to us graphically today how we got the "predetermined," fixed mind-set, the expectations and presuppositions, of affluent Western middle-class Christians.

It is less a question of finding out where our "roots" are than it is discovering the ground we grew in, the costliness of the manure, the degree of light, what other trees were around, what we were assumed to be there for.

Four elements come to mind, as I reflect on my own backwards journey. First: my existence has been all but entirely determined by economic factors - in my case, the coming of a poor Suffolk country lad, without parents alive in his youth, to the industrial North West, where his industry and pride made him scrimp and save to send his three sons to grammar school. Second: the existence of that milieu in which there was a grammar school available for me was all but entirely determined by the industrial revolution, bringing to Manchester the harvest of a world-wide trade network. Third: the existence of that world-wide trade network that gave Manchester its wealth was inextricably bound for a hundred years to slave trade, whose ships brought the cheap products of Lancashire factories to Africa, to be emptied and filled up with African slaves and brought to America, to be emptied and filled up with cotton or tobacco and brought back to Manchester, where the whole cycle started all over again. So my fourth element is that I came under the influence of the local Methodist Chapel in Hale, and there was a local Methodist Chapel there because the mill-owners and entrepreneurs of 19th century Lancashire were Wesleyans, and built chapels for the worship of their God.[31]

My journey backwards shows that I am the result of four elements: entrepreneurial parents, a grammar school deriving from the industrial revolution, the slave trade back of the industrial revolution, and the Methodist chapel the product of it. I am what I am because of the alliance of entrepreneurship, grammar school, industrial revolution, slave trade, and cultural Christianity.

If I want now to consider myself, I have to consider myself in the light of this. And if I want to consider what the Gospel or Christ might say to me, I have to know that it will be said to me as a person with such a background. So I will expect the Gospel to address me in terms of entrepreneurship, education, industry, slave trade, and cultural religion. And my hunches are that the Gospel will have a great deal to say to me about those things. But if I want to "change," or "be converted," or "be born again," or "be a new man in Christ," it will be by the radical change, reversal, conversion, or death of precisely those things which have put me where I am and determined that I am who I am. So that my new being in Jesus Christ will be a new being decisively determined by the limitations and possibilities of what I have been made. It will not be an "inner" change, that merely alters my "attitude" to these things, or my mind-set in the light of them. It will be a new being which in some sense will celebrate the Jubilee, which will be a restitution to what was there before.

Where will I find myself? I am daily discovering! But for a start it will mean a reversal of the entrepreneurial assumption that with or without the help of God I am free to exercise my innate instinct towards "getting on" and "doing something." It will mean that I have to find a way to live as though the "advantages" of education were, in some senses, not there. I have to find alternatives to the industrial revolution which will provide new possibilities for my own and others' enrichment through work. I have to live as someone whose wealth was purchased by black slavery. I have to discover a Christianity which frees me from cultural religion. Thus, the lines of my future discipleship are already clear as the "restitutions" which Jesus proclaims and which Jubilee promises.

It is not for me to say what the Journey Backwards means for Christians in <u>North America</u>. The country with six percent of the world's population and using thirty percent of the world's resources is so tied into an economic framework of injustice and exploitation that will not be an easy journey. The assumption has been made for so long that progress is inevitable (which it isn't), that every rise in living standards benefits the poor (which it doesn't), that everyone needs to rise to the level of their own competence (which they don't), that God has given us the good things of life to enjoy (which he hasn't, for we cannot have most of them save by theft from others).

Somehow, the impossible steps must be begun backwards, for a Jubilee, for the sake of the poor of the world as well as the poor of the land. The 1976 Fourth of July Jubilee Inter-religious Service at the Jefferson Memorial invites us to commitment:

> We have assembled here to rededicate ourselves to building a community of love and concern for each other and for all God's peoples. We realize that God's love requires us to strive for peace, for justice, for liberation. Therefore: we commit ourselves to the equitable distribution of wealth and economic power, and to the attainment of true equality of condition in our society. We commit ourselves to begin to work out the specific steps that will bring about an American Jubilee. We commit ourselves to begin to work out in our homes, our schools, our workplaces and our communities the

programs and changes that will create the renewal of body and spirit that is the Jubilee... for our generation and those who will follow. We commit ourselves to transform our relationship toward the land and toward each other so that we can be renewed in our relationship with God.

We will therefore strive for material change, by treating the land with dignity, by sharing the resources of life with all peoples. We will therefore strive for spiritual change, where hatred, possessiveness, prejudice, war, competition, and oppression will be replaced by love, peace, cooperation and community! We know that when we see God in the face of every human being our American Jubilee will already be at hand.

Let the ancient ram's horn sound! Let our liberty bell ring out! In the harmony of common purpose to proclaim Jubilee throughout our land unto all the inhabitants thereof.[32]

The Journey Backwards, the Jubilee which epitomizes it, and Jesus of Nazareth who proclaims and creates it, can be, I believe, powerful paradigms for our faith-action in the future. They cannot, of course, be assured of "success," but they might assure us some faithfulness.

Christian theology, I might add, will be somewhat desperately required by people journeying backwards. Who else has paradigms and stories, and a community, for it? So we at last might have an existential situation in which people are clamoring for our story as one that can sustain them in such an impossible, vital path.

## V. A JOURNEY SIDEWAYS

The Journey Backwards is a call to all society, to find a new lifestyle. But soon there have to be special vocations.

So, Jesus proclaims the Jubilee, and people here and there get into it. But soon he cannot be alone. He can only be in one place at a time. So he calls disciples. First, Simon, James, and John "brought their boats back to land, and left everything and followed him" (Luke 5:11), then Levi the tax collector "leaving everything, got up and followed him" (Luke 5:27), then the disciples were brought together and twelve of them were picked (Luke 6:13). Then, (Luke 6:20) with a great crowd all round him, Jesus fixing his eyes on his disciples said:

> "You poor beggars are the happy ones;
>   God's kingdom is your property.
> You hungry beggars are the happy ones,
>   Satisfaction is your lot.
> You weeping at losses,
>   Laughter shall be yours.
> You hated, driven out, abused, denounced as criminals,
>   all for the son of man's sake,
>   Rejoice in that day,
>   Dance for joy
>   Your reward in heaven is stupendous.
> They always treated prophets like that!

To the rest, standing by, Luke has Jesus deliver curses on the rich; and then the more general instructions to everyone to "Love your enemies," etc.[33]

The disciples were called to the first and classic alternative society. They made the first, classic "Journey Sideways." They moved from home, profession, status, relatives, religion, and nation into the insecure, status-less, new family of Jesus, the alternative Israel.

The biblical paradigm of the Journey Sideways is especially relevant today. Let me give an example. Inspired by blasé assurances that "when one door closes, another door opens," my wife Grace and I, at a particularly bloody, rejected and unprofitable period of our ministry, coined the slogan: "when one door closes, another door shuts." Sometimes, you come to a place where all doors are closed. You have arrived at a situation in which there is no exit. How do you get out of it? Only by getting out of that wretched room altogether, and starting again, even if only out in the open, or perhaps in a tent, alongside it.

The Journey Sideways means chaos. Order and uniformity, security and predictability, are gone forever. Being disciples, we shall all receive different calls from the Gospel, and find ways to support each other in them. Being human, we are all going to move in different directions. When we were all in the same room, we were blocked and frustrated beyond words, but at least we were together. Now, we have got to go out into the unknown, holding hands with whomever we can find.

The Church today desperately needs to discover the Journey Sideways. Our special temptation is to imagine that a ministry of acceptance, support, and love in personal and interpersonal life can decisively affect or change lives and communities which are basically determined by socio-cultural mores and expectations which have never been brought to judgment by the gospel. We know in our hearts that it will not do. Conversion in the synoptic gospels means radical, significant, secular change in one or more of the areas of housing, money, career, lifestyle, relations (not relationships!), possessions, and families.

If we wish to have persons converted to Christ, we must provide challenge-and-maintenance groups to sustain and expect such conversion responses and life-changing faith-moves. Consequently, the purpose of Church should be to expose people to situations and communities which have succeeded in making radical shifts in the areas just mentioned. Such situations and communities would exist in otherwise unused parsonages and church plants. They would be food co-operatives, house-sharing communities, radical finance-sharing groups, co-operative industries, alternative career structures, and so on. They would be both experiments involving full-time and permanent involvement, and also those involving part-time or spare time and temporary involvement.

The Church itself as institution is already producing its own people taking lonely Journeys Sideways in the Para-Church and the Alternative Church.[34] Indeed, the Para-Church may be an example useful to the whole community of Christ concerning how change occurs. Often, big organizations or institutions have too large a vested interest in the continuation of the past to be able to throw in their lot with the new, the untried, and that which might well fail. Perhaps the institution ought not always to change. In our times, the small nuclear group may be the way to change things. It may be only when there have been many more alternatives, para-institutions, experiments, uncontrolled projects, and risky undertakings, that the institutional churches will see that they are not in fact the only or the indispensable custodians of the truth, and that alternative methods and structures are not only possible but necessary.

The nature of humanity itself constantly demands alternative institutions. Human groupings have ways of providing rituals to keep societies cohesive and "holy." Rituals require priests, so the institutional churches must go on providing priests and exercising priest-craft. Established churches exercise priest-craft for society, and act as chaplains to society and to people who desire styles in line with society. But we also need prophets, people who are not priests, but are "called" out from the world and God, who provide rituals and cohesion and holiness for people who are looking for or already living alternative styles. Many who are paid to be priests just cannot do this task, and probably should not try.

Is not Theology called to a Journey Sideways? W. A. Visser t'Hooft has always been the father of my own search for alternative theological education. He it was who, some ten years ago, called for some" theological action-stations based on a charismatic Socrates." That is to say, what you wanted was: first, an action-station; second, a man who was working practically, and also thinking and talking; third, a bit of flair (the "charismatic" bit!); and finally the theology. Even so did theological education begin in the early church. The model was the student walking behind the rabbi, hearing him, learning his words oft by heart, occasionally asking questions, learning to imitate his actions, his tricks-of-the-trade (like mnemonics), his way of dealing with things. And to this the early church added only one decisive and determinative thing: that the one you learn from is not really any more than you are, but just a learner of Christ. He is not to be called Rabbi or Lord, for he and you have only one Rabbi and Lord, who is Christ (Matt. 23:7-12). So, in our time, has the Urban Theology Unit in Sheffield sought to work at an "alternative," more modest, more down-to-earth, style of theological education.[35]

Especially today, main-line church people flee the Journey Sideways. We cannot conceive of alternatives to getting what "the people at the top" have got. So, "liberation" in affluent societies always means people who are in one way or another disadvantaged, learning how to get a larger slice of the cake. The only model the blacks or the women have to go on is affluent, white-dominant entrepreneurial self-indulgence and success-orientation. It is therefore no surprise that blacks and women when they get "liberated" end up as objectionable as the dominant group it was hoped they might replace. An affluent, educated, dominant, entrepreneurial, self-indulgent, and success-oriented black or woman is no more "liberated" than the white male they assimilate.

Can there be real "liberation"? - liberation which is not what Segundo calls merely "over-simplification" and "immediatism"?[36] It is ironical, though typical of history, that just at the time when a radical discovery of the relevance of poverty, chastity, and obedience are the requisites for a new form of Christ in our world, the main-line monastic communities have run helter-skelter into main-line culture. "Let us in on the world of possessions, sexual wholeness, and self determination (is it called "liberation"?) that the rest of affluent society has." Yet here and there new communities are discovering that there was something in the old "evangelical counsels," despite all the perversions.[37] It is ironical again - and typical of history? - that just at the time when a radical rediscovery of the essential diakonal, priestly, and representative roles of every man and woman in Christ is becoming mandatory, the Church should be confirmed in its professional, full-fire, specialist clergy stereotypes by the arrival of women to fill the ranks of the clergy. Yet here and there are new experiments in ministry emerging - as at the Church of the Savior in Washington, D.C., where all church members are trained and ordained as ministers.[38]

So, then, what do we need for the Journey Sideways?

1. Models of Alternatives, alongside life at every conceivable point - church, professions, industry, education, health, social service, agriculture.

2. Availability of Places, where people can give sustained thought and study as to the possibilities open to them, aided by people who have themselves made radical faith - moves.

3. Alternative Myths, which will invite the imagination and vision to see oneself in a different place. Here the Entrapment of our Language - Success, Responsibility, Security, Standard of Living, Proper Expectations - needs to be overcome by the power of alternative myths and alternative language.

4. Communities of Trust and Support, so that people do not have to make their faith-moves on their own.

## VI. A JOURNEY DOWNWARDS

The last paradigm I want to propose is a Journey Downwards. The Jubilee is there through Jesus' ministry. The alternative group is there in the Disciples' Community. But what of the masses? To them must the disciples go. So Luke 9:16:

> Jesus called the twelve together, and gave them power and authority over all demons, and to cure sickness. And he sent them out to proclaim the Kingdom of God, and to heal.

And he said to them:
Take nothing for the Journey;
No staff, no pack, no bread, no money.
No one takes a second tunic,
Whatever house you enter, stay there.
When you leave, go from there.
If people do not welcome you,
Shake off the dust from your feet
When you leave the town,
As a sign against them.

So they set out and went from village to village proclaiming the Good News, and healing everywhere.

So the first mad, unapologetic mission of the Church gets underway. The penniless disciples, scrounging whatever they can are the proleptic embodiments of the Kingdom in which no one shall lack anything, because each shares with the other whatever they need. They are the acted parables of the new community of sharing in which all is held in common.[39]

The mission of the kingdom is always for people at the bottom, and we must learn the meaning of the Journey Downwards to be with them. And then we must begin to <u>learn</u> from people at the bottom.

May I use an example from my own little bailiwick? My colleague, Ray Crowder, is working on a paper called "The Long March of Mao Tse-tung as a Paradigm for Adult Education." You will recall the story of Chairman Mao's "Long March," which Edward Rice describes as follows:

The main body gathered, one morning in the middle of October 1934, for the beginning of the march. Those who were setting out could not know that the retreat they were beginning would last a whole year, that they would have to travel five to six thousand miles to reach their destination, and that only one in ten would complete the journey.[40]

The Long March, remember, was a <u>retreat</u>, a journey backwards. It was also a Journey Downwards - down to the grass-roots again. But it was an experience in which the future doctrines of the Chinese nation were forged. It was then that a tiny minority learned how to function against an enormous hostile majority. It was then that Mao Tse-tung taught "our strategy is" pit one against ten, and "our tactics are" pit ten against one - that is, use your overall numerical inferiority by concentrating superior forces at selected parts of the enemy's total forces.[41] That is, learn at the bottom how to function as a nucleus for radical change.

Theologians are not often at the bottom. Moltmann has claimed that, often, liberation theologians are isolated from a vital community, and do not belong to the oppressed, exploited people themselves.

> The intellectuals and the students are certainly not the subject. They can at most throw the revolutionary sparks into the dried-up and parched woods. But if the people are not "burning" and do not rise up, the most beautiful sparks are no use. The sparks then become sectarian candles around which elite circles gather ceremoniously in order to confirm themselves.[42]

James Cone has rightly stated it: "One's social and historical context decides not only the questions we address to God but also the mode or form of the answers given to the questions."[43] As Jose Miguez Bonino has claimed, a Christian assessment of Marxism leads to affirmation of four basic assumptions:

> 1. The class struggle is the prime story of human history.
> 2. History is ultimately dependent on production to satisfy human need.
> 3. There is a structural and ideological unity between individuals and communities.
> 4. Action itself is the test of theory, leading to new praxis.[44]

Whoever we are, if we wish to serve the Kingdom, there is no substitute for going from village to village, living among local folk, healing, and proclaiming the Kingdom. Only so can there be the constant infusion of committed people into life at the bottom, where transformation must begin and be sustained. And do not be afraid of elitism. Segundo asks:

> Was the original Christian message aimed at masses as such, so that it must be thought out and propagated in those terms; or was it rather aimed at minorities who were destined to play an essential role in the transformation and liberation of the masses?[45]

Segundo rightly sees the constant transmission of new engagements of committed people among the masses of society as the only way whereby mission can take place and people become transformed.

What this all may take us into, only time will tell. It is a matter of vocation. But now we will expect people in Christ to be called downwards instead of upwards. We will expect that Jesus' "The top shall be the bottom - and the bottom shall be the top," will be the way in which people will see their vocations in Christ. We will structure for failure instead of success; for constant division and reduction, not for constant unification and expansion; for losing ourselves, not for confirming ourselves.

Whoever hears must decide what it means for them. The call is to lifetime commitment to constant self-emptying. It will take us where it will take us.

And even for middle aged people stuck in professions, there is always the chance to move out or move down. Wouldn't it be great if Drew rejoiced in its smallness and became the first University in America where everyone accepted reduced salaries, reduced expectations, and reduced classes as a prophetic contribution at least to the declining national future, if not to a downward affirming lifestyle?[46]

Even church and ministry could get in on the Downward Gospel Spiral. The church and ministry have been late entrants into the high-technology race. Let's hope they may now be allowed the privilege of not entering it at all. Industrialists, educators, and doctors are now questioning the high-technology machines which take as the norm the costly combination of vast experimentation, complete industries, large bureaucratic organizations, enormous ongoing maintenance costs, and constant attention by highly paid specialists. The skills of industry, education, and medicine become lost or irrelevant in the face of high technology. Neither humanly nor economically can we afford it. Already, there are people everywhere moving in new directions. They are a mixed and unconnected group - the living religious and humanist people, those interested in social goals and values, the potentially committed but non-religious (i.e., not worshipping some past figure), the divergers rather than the convergers, the world development campaigners, the ecologist, the environmentalists, the conservationists, the hikers, bikers, and joggers.[47]

In this context, Church and ministry may rejoice at their odd, but undeniable survival of the bumbling virtues. The human-scale, the small minded, the conservative, the jog-along, the modest, the incompetent, the do-it-yourself, the improvised, the penny-saving, the time-wasting. "Why should Church and ministry not learn from the management techniques, the control systems, the supervisory methods, the economic rationalizations, the labor-saving devices, the prepackaged shortcuttings of the secular world?" they used to ask us. Something in Church and ministry made us hesitate. Partly it was our obstinacy - get our wisdom from on high. Partly it was our omnicompetence - nobody can tell us what to do. Partly it was our neurotic need to fill every minute with labor unto the Lord - for we had to ensure to ourselves if not to others that the preacher was worth his hire. Partly it was sheer lack of trust in technology - we had mainly come up through psychology, sociology, classics, or the lesser known mysteries of the early Greek fathers. Partly - or probably largely - it was lack of finance - the church of Jesus has to travel light. So, for one reason or another, we missed the high technology revolution. We had duplicators but not photocopiers, part-time secretaries but not stenographers.

We got landed a bit nearer the bottom, and became parables in a tiny way of the Gospel Journey Downwards. And it wasn't all that hard, for the clergy still live till eighty, and are among the healthy and the well-balanced! And so by accident ended up prophetic of the coming century of Journey Downwards.

## VII. CONCLUSION

Such, then, are three possible biblical paradigms, Gospel dynamics, for us today.

There is no way of knowing whether they are the "right" ones, save by a few of us trying them out. Paradigms and dynamics we have worked on in the past have not landed us anywhere, so we have nothing to lose - except, that is, our journey forward, and journey straight ahead, and our journey upwards! But precisely those journeys are the ones leading us and those around us into death and despair - as we began by observing. Precisely those "challenges" we must pass by if we are to discover rebirth or change.

So: the debate is about what we now do with our history, what we do with our freedom, what we do with the Christ events. It is a debate which is vital to the survival of Christian theology in any form other than the culture-affirming one we are slowly moving out of.

So, theology hangs on people making the Jesus story again; and a new theology will be the result. Writing of the way the Christ stories got down in the New Testament, John D. Davies says in Stirrings:

> The most urgent mandate to the church is surely to enable God's story to continue to happen in the world.... The New Testament is the story and the evidence of the effect of Christ on people, not only through the activities of Jesus of Nazareth but through the community of faith which derived from his activities.......

> This is how faith was transformed into story; later, men came along with their words and pens, and put the story into the form in which

we have received it. But the writing always comes after the happening.

One day, someone may be able to write down the story of how faith happened amid the disorders and despairs of our contemporary society. But, before the story can be told, it must be acted: and that is the activity of faith. Our task is to get on with making the story.[48]

All this century, we have tried to make Jesus our man, our person. We tried to make him the leader for us when we wanted to campaign. We tried to make him the whole person, when we wanted to become whole. We tried to make him the ethnic neutral when we wanted to affirm the blacks. We tried to make him a community developer when we wanted to build relationships. We tried to make him an asexual being when we wanted to liberate our sisters.

But he is not our man. He is for my breaking before he is for my making. He is always for me, because he is flesh of my flesh and bone of my bone. He is my brother, and he is cut with every shaft that cuts me, he is pierced with every word that pierces me, he is broken by every act that breaks into my being, he is divided by every division that cuts me from all others. He is my brother, who alone is always for me.

But from somewhere within me, I welcome him not as the one who is for me but as the one who is never for me. I am for me, my loved ones are for me, an astonishing number of people are for me. He perhaps alone can really be for me by never being for me, by being outside me, over against me, apart from me, my enemy, my stone of stumbling, my adversary, my alternative.

He in this time is uniquely and sufficiently the one who is behind me, calling backwards, who is next to me, calling me sideways, who is beneath me, calling me downwards. Somehow or other, we'll get to follow.

ENDNOTES

1.      Charles Courtney, Olin M. Ivey, Gordon E. Michalson, eds., Hermeneutics and the Worldliness of Faith. An issue of the Drew Gateway 45, 1974-75.
2.      In many ways, the articles in Hermeneutics and the Worldliness of Faith already do this. Yet everyone - like me in this lecture! - has "taken off" from Michalson in his own direction. It was part of his greatness to encourage and expect that his students would do this. Yet there might be a project to put together the various pieces and attempt a "systematic" (would he like it?) on the lines of what he wrote, and perhaps even more on the lines of his lecture notes, still in some books and tapes. Especially, so much of his writing was prolegomena, was getting off the ground. But I gather from many who recorded him towards the end that it was all getting together in a more thorough and detailed way. And that is certainly worth a few people giving a few years to.
3.      Carl Michalson, Worldly Theology; NY: Scribners, 1967, p. 19.
4.      Ibid, pp. 19-25; 24f.
5.      Ibid, p. 25.
6.      Ibid, p. 188.
7.      Ibid, p. 220. He saw the line as running from scripture to theology to preaching. Preaching is "the grammar of assent to the new age of freedom" (p. 180).
8.      John J. Vincent, Secular Christ; NY/London: Abingdon/Lutterworth, 1968, pp. 209-210.
9.      Ibid, p. 206.
10.     Op cit., p. 159.
11.     Op cit., pp. 160, 161.
12.     At this point, Michalson is not so clear. Though perhaps his unpublished lectures on Christology should be researched.
13.     Op cit., p. 218.
14.     I have developed this understanding of Christian Theology in an essay, "God as Possibility," in Stirrings: Essays and Radical ed John J. Vincent; London: Epworth, 1976, pp. 15-31, esp. pp. 23-26.
15.     Ortega y Gasset, History as a System; NY: Norton, 1964.
16.     I do not wish to say that this task is not important, but that it is not the first task. I am aware of what has been written in this area by Amos N. Wilder (Theopoetic: Theology and the Religious Imagination; Philadelphia: Fortress, 1976), but feel that in Christianity "the recovery of the sacred" hangs on the recovery of his discipleship.
17.     The literature on this is vast. See the critiques by Thomas C. Oden (The Intensive Group Experience; Philadelphia: Westminster Press, 1972) on Encounter Groups, and Game Free (NY: Harper & Row, 1974) on Transactional Analysis.
18.     Cf. two issues of New City. The first, No. 11, Doing Theology in the City, describes the practical experiments in Sheffield and elsewhere in this area. The second, No. 12, Urban Gospel, works at the New Testament end of it. ($2.00 each from Urban Theology Unit, 210 Abbeyfield Road, Sheffield S4 7AZ.)
19.     W.H. Auden, The Age of Anxiety; NY: Random House, 1947, p. 134.
20.     Ernest Becker, The Denial of Death; NY/London: Free Press/Collier Macmillan, 1975, p. 5.
21.     Ibid, p. 7.
22.     The method of "snap" is in my article, "Ways into the Gospel," in Urban Gospel.
23.     We could use a thorough and wide-ranging study of various, alternative biblical paradigms and their use in contemporary theology. It might show, as Paul Minear's Images of the Church in the New Testament (Philadelphia: Westminster, 1960), showed with

reference to the Church, that we get hung up on one or two paradigms instead of using the wide biblical variety.

24.    Robert McAfee Brown, Is Faith Obsolete? (Philadelphia: Westminster Press, 1974, pp. 137-140), calls us to "the Abrahamic Venture" as a prescription for contemporary "going out not knowing where we go." But we do know only too well, as his preceding chapter has made plain!

25.    Richard L. Rubinstein, After Auschwitz; NY: Bobbs-Merrill, 1966.

26.    See the comments of William R. Jones, Is God a White Racist? (Garden City, N.Y.: Doubleday Anchor, 1973), on the work of Albert Cleage, The Black Messiah (NY: Sheed P. Ward, 1969), and James Cone, A Black Theology of Liberation (NY: Lippincott, 1970).

27.    So Michalson, Worldly Theology, p. 219. We simply have to choose, in faith, between them and then live by them.

28.    See especially Martin Noth, Leviticus: A Commentary; Philadelphia/London: Westminster/SCM Press, 1965, pp. 183-189.

29.    For the passage as referring to Jubilee, see August Strobel, "Die ausrufung des Jobeljahrs in der Nazarethpredigt Jesu," in Jesus in Nazareth ed Walter Eltesker; Berlin: Walter de Gruyter, 1972, pp. 38-50.

30.    Saul D. Alinsky, Rules for Radicals; NY: Vintage Books, 1972, p. 185.

31.    This is not an exhaustive history of "origins." I seek to hold up decisive elements which one can do something about. Especially, I name characteristic elements which might also be suggestive for Americans doing a "Journey Backwards."

32.    People's Bicentennial Commission. There is a continuing Jubilee Group. Contact Arthur Waskow, Institute of Policy Studies, Washington, D.C.

33.    I believe this differentiation of audience is clear in Luke. On the consistency of Luke's teaching as applying mainly to the disciple group, cf. Edward S. Kessler, "A Jubilee and Disciples," in Stirrings, pp. 47-68, especially pp. 52-61.

34.    For some recent examples from Britain, and some theological and ecumenical assessment, the reader may care to see my Alternative Church; Belfast: Christian Journals, 1976.

35.    Cf. Doing Theology in the City (New City, No. 11).

36.    Juan Luis Segundo, The Liberation of Theology; Maryknoll, NY: Orbis Books, 1976, pp. 218, 220, following Lenin in What Is To Be Done?

37.    Cf., for example, the communities described in Richard Rodes, Running Free; Valley Forge: Judson, 1975; and the journal Sojourners.

38.    Cf. Elizabeth O'Connor, The New Community; NY: Harper & Row, 1976; Gordon Cosby, Agenda for Mission Groups; Waco: Word, 1975.

39.    This understanding of Luke 13 is indicated, for example, by John H. Yoder, The Politics of Jesus; Grand Rapids: Eerdmans, 1972.

40.    Edward E. Rice, Mao's Way; Berkeley: University of California, 1972, p. 83.

41.    Ibid, p. 74.

42.    Jurgen Moltmann, "An Open Letter to Jose Miguez Bonino," Christianity and Crisis, 29 March 1976.

43.    James H. Cone, God of the Oppressed; NY: Seabury, 1975, p. 95.

44.    Jose Miguez Bonino, Christians and Marxists: The Mutual Challenge to Revolution; Grand Rapids: Eerdmans, 1976.

45.    Segundo, Op cit., p. 209.

46.    The relationship of the small prophetic act to the historical movements of society in general deserves further study than it has so far received.

47.    I am aware of the criticisms of many against what has been called "de-modernisation." But the critics propose no alternatives in a world running short of resources and initiatives, compassion and real sharing. Peter Berger, Brigitte Berger and Hansfried Kellner, in The Homeless Mind: Modernisation and Consciousness (NY: Vintage, 1974), who criticize

de-modernisation finally concede: "one might even envisage a situation in which there would be parallel career systems in society, some within the technological-bureaucratic structures, others outside them" (p. 226), though they are not optimistic.

48. John D. Davies, "Faith as Story," in <u>Stirrings</u>, pp. 33-46, especially p. 46.

# V.

## GLOBAL INTERPRETATION

# RELIGION IN THE GLOBAL VILLAGE

## Kosuke Koyama

At the outset of this lecture I would like to say a few words about the journey this paper will take. On the subject of "Religion in the Global Village," I shall argue that we live today under overlapping ambiguities, found in both technology and in religion. The peril in which the world finds itself is a consequence of this situation. At no other time has religion been so severely tested. Technology has given us brilliant efficiency; but this very gift is threatening the meaning of human life. Religion has inspired humanity towards the values of humility and creativity; but this very inspiration often conceals the truth about humanity. The combination of these two ambiguities incites within us a drive towards human self-worship (idolatry). Our global village is paralyzed in the grip of this idolatry.

The world has become a small village because of the unprecedented advancement of science and technology. The great Jesuit missionary Francis Xavier left the city of Malacca, on the West Coast of Malaya Peninsula, on June 24, 1549, and after a series of dangerous sea voyages arrived in Kagoshima, Japan, on August 15. It took nearly eight weeks to go from Malaysia to Japan! The same distance can be easily travelled by air in less than ten hours today. Today even the Pope travels all around the world by jet planes. In its first adventure, Columbia, Americas's space shuttle, made thirty-six global orbits in fifty-four hours. Living in New York, I can speak with my brother in Tokyo instantly by picking up the telephone.

Ideas conceived and events occurring even in the remotest corner of the world can be immediately shared by the world's community because of our science based technology. The world in 1981 had a population exceeding 4.5 billion people. Demographers tell us that in the year 2000 the world population will reach 6 billion. In terms of population growth, the world is getting very small. And these billions of people are all in one way or another affected by the ever increasing "speeds" (efficiency) that technology is giving to them. Technology is represented by straight lines. The world has been increasingly "straight lined" as it became an information planet. Never before has humanity experienced such a drastic shrinkage of the size of its habitat, earth.

In Southeast Asia, where I have lived for more than a decade, the image of the village is that of a religio-cosmologically structured space, at the center of which is a Buddhist temple, in Thailand, a mosque, in Indonesia, or a church, in the Philippines. Round about such religious centers one may find the village administration building, post-office, shopping area, and sometimes a railway station. The village is a small and intimate unit of information, religiously, cosmologically, and economically. The village is a manageable one where "everyone knows everyone else." Such a self-contained and informationally satisfying image of village space and the human life in it cannot be applied to the world as we experience it today. The world has become a global village. But is not a peaceful village. Ours is a dangerously chaotic world in which the traditional value system of humanity has been convulsed by the ambiguities we see in technology and in religion. In short, ours is a global village in convulsion.

It is true in general that we who live today are far more informed about "other peoples" and "other cultures" than any generation before us has been. Technology has facilitated the traffic of thoughts in philosophical, cultural, political, ideological, and religious areas. Everything, including nuclear know-how, political ideas, medical technologies, proliferates. The locally defined historical cultures are disappearing, either rapidly or slowly, and the culture of the dominant Western civilization, the culture of technological efficiency, is emerging as a universal culture. Again, this "shrinking" has been accompanied by a great deal of painful alienation, that is to say, "distancing." The twentieth century world is most tragically torn asunder and mutilated. The global village is full of all kinds of confusing misunderstandings, mistrust, intolerance, and hostilities. While diversity is disappearing, conflicts are increasing. Or I should say that the kind of diversity which encourages conflict is increasing, such as economic discrepancy and racial prejudice. The unprecedented technological advances have introduced a frustrating unmanageability into the world. As the world has become smaller, it has become more violent. The same technology that has made the world smaller is used by us to make the world more violent. The speed in which we come together can become the speed in which we go away from each other. It works in both ways. Technological efficiency is most outstanding in the area of military technology, the technology of violence.

> One megaton nuclear explosive is equivalent to exploding one million tons of TNT. One million tons of TNT would fill a very long freight train. The string of box cars would be 300 miles long. The train would take six hours to pass at full speed.[1]

One megaton bomb! What efficiency! Let me quote two lines from order to illustrate this demonic efficiency:

> The World War II submarine could sink only passing ships; now a single sub can destroy 160 cities as far away as 4000 miles.

> A nuclear war which could snuff out 800 million lives in a few hours could be launched on the decision of a single individual.[2]

The world spends $550 billion annually for weapons! May I suggest that this staggering sum means about one million dollars a minute! We might wonder whether we must not call this a Global Military Installation rather than a village. Can such a dehumanized world be called a village?

We continue to be appreciative of the countless good things that technology has given us. Technology at work in the areas of transportation, education and medicine, for instance, has eliminated a great deal of human misery. Technology means an ability to duplicate almost indefinitely. Humankind is free from the labor of "duplicating." We are freed to engage in creative work that seeks to enrich the meaning of our life. It is true that technological efficiency has resulted in enhancement of human meaning.

The mighty technology, however, is ambiguous. Its tremendous efficiency can be used in two opposite directions, humanization and dehumanization. Technology mobilized to disseminate a sound body of knowledge would contribute to the enhancement of human meaning, while technology that broadcasts a view destructive to the welfare of humanity would paralyze the construction of human meaning. Technological efficiency can both enhance and destroy human meaning of life. There is no neutral technology because all technologies are in the hands of people, the creators and users of technology. Technology has contributed to producing a shrinkage as well as a distancing (alienating) world.

I must now proceed to the subject of "religion."

I am at once faced with the difficult task of defining religion. I think immediately of the great historical religions such as Judaism, Christianity, Islam, Taoism, Confucianism, Hinduism, and Buddhism. The aggregate of the numbers of adherents in all these faiths would be about 2.5 billion out of the total population of the world estimated at 4.5 billion. There is a "religious orientation" in communism and fascism. Scholars such as Paul Tillich have spoken of them as quasi-religion. Perhaps we may add to this list technologism as a quasi-religion. No simple words can adequately describe the substance and scope of the historical religions and quasi-religions.

I wish to suggest religion is our reception of authoritative words on human salvation. I think this can be said of all these historic religions mentioned above, including the quasi-religions, and also of religions of primordial nature-myths and symbols. This is not, however, a definition of religion. It is merely a description of religion at work. But what, then, is "salvation?" It is an antonym to "alienation." What is alienation? This will be answered differently by the different religious traditions. In general, I believe I can say that religions are concerned about human deliverance from alienation. All religions in one way or other would appreciate the human sentiment expressed in the first line of the Psalm 121 of the Hebrew Bible; "I lift up my eyes to the hills, from whence does my help come?"

Professor Louis Finkelstein writes: "The heart of Judaism and its chief contribution to religion is the doctrine of the One living God, who rules the world through law and love."[3] The thrust of this doctrine is also present in Christianity and Islam. Alienation can be described here as living at a distance from or at enmity with the "One living God who rules the world through law and love." Such a characterization of alienation contrasts generally with the Indian religious orientations such as Hinduism, Jainism, and Buddhism. The Vedanta Tradition (The Upanishads) speaks about the deliverance from alienation as our personal experience of the union between the outer world (Brahman) and the inner world (Atman). Here comes the importance of "breathing" (at-man from the root an, "to breathe"). When such a union takes place within oneself, one is freed from dualistic contradictions and attains the mystical peace described in the famous saying of the Taittiriya Upanishads; "I who am food, eat the eater of food" (III 10:5). Alienation is the discrepancy or conflict between the observer (eater) and the observed (food).

Buddhism teaches deliverance from alienation in terms of the destruction of dukkha (suffering) by way of the elimination of tanka (thirsting greed). This is the way of true knowledge (vijja). Jainism encourages us to wage a relentless battle against the power of the destructive karma (action-reaction). Of the founder of Jainism the Venerable Mahavira has written:

> This is the rule followed by the Venerable One; When the cold season has halfway advanced, the houseless one, leaving off his robe and stretching out his arms, should wander about, not leaning against a tree-trunk. When a cold wind blows in which some feel pain, then some houseless monks in the cold rain seek a place sheltered from the wind. "We shall put on more clothes; kindling wood, or well covered, we shall be able to bear the very painful influence of the cold." But the Venerable One desired nothing of the kind; strong in control, he suffered, despising all shelter. Sometimes in the cold season the Venerable One was meditating in the shade. In summer he exposed himself to the heat, he sat squatting in the sun. The Venerable One did not seek sleep for the sake of pleasure; he waked up himself, and slept only a little. Purgatives and emetics, anointing of the body and bathing, shampooing, and cleansing of the teeth do not behoove him.[4]

May I add here that the quasi-religions, such as Communism and Fascism, also speak of their versions of the deliverance from alienation. If I may use medical language, religions give us diagnosis (dia, "through," gignoskein, "to know") and suggest a therapy (therapeuein, "to nurse").

Religion must make its diagnosis and recommend its therapy authoritatively. It must speak carefully the words of truth. Of Jesus Christ the New Testament says, "The true light that enlightens every man was coming into the world" (John 1:9). Such truth must show its reality and power by being truth and as such must come to us as something we cannot simply ignore. If we ignore it, we will be still judged by its reality, as we will be dead if we refuse to inhale oxygen.

"The truth will make you free" (John 8:32) of Christianity is echoed in Buddhism's "Heedfulness (appamada, non-infatuation, constant mindfulness or watchfulness in doing good) is the path to the deathless" (The Dhammapada II Appamadavagga). The Greek word for truth, aletheia, which appears in the Greek and Hellenistic literature and in the New Testament means "non-concealment." Truth is the moment of judgment (krima, "to sunder," "to divide," "to select") that comes when the cover of falsity is eliminated. The Hebrew word emeth, which appears in the Hebrew Scripture (and in the Christian Old Testament) about 126 times, denotes a "reality which is to be regarded as 'firm' and therefore 'solid,' 'valid,' or 'binding.' It thus signifies what is true."[5] The Greek translation of the Hebrew Bible, the Septuagint, uses words such as pistis ("faith"), dikaiosune ("righteousness," "justice") and aletheia ("truth") to convey the rich meaning of the Hebrew emeth. One of the Sanskrit words that signifies truth, tatha, means "as it is," which in Japanese Zen Buddhism is expressed as sonomama. The Buddha is called tathagata, the one who comes ("as it is," sonomama, without falsehood).

Religions compel us to engage in honest discussion about diagnosis and therapy of the human condition. They seek the elimination of falsity and try to locate and affirm that which is "firm." Abraham Lincoln spoke of the power of the truth with these words: "You can fool all of the people some of the time, and some of the people all of the time, but you cannot fool all of the people all of the time." The moment of "non-concealment" will come eventually. Religion is the power at work in this world towards "non-concealment," towards revelation.

Thus we understand that the question of the truth (diagnosis and therapy) is a central concern of religion. But this primarily positive understanding of the significance and role of religion in the global village is not free from its own ambiguity. I am suggesting that religion does not always function positively. It is possible for religion to occasion or to inspire us to work against the "true" diagnosis and therapy.

Religion names deception as deception. But it can also name deception as truth. A classic case can be taken from the Book of Jeremiah (7:1-15), which is usually called Jeremiah's "Temple Sermon." In this sermon Jeremiah warns the people of Judah that their protection from the impending Babylonian invasion will not come by simply reciting the sacred formula, "This is the temple of the Lord, the temple of the Lord, the temple of the Lord". "Do not trust in these deceptive (religious) words," says Jeremiah. Not by the recitation of the holy name of the temple of Jerusalem, but by practicing social justice ("If you truly execute justice one with another, if you do not oppress the alien, the fatherless or the widow, or shed innocent blood in this place...") the nation will survive and prosper.

For Jeremiah a sacred subject, indeed as holy as the temple of Jerusalem itself, can become an occasion for deception. It was the religion of the holy temple that falsified diagnosis of the historical situation. For this unpatriotic sermon, Jeremiah was nearly lynched (26:1-15). In this juncture I would like to introduce the Sanskrit word maya, which means "marvelous power, artifice, device, trick, deceit, fraud, jugglery, witchcraft, illusory image, phantom, illusion." The ancient Hindu people detected the hidden connection between marvelous power and illusion. The Jerusalem temple is the center of the "marvelous" presence of God among the people. But it can become an occasion for illusion!

And that is exactly the point of ambiguity with religion. It was, in the case of Jeremiah, the religious community which opposed the view of "religious" Jeremiah. That "Jerusalem is safe because it has the temple of God in it" was seen by Jeremiah to be a deception, though it was thought to be saving truth by other religious people. There was a conflict between the two opposing religious perceptions on the subject of national security and the temple. The diagnoses were different. But which was true? Thus the questions relating to religion are always tied to the question of "false prophets." For Jeremiah the opposition party was the false prophet, while for them Jeremiah was a false prophet. Or is it possible that both were right? Or perhaps that both were wrong?

In today's language Jeremiah would be saying something like this: "The national security of any nation, including the mighty United States of America, will be established only when the nation pays far more attention to the welfare of the marginal people within its borders and beyond. National security will not come by simply reciting "The United States of America is a Christian Nation, Christian Nation, Christian Nation". The opposing view would say that helping the poor, the widows, the orphans will not give a nation fundamental security. Security comes with the massive build-up of arms in the name of God. God approves nuclear buildup, but God disapproves communism. God approves assistance to the rich and fewer handouts for the poor. Let me quote a sentence from Abraham Lincoln's Second Inaugural Address (1865): "Both read the same Bible, and pray to the same God; and each invokes His aid against the other." One party was for the continuation of slavery, the other for the abolition of it. Could both be right? or wrong? And each "invoked divine aid against the other."

Religion would speak the language of "thus saith the Lord..." (Thus saith the Bible, Thus saith the Qu'ran, Thus saith the Buddha, Thus saith Zoroaster, Thus saith Luther, Thus saith Wesley, Thus saith the Emperor, Thus saith Karl Marx, Thus saith Technology...") In the Republic of South Africa the racial policy of apartheid is both rejected and supported by Christians who quote "Thus saith the Lord..." It is the will of God, the one party says, that the races should live together in mutuality of trust and sharing. The other party says it is the will of God that the races should not be mixed and live together. In the United States Christians are taking completely opposite views on nuclear armaments. Religion is capable of occasioning and inspiring different views and attitudes towards human life in this world. It has inspired both peace and violence, both apartheid and opposition to apartheid. "What father among you," Jesus said, "if his son asks for fish, will instead of a fish give him a serpent?" (Luke 11:11). Religion must not give a serpent to the people. It must consistently give fish to them. But religion tragically gives us both fish and serpent. The same strength that reveals truth can be the strength that conceals the truth, and vice versa.

We have a difficult passage in the Book of Samuel:

> Thus says the Lord of hosts, "I will punish what Amalek did to Israel in opposing on the way, when they came up out of Egypt. Now go and smite Amalek, and utterly destroy all that they have; do not spare them, but kill both men and women, infant and suckling, ox and sheep, camel and ass." (I Sam 15:2-3)

Here a complete annihilation of the population was commanded by God. This kind of passage in the Bible reflects an understanding of that time that wars were of God and that booty was sacred and belonged only to God (doctrine of herem). Better portions of the Bible dispute such a command to destroy. "I desire steadfast love and not sacrifice, the knowledge of God, rather than burnt offerings" (Hosea 6:6). "What does the Lord require of you but to do justice, and to love kindness, and to walk humbly with your God?" (Micah 6:8).

I believe that "killing both men and women, infant and suckling, ox and ass" is less-truthful than the attitude expressed by God who desires "steadfast love and not sacrifice." If we apply the revengeful theology of I Samuel 15:2-3 all of us would in one way or other be decimated, because some time in the past our ancestors must have done something terrible to other ethnic groups. Japanese would be utterly destroyed for what they did to the Koreans. White Americans would utterly be destroyed for what they did to the native Americans. Koreans also would be annihilated for what they had done to some groups of people in the past, and so on. Such theology could not create a breakthrough to a new beginning for humanity. It would conceal the truth about human life on this planet and thus destroy all life, including human life.

War is terrible. But holy wars can be far worse. Professor Bainton writes that "war is more humane when God is left out of it."[6] There is a difference between saying "I do not like you" and "I tell you that God does not like you." The former is simplistic while the latter is neurotic and sinister. When soldiers go to war quoting the name of God (gods), the wars become very brutal. This was demonstrated when Japan went through the last war (1941-1945) against the United States, Britain, and Netherlands (in 1945 Japan was in hostility with 50 nations!). Japanese soldiers fought viciously in the name of the divine emperor. Japan was to punish the United States in the name of Heaven. Hitler was not called President, Chancellor, or Prime Minister. He was the Leader, the one who transcended the realm of the human. Today we hear of Christian leaders in the United States who believe that the God of the Bible is on their side against the atheistic Soviet Union. A Christian nation such as the United States, they believe, must be protected even with nuclear arms.

I am saying that it is difficult to separate war from some kind of "God-talk" (or gods-talk). The psychology of self-righteousness and war are intimately related. War usually begins with the prayer of the Pharisee, "God, I thank thee that I am not like other men, extortioners, unjust, adulterers, or even like this tax collector..." (Luke 18:11). Let me quote a few paragraphs from Howard Zinn. The following views were expressed in 1847 with regard to the United States' policy toward Mexico:

A letter appeared in the New York Journal of Commerce introducing God into the situation: "The supreme Ruler of the universe seems to interpose, and aid the energy of man towards benefiting mankind. His interposition...seems to me to be identified with the success of our arms...That the redemption of 7,000,000 souls from all the vices that infest the human race, is the ostensible object... appears manifest.

Senator H. V. Johnson said: "I believe we should be recreant to our noble mission, if we refuse acquiescence in the high purposes of a wise Providence. War has its evils. In all ages it has been the minister of wholesale death and appalling desolation; but however inscrutable to us, it has also been made, by the Allwise Dispenser of events, the instrumentality of accomplishing the great end of human elevation and human happiness...It is in this view, that I subscribe to the doctrine of 'manifest destiny'."[7]

Every nation has its own version of the doctrine of manifest destiny. It is an expression of national aspiration. But it can become a dangerous pagan ecumenism, as it did in the case of Japan and the United States. The manifest destiny ideology goes hand in hand with the ideology of national sovereignty, the creed that there is no principle of judgment higher than national interest. That, too, is pagan ecumenism.

Ambiguity of religion expresses itself in the most subtle and dangerous way in the dividing of humanity into two sections: the pious people and the impious people. Let me briefly address this point. Great religions are convinced of the presence of the universal value in humanity. In Buddhism all humans are declared to have buddha-quality which will lead to the highest value of reaching the nirvana. In Judaism and Christianity, all humans participate in the image of God. In Islam all humans are servants of the mighty Allah. In Hinduism there is a kernel of salvation-possibility in all of us. Here is a strong expression of this line of universality in St. Paul's letter to the Galatians: "There is neither Jew nor Greek, there is neither slave nor free, there is neither male nor female, for you are all one in Christ Jesus." (3:28) This is a great breakthrough that the great religions have given to us. But this breakthrough, which was able to obliterate many "distinctions" and "divisions," unfortunately set up a new powerful distinction, namely, between believers and non-believers.

Though religions proclaim the universal principle of value that is in humanity itself, they also introduce the distinction between "insiders" and "outsiders," "saved" and "unsaved," "Buddhists" and "non-Buddhists," "Christians" and "non-Christians." This is the source of the powerful formulae of "we and they," and "good boys and bad boys." Tragically, it is impossible to understand the tension between the United States and Soviet Union today without taking cognizance of this "we-good-boys and they-bad boys" scheme which is fundamentally religious in nature.

Here is a delicate point, the point at which we must decide to walk either towards militarism or towards evangelism. If we are convinced that "we" are good and "they" are bad, we go to militarism. If we come to know that we and they "fall short of the glory of God" (Romans 3:23) and need more mutual understanding in order to locate the whereabouts of the real evil, then we move towards evangelism. This distinction is delicate. Let me quote one paragraph from the writing of Thomas Merton:

> "War never again!" cried Pope Paul addressing the United Nations in October, 1965, and many who solemnly assented to his plea as reasonable and right, assented with equal solemnity a few weeks later when a retired Air Force General suggested that the way to bring peace to Southeast Asia was to "bomb North Vietnam back into the stone age." It was in this atmosphere that Cardinal Spellman, addressing troops in Vietnam, deplored the protest against the war articulated at home and summed up his view with, "My country right or wrong!" All of which goes to show that when war is actually being waged, emotional cliches come easier than creative thinking.[8]

We must reflect carefully on the words, "you are all one in Christ Jesus." We are all one in Christ Jesus "who has broken down the dividing wall of hostility" (Eph 2:14). The mind of Jesus Christ is far wider and deeper than ours (Romans 5:6-8).

Thus religion criticizes the divisions and at the same time introduces the major division. It is an ambiguous spiritual force working in the world. Religion destroys the idols and sets up idols. And none of us, including the most secular and pious among us, is free from this power of religion. All of us live between the destruction of idols and the setting up of idols. That is what history means. The same ability that can criticize idols can, if misdirected, set up new idols. When a certain group of people think that they are unquestionably "good-boys," then they must have set up a new idol. Violence emanates from such self-idolatry. Do not trust these deceptive words that you are good-boys and they are bad-boys! For Billy Graham the war in Vietnam was a "spiritual war between good and evil."[9] The truth (the unconcealed state of affairs) is that both "we and they" are idolatrous, and for both "we and they" to foster such a division based on self-righteousness really does not contribute to the health of humanity.

Idolatry is a spiritual and intellectual operation that goes through two stages: first the world is divided into good and bad sections; the second stage identifies ourselves with the good and our adversary with the bad. Idolatry can generate great power. There may be no greater generator of human power than self-righteousness. Idolatry, moreover, is not just a religious concept. It is actively at work in the realms of economics, politics, and in particular in the military. But it has its origin in the world of religions in which the name of God (of gods) is quoted. There is no idol apart from some kind of God or gods. And we must make a "graven image" of our God in order to preserve this destructive tension. "You shall not make for yourself a graven image!" (Exodus 20:4).

We have seen two sets of principal ambiguities in which we live today: the ambiguity of technology in which technological efficiency can suffocate the human meaning, and the ambiguity of religion in which our dedication to truth can distort truth, producing destructive idolatry. Our global village is shot through with these two ambiguities. Confusions produced by them has resulted in what I call a Global Military Installation. This compels us to ask several questions: What is meaningful technology? What is true religion? Where can we find technology which will enhance human meaning? Where can we find religion which will save us from idolatry? That is to say, how can we nurture the creative side of technology and religion instead of the destructive side?

If technology is to enhance human meaning it must not be used in support of the idolatry of self-righteousness. It must be used against that orientation. In this context, technology and religion are not to be thought of as two separate subject matters, but in reality very much one when they come to us. Rather we should say that we live in the very interaction of these two realities. In short, the problem of humanity in this global village is the problem of idolatry, the use of religion and technology for one's own self-aggrandizement. The world has become too small a place for such self-aggrandizement.

242

FOOTNOTES

1.      See p. 310 in Roger L. Shinn, ed., <u>Faith and Science in an Unjust World. Vol. 1:</u>
<u>Plenary Presentations</u> (The World Council of Churches); Philadelphia: Fortress, 1980. 408
pp.
2.      See p. 5 in Ruth L. Sivard, <u>World Military and Social Expenditures 1981</u>, 6th ed;
Leesburg, VA: World Priorities, 1981.
3.      See p. 486 in Louis Finkelstein, "The Jewish Religion: Its Beliefs and Practices." pp.
469-531 in <u>The Jews, Their Religion and Culture</u>, 4th ed, ed Louis Finkelstein. NY:
Schocken, 1970. xv + 554 pp. (original 1949)
4.      F. Max Muller, ed., <u>Sacred Books of the East. Vol. XXII.</u> Jaina Sutras, Part I. The
Akaranga Sutra; The Kalpa Sutra tr from Prakrit by Hermann Jacobi. UNESCO Collection
of Representative Works, Indian Series. Delhi: Motilal Banarsidass, 1980. (original, Oxford
University Press, 1884)
5.      Gottfried Quell, <u>aletheia</u>, "A. In the Old Testament," Vol. 1:232-237 in <u>Theological</u>
<u>Dictionary of the New Testament</u> ed Gerhard Kittel.  Grand Rapids: Eerdmans, 1964. Cf.
also, Gerhard Kittel, "B. Rabbinic Judaism," pp. 237-238, and Rudolph Bultmann, "C. The
Greek and Hellenistic Use of <u>aletheia</u>," pp. 238-241, "D. The Early Christian Use of <u>aletheia</u>,"
pp. 241-247, and, <u>alethes</u>, <u>alethinos</u>, <u>aletheuo</u>.
6.      See p. 49 in Roland H. Bainton, <u>Christian Attitudes Toward War and Peace. A</u>
<u>Historical Survey and Critical Re-evaluation</u>; Nashville: Abingdon, 1979. 299 pp.
7.      See pp. 152f in Howard Zinn, <u>A People's History of the United States</u>; Harper &
Row, 1980. 614 pp. 2nd ed, 1990.
8.      See p. 40 in Thomas Merton, <u>Faith and Violence: Christian Teaching and Christian</u>
<u>Practice</u>; Notre Dame, IN: Notre Dame University Press, 1968. x + 291 pp.
9.      Ibid., p. 91.

# VI.


# FINAL INTERPRETATION

# THE DEATH OF DEATH

## Paul S. Minear

In selecting this topic I have wanted to touch on matters that were of prime concern to Professor Michalson: his early and continuing fascination with existentialism; his insistence on dealing with the panorama of human history from the perspective provided by its "hinge"; his penchant for delving deeply into hermeneutical riddles; his pastoral instinct for wrestling with personal crises. Several of these concerns converge in the need for us to think more coherently about death, and about the one who, for Christian believers, holds the key of death.

Carl Michalson's concern for death is illustrated by his citation of Baudelaire: "Time eats up all things alive. Time blots me out as flakes on freezing waters fall. Time is the gambler that need not cheat to win."[1] And Carl's concern with the keys of death is illustrated by his statement: "Existentialism is at least a road to Calvary.... But at the end of that road one may as easily find...two thieves as find the suffering savior."[2]

I have a second reason for exploring this topic. I want to examine the distance between the early Christian movement and the pictures of that movement conveyed by current historical scholarship. What I have in mind here will become more apparent if I make two observations. The first observation is this: few movements in human history have demonstrated such explosive power as early Christianity. Within a few decades it had spread (without benefit of airplanes) throughout the worlds of western Asia, northern Africa and the shores of the Mediterranean. This expansion (without benefit of television) triggered volcanic enthusiasms and murderous hatreds. At each step the devotion of martyrs was matched by the violence of their murderers. What to martyrs seemed the best of news seemed to their enemies the worst of news. My second observation is this: no current reconstruction of that ancient history produces comparable excitement or comparable hostility. Does the best recent portrait of Jesus make intelligible either response - or produce either response? Does any recent picture of Paul evoke comparable devotion or venom? Martyrdoms, of course, continue to occur, but not as a result of scholars' versions of the Gospel. In short, there is a vast distance between the original events and our best academic descriptions of them.

If we are to gauge this distance with some accuracy, we need to think about the keys of death, for those ancient martyrs and their murderers had one thing in common: death. The execution of the martyrs signalled the power of a revolutionary gospel and the power of counter-revolutionary resistance to it. Both murderers and martyrs claimed to hold and to use the keys of death. One set of keys produced death; the other was designed to accomplish the death of death. Here, then, is an area of reality that demands exploration.

Of one thing we may be sure: the apostles and prophets would not have encountered such love or such hatred had they not made contact with the most elemental of hungers and the most universal of fears. And another thing is equally sure: these responses would not have been evoked had those messengers not spoken with the highest degree of authority. It was as spokesman for the risen Lord, as recipients of the Holy Spirit, that they addressed the most universal of fears - the fear of death - and the most elemental hunger for victory over death. It was their claim that a crucified King held the keys of death that aroused both irresistible enthusiasm and implacable hatred. Just here may we locate the epicenter of the earthquake that sent shock waves in all directions. We will not understand the ancient story until we understand why this use of the keys of death proved to be so revolutionary. And since we are interested in measuring distances between ancient events and their modern reconstructions, we must compare modern perceptions of death with ancient ones. Is our current situation in this regard greatly different from the situation in New Testament times? So this is what I shall attempt to do: I shall outline a set of modern perceptions about death. Then I shall use that set of perceptions as a foil against which to outline early Christian perceptions.

I

As a representative of the modern perceptions, I shall use the book of Ernest Becker, The Denial of Death. At some risk of oversimplification, let me summarize his central convictions.

First of all, Becker describes man as "a worm and food for worms."[3] Man is a part of nature, whose mortality links him to all other animals. This mortality is all inclusive, extending to every institution and every society. According to Becker, the soberest conclusion we can make on what has been taking place on the planet for three billion years is that "it is being turned into a vast pit of fertilizer."[4]

Yet man can be distinguished from other animals in this: he is conscious of his own mortality. In becoming self-conscious of his own identity, his own life story, he becomes conscious of its certain end. He knows that whatever he does "on this planet has to be done in the lived truth of the terror of creation, of the grotesque, of the rumble of panic underneath everything."[5]

So an inevitable result of this consciousness of mortality is the fear of death, a fear that further distinguishes man from other animals. This fear is truly universal, and no one is immune to it. Carl Michalson quotes Luther's axiom that "the fear of death is death itself."[6] Such fear lies at the root of many other fears, hiding within them and influencing them all. To use the words of John Donne, "So does fear insinuate itself in every action and passion of the mind." Or to cite the text of Benjamin Britten's St. Nicolas, "Poor man. I found him solitary, racked by doubt: born, bred, doomed to die in everlasting fear of everlasting death - the foolish toy of time, the darling of decay...."[7]

This fear has many results, among which is the persistent effort to immunize ourselves against the terrors of death. We devise countless ways to repress the fear, one form after another of anesthesia: psychological tricks, aesthetic diversions, personal preoccupations, social games. We locate the windows of vulnerability one after another, and then nail them shut. But to be effective, our immunization systems must be kept hidden, secret even from ourselves. Professor Becker argues that the most effective security systems are constructed in the area of morality and religion. By its standards of "the mature character" and of moral excellence, a community develops types of anesthesia by which to keep the fear of death under control. Not unexpectedly, a community succeeds best among its most respected members. The greatest immunity is awarded to its leaders, along with the self-assurance that accompanies moral excellence. Many of these leaders can even claim to be quite free from the fear of death.

The success of the security systems depends upon success in self-deception. The greater the sense of moral achievement the easier the deception. The practice of religion becomes a conspiracy in which the individual's illusions are reinforced by communal systems of hypocrisy, subtly designed to deny the power of death and to stifle the fear of it. But the more successful the immunization process the more disastrous the results. As Becker states the cumulative consequences, "the briefest explanation of all the evil that men have wreaked upon themselves and their world (is)... not in terms of man's animal heredity, his instincts and his evolution...but in the toll that his pretense of sanity takes, as he tries to deny his true condition."[8]

Because moral standards and religious achievements function in this way, anything that threatens them is immediately feared as representing a threat to the very foundations of the community's existence. Once an immunity system has been sanctified, any attack on that system will be viewed as worse than death itself. This fact serves to explain the violence that accompanies religious wars (and in the modern age, the claims of nations and classes are inherently religious). The deaths of some of its members becomes the price paid by a community to safeguard its methods for repressing the fear of death. Here I may add a note to Becker's analysis. When such an attack takes place, the death of martyrs becomes a signal that an ultimate conflict has broken out between the heretics and the hypocrites. Here, as I have said, can be located the epicenter of an earthquake. The hypocrites are persuaded to kill the heretics in order to protect their own immunity. The heretics, on the other hand, in accepting death, celebrate their liberation from the conspiracy, the illusions, the hypocrisies that have repressed the fears of death.

Returning to Becker, we note his appraisal of the role of Christianity. He draws a distinction between its initial role and its latter-day perversions. With a trace of nostalgia he recalls the time when "man lived securely under the canopy of the Judeo-Christian world picture....He came from the invisible world into the visible one by the act of God, did his duty to God by living out his life with dignity and faith, marrying as a duty, procreating as a duty, offering his whole life, as Christ had, to the Father. In turn he was justified by the Father and rewarded with eternal life in the invisible dimension....The Christian world picture...could take cripples, imbeciles, slaves, the simple and the mighty and make them all secure heroes, simply by taking a step back from the world into another dimension of things, the dimension called heaven."[9] But all this has changed. The Christian option ceased to be viable as soon as "man no longer had God." God has become "no more than an abstraction," an illusion that "has reinforced the regressive transference into a more choking bind."[10] By such statements I believe Becker is accusing contemporary Christianity of becoming a chief source of communal self-deception in denying the realities of death.

## II

Now I want to use Becker's analysis as a foil against which to examine the attitudes toward death on the part of the earliest prophets and apostles. And the first point, naturally, is to observe that these writers fully agree with Becker in recognizing the universal power of death. A base line for New Testament thought is Isaiah's axiom: "All flesh is grass and all its goodliness is as the flower of grass."[11] There can be no immunity or exemption from mortality. Paul was typical in tracing death to its beginning - "As in Adam all die" - and in anticipating a future in which the last enemy to be overcome is death.[12] By treating Death as one of the heavenly principalities, by capitalizing it as a mythological entity, by viewing it as an enslaving potentate, prophets exceeded even Becker in the austere realm of their thought. Any inclination to diminish the power of death results in diminishing the power of God at work through the Gospel.

We can be equally confident that the prophets were fully aware of the subtle union between death and the fear of death. Death merits and produces this fear because it is the ultimate index of captivity, of weakness, futility, vanity and separation from the land of the living. As death is the last enemy, so terror in the face of its power is the almost universal reaction. That the Christian prophets were more emphatic on this point than Becker is indicated by their tracing of this fear to a superhuman source - the Devil. The Devil wields the power of death by using man's fear of death to subject him to "lifelong bondage" (Heb 2:14). The last things which the divine judge is to consign to the lake of fire will be death and the Devil. Any inclination to minimize the power of this fear results in emasculating and trivializing the Gospel.

Nor is Becker the first to discover the human penchant for hiding the fear of death. Early Christian prophets, beginning with Jesus, were alert to the multiple forms of self-deception, which again they traced to the work of Satan. The devil is a liar and the father of all lies. He is an expert in using the good to hide the evil and in turning the best intentions into the worst deeds. His slaves are always deceived and self-deceived by their conscious goodness. Paul, for example, was forced to recognize the linkage between death and sin because his own self-confident persecution of "the church of God" has made him "unfit to be called an apostle" (I Cor 15:9). He knew what it meant to say, "the sting of death is sin." Or to quote a modern novelist: "Only the devil could have thought up all the deceits and guises under which death masquerades."[13] Among the guises are these: God, America, the happy life, new life in California, liberalism, Christianity, the new Christendom, love, etc. However attractive the mask worn by the devil, the mask illustrates the Pauline law: "the sting of death is sin."

It is only a small step to the next half of that axiom: "the power of sin is the Law" (I Cor 15:56). The New Testament provides ample documentation for Becker's thesis concerning the use of morality and religion as the means of immunizing a community against the fear of death. For the prophets this was not a matter of abstract theory but of personal experience. The most highly respected servants of the Law had become their deadly enemies, illustrating the depth of the self-deception. As John writes: "The hour is coming when whoever kills you will think he is offering service to God" (16:2). Perhaps the most succinct epitome of this blindness is the cry, "We have a law and by that law he ought to die" (John 19:7). And the motivation behind that cry is underscored by the saying of Caiaphas: "It is expedient for you that one man should die for the people and that the whole nation should not perish" (John 11:50). Northrop Frye has recently remarked that "there has never yet been a society that has not agreed with Caiaphas."[14] Here one can see disclosed the deadly result of the fear of death when channeled through loyalty to God's law. Death and the fear of death have spawned a conspiracy that justifies a constellation of Pauline images: Adam, the devil, the world, sin, flesh, the Law, hypocrisy, blindness, the night....It is not strange that Jesus' disciples, when liberated by his death from the immunity systems of Judaism, should have directly attacked continued reliance upon those systems: reliance on the Sabbath, circumcision, the festivals, Abrahamic lineage, Mosaic revelation, the accepted criteria for measuring holiness and uncleanness, salvation and damnation. Nor is it strange that the disciples' adversaries should have emerged from among the leaders of the synagogues and the temple, established defenders of the Law and the nation. The death of the martyrs became the measure of both slavery and liberation: slavery to the established immunity systems and freedom from those systems. Yet what the murderers called death the martyrs called life. And behind this contradiction over words lay the ultimate conflict between the power of God and the power of the Devil. Becker's analysis may be of genuine value if it reminds us again of the issues central to the New Testament.

### III

I want now to explore some of the reasons why early Christian prophets and apostles could announce the death of death, claiming the authority of the risen Christ. How had they been liberated from the conspiracy that still blinded their opponents? None knew better than they the power of the law of sin and death. Whence came their confidence in a greater power? A complete answer would of course require citing virtually the entire New Testament. We must be content with the briefest of summaries. Any summary must do justice to two essential components, the

crucifixion of Jesus and the share in that crucifixion on the part of every
believer. We will discuss two components in that order.

In the New Testament the term death has many resonances and
connotations. Consider just a few of them:

> the death he died, he died to sin,
> sin revived and I died,
> I die every day,
> death is at work in us, but life in you
> whoever believes in me shall never die,
> this is the second death,
> God is "ready to judge the living and the dead"
> light to those who sit in the shadow of death,
> death reigned from Adam to Moses,
> whoever does not love abides in death,
> put to death whatever is earthly in you,
> we have been united with him in a death like his,
> I died, and see, I am alive forever,
> if we die, we die to the Lord.

That is only a sample of the range of meanings of death in the New
Testament. But that sample is enough to show that all variations of meaning
in the word "death" have been influenced by the story of Jesus. And of
decisive importance in that story is the story of his death. It is not simply
that in his death Jesus won a personal victory over death. That is of course
essential. But his victory produced continual and radical revision in the
entire lexicon of meanings. The Gospel of John uses the clause "if I be lifted
up" three times to indicate the character of that victory. The same clause
could be followed by many result clauses. When he was lifted up on the
cross, Jesus transformed previous ideas of death, previous fears of death,
previous ways of controlling these fears. In being lifted up, he freed his
followers from bondage to the law - a bondage by which he was judged to
be worthy of death. He freed his followers from bondage to the sin which
had established its hold on religious folk through the law. He freed them
from the blindness endemic among self-confident defenders of the law. He

freed them from being deceived by the Tempter who since Eden had used the fear of death to create a slavery worse than death itself. In dying Jesus established a kinship with all who had died and all who would yet die, to use the language of First Peter, with all the "spirits in prison." In thinking of Christ as the Alpha and the Omega, his followers also thought of his cross as directly linked to both the origin of death and to its ultimate banishment. Richard Roberts was no alien to this mode of thought in saying: "The whole world is Calvary writ large....A man's soul is Calvary writ small."[15] It is a minimal statement of the truth to say that after Jesus' death, death would never again be the same - at least never to those who called him "Lord." Yet every version of the Gospel insisted upon the horrible actuality of his execution as a criminal by the people to whom he was sent.

We should be forever curious, more curious than we usually are, about how people could accept such a revolution in their thinking about death. No answer can be fully credible that ignores their own confessions - that this revolution was a direct result of God's revelation of his presence in the "lifting up" of Christ. I find it hard to forget the observation of Karl Barth that modern Christians take the state a hundred times more seriously than they take God, because I find it hard to avoid extending that observation to many other things that we take more seriously than we take God. We know very little of that fear of God that is the beginning of wisdom about all things, including death. But as we ponder the ancient option, we can say that the early Christian martyrs, like their Jewish murderers, took their relationship to God more seriously than any other relationship. But while these martyrs and these murderers both took the death of Jesus seriously, they viewed God's relationship to his death in opposite ways. When the apostles and prophets say the risen Lord, heard his voice and obeyed his commands, they were induced to take God more seriously than they had taken all their prior attitudes toward death, as well as this particular death. That is why they came to recognize that acceptance or rejection of this revelation marked the most profound distinction between human beings. Belief in God's glorification of the crucified Jesus formed the boundary between the two religious communities, both of which thought of themselves as God's people. But only one community viewed itself as summoned to share in Christ's death, and more specifically to die for the sake of those very enemies who viewed the cross as proof that Jesus had <u>not</u> been God's messenger. It is the normative view of New Testament writers that the valid confession of Christ's victory over death can be given only by those who share that victory through dying with him.

Consider Jesus' rigorous teaching about losing and saving one's life, and the reiterated demand that every follower must carry his own cross, whether in daily self-denial or in martyrdom.

Consider the Johannine pictures of how disciples are to imitate Jesus by washing one another's feet, by walking the same road, by sharing the same hostility from the world, by falling, like seed, into the ground and dying.

Consider the conception of baptism as dying with Christ and being buried with him, and the connection that this death is far more decisive than any death that might be anticipated in the future.

Consider the conception of the Eucharist as proclaiming the death of the Lord, as eating his flesh and drinking his blood, as sharing in the giving of flesh for the life of the world.

Consider the Pauline picture of what God's exhibit to the world looked like: "men sentenced to death... a spectacle... fools... weak... reviled... homeless... the offscouring of all things" (I Cor 4:8-13). "Dying, but see, we live."

Consider the many ways in which dying with and to the Lord transformed the most intimate relations, husband and wife, parents and children, masters and slaves, rulers and subjects, teachers and taught.

Consider the new idea of priesthood according to which every priest has an altar "outside the camp" where his liturgical exercise must be to "bear the abuse he endured" (Heb 13:13).

Consider Paul's testimony that in the cross of Christ "the world has been crucified to me, and I to the world" (Gal 6:14).

So the early testimonies of faith in the victory of the crucified Lord were tightly bound together with recognitions that the only way to share in that victory was to share the same sufferings. It is often overlooked that in the famous defense of the resurrection in I Corinthians 15 the apostle speaks of his own daily dying as a corollary of that resurrection (15:31). Such an assertion may be taken as a homiletic hyperbole, a melodramatic exaggeration, but to do so would be a vast mistake, since the assertion is supported by Paul's martyrdom. No, Paul meant to say that apart from this daily dying, any confession of Christ's resurrection is a grotesque self-deception.

These considerations linking the death of Jesus to the dying of his followers stress ever more clearly the boundary between two religious communities, a boundary which, as we have noted, separates two opposing conceptions of life and death. Although that boundary is absolutely firm, it is also entirely provisional. At any moment, a Pharisaic persecutor may become an apostle: at any moment, an apostle may ignore or betray God's revelation of the life that is hidden in death. The Gospel can all too easily become an immunity system repressing the fears of death and encouraging hypocrisy and self-deception. Surely Northrop Frye is justified in saying that "What Jesus condemned in Pharisaism is as common in Christianity as in any other religion."[16] Our churches no longer fully understand the death of death that took place on Calvary, no longer live as if their Lord holds the keys of death and Hades, no longer can say that they have been crucified with Christ, dying to the law, to sin, to the world, and to the fears by which the devil holds them captive.

In these observations we may find an answer to my initial questions concerning the radical contrast between an early Christian movement which released volcanic enthusiasms and murderous hatreds and modern reconstructions of that movement which evoke neither comparable excitements nor similar hostilities. If that judgment is even partially true, what does it is suggest about our own roles as teachers and preachers in churches, where so many celebrations of Easter have become new forms of the denial of death, and therefore a denial of the victory over death?

I suggest that our role might be compared to that of a volcanologist whose specialty is knowledge of the volcanic power of the Scriptures. That volcano appears to be dormant. We are surrounded by former lava flows which have hardened. But we should keep our eyes on the seismograph. There are earth tremors to be measured and watched. Wherever we now live, it is not far from what a geologist might call the Gethsemane crater. An eruption may take place at any moment. So be careful when you open the Bible, when you celebrate baptism, when you distribute the bread and the wine. Beware of what might happen! That word of God might again announce immediate liberation from the law of sin and death. And that liberation might again arouse murderous hatred against those so liberated. Whenever we let the Gospel be the Gospel it makes contact with elemental hungers and universal fears. Don't ever underestimate the power of those hungers and fears. Any revelation of God in a society where God is dead is bound to be explosive. So in this regard, our vocation should make us appreciate the poem of Emily Dickinson:

> On my volcano grows the grass,
> A meditative spot,
> An area for a bird to choose
> Would be the general thought.
>
> How red the fire reeks below!
> How insecure the sod!
> Did I disclose, would populate
> With awe my solitude.[17]

258

## ENDNOTES

1. Carl Michalson, <u>The Hinge of History</u>; NY: Scribners, 1959, p. 185.
2. Carl Michalson, <u>Christianity and the Existentialists</u>; NY: Scribners, 1956, p. 20.
3. Ernest Becker, <u>The Denial of Death</u>; NY: Free Press, 1973, p. 161.
4. Ibid., p. 283.
5. Ibid.
6. Carl Michalson, <u>Faith for Personal Crises</u>; NY: Scribners, 1958, p. 161.
7. Benjamin Britten, <u>St. Nicolas</u>, 1948.
8. Becker, op. cit., pp. 29-30.
9. Ibid., pp. 159f.
10. Ibid., pp. 160, 204.
11. Isaiah 40:6.
12. I Corinthians 15:22, 27.
13. Walker Percy, <u>The Second Coming</u>; NY: Farrar, Straus, Giroux, 1980, pp. 271f.
14. Northrop Frye, <u>The Great Code</u>; Toronto: Academic Press, 1982, p. 133.
15. Richard Roberts, <u>That Strange Man Upon His Cross</u>; NY: Abingdon Press, 1934, p. 122.
16. Frye, op. cit., p. 133.
17. Emily Dickinson, <u>The Poems of Emily Dickinson</u>; Cambridge, MA: Belknap Press, 1955, Poem 1677, p. 1141.

Bernhard Word Anderson is Professor of Old Testament Theology Emeritus at Princeton Theological Seminary (1968-82) and Adjunct Professor of Old Testament at Boston University School of Theology. He was Dean (1954-63) and Henry Anson Buttz Professor of Biblical Theology (1954-68) at The Theological School of Drew University and a colleague of Carl Michalson until the latter's death in 1965. While at Drew, he helped organize the Drew-McCormick archaeological expedition to Tell Balata, ancient biblical Shechem, with G. Ernest Wright and faculty of both schools (it later became a "joint expedition" involving a number of other schools). Earlier Dr. Anderson taught at Colgate University (1946-8), University of NC, Chapel Hill (1948-50, James A. Gray Associate Professor of Bible), and Colgate-Rochester Divinity School (1950-54, Joseph B. Hoyt Professor of Old Testament). He was born (1916) in Dover, MO, holds the B.A. (1936) from the University of the Pacific and the M.A. (1938) and B.D. (1939) from the Pacific School of Religion. His Ph.D. (1945) is from Yale. He was ordained in 1939 (The Methodist Church, now United Methodist) and served churches in CA, CT and NY. His most well know work is Understanding the Old Testament; Englewood Cliffs, NJ: Prentice-Hall, 1957, 551 pp. (4th ed, 1986, 672 pp.). Earlier he published Rediscovering the Bible (NY: Association Press, 1950) and The Unfolding Drama of the Bible (Association, 1953; rev, Piscataway, NJ: New Century, 1971). Other volumes followed: The Beginning of History (Nashville/London: Abingdon/Lutterworth, 1963), Creation vs Chaos (Minneapolis: Augsburg/Fortress, 1967, 192 pp), Out of the Depths (NY: Board of Missions, Women's Division, United Methodist Church, 1970; 3rd ed, Philadelphia: Westminster, 1984, 254 pp), The Eighth Century Prophets (Philadelphia: Fortress, 1978) and The Living Word of the Bible (Westminster, 1979, 118 pp). He edited The Old Testament and Christian Faith (NY: Harper & Row, 1962; Herder & Herder, 1969), Israel's Prophetic Heritage: Essays in Honor of James Muilenburg (Harper, 1962; with Walter Harrelson), Faith Enacted as History, Essays in Biblical Theology (Westminster, 1976; the essays of Will Herberg), Creation in the Old Testament (Fortress, 1984, xiii + 178 pp) and The Books of the Bible (NY: Scribner, 1989, 2 vols). He has also written numerous articles, books reviews, sermons and curriculum material. For a complete listing to 1985, see his festschrift: Understanding the Word: Essays in Honor of Bernhard W. Anderson, ed James T. Butler, Edgar W. Conrad and Ben C. Ollenburger; JSOT Supplement 37; Sheffield, England: JSOT Press, 1985. 389 pp. Professor Anderson has held numerous lectureships, e.g., Lund, Burns, Haskel, Vosburgh, etc. The Pacific School of Religion (1960) and Colgate University (1965) each awarded him a D.D. and the University of the Pacific gave him an S.T.D. (1961).

James Pearce Carse is Professor of Religion at NYU (1966-  ). He was born (1932) in Mansfield, Ohio, graduated from Ohio Wesleyan (A.B., 1954) and Yale (B.D., 1957; S.T.M., 1962) and studied with Carl Michalson for his Ph.D. from The Graduate School of Drew University (1966). His dissertation was published as Jonathan Edwards and the Visibility of God; NY: Scribner, 1967, 191 pp. He published The Silence of God: Meditations on Prayer; NY: Macmillan, 1985. He served as University pastor (1957-60) at the University of NC (Chapel Hill), and at the University of Connecticut (Storrs, 1960-62). As part of his teaching at NYU, he taught an interdisciplinary course on death, drawing on secular social, philosophical and theological viewpoints. The course attracted large numbers of students from various university disciplines. He edited Death and Society (NY: Harcourt Brace, 1980) and authored Death and Existence: A Conceptual History of Human Mortality; NY: Wiley, 1980, xiv + 473 pp. The latter traces human reflection on death from ancient Greek philosophers through mysticism, modern science, Freud, world religions, Hegel, Nietzsche, Heidigger, Kierkegaard. More recently he published Finite and Infinite Games; NY: Free Press, 1986, 152 pp (Ballantine, 1987, 192 pp). He has hosted a Sunday morning TV show,

"The Way to Go" which considers religious and various other human concerns. He has also taught in the NYU TV educational series, "Sunrise Semester."

Dr. Karlfried Froehlich is the Benjamin B. Warfield Professor of Ecclesiastical History at Princeton Theological Seminary. He was born in Schmeckwitz in Saxony, the second child of Hanna (Ruettger) and Karl Froehlich. His father was a pastor in the evangelical Lutheran church. After the gymnasium years, he attended the Kirkliche Hochschule Wuppertal and then Basel and Goettingen. At the University of Basel where he studied for his Th.D. with Oscar Cullmann (major professor) and Karl Barth (member of his examination committee), he passed his examinations summa cum laude. He edited a collection of Cullmann's essays: Oscar Cullmann: Vortraege und Aufsaetze (Tuebingen: Mohr-Siebeck, 1967), and a festschrift for his teacher: Testimonia oecumenica in honorem Oscar Culmann octogenarii (Tuebingen: Vogler, 1982). Dr. Froehlich holds a Master's degree (1961) from Drew University where he was a colleague of Carl Michalson before the latter's death and Froehlich's own move to Princeton in 1968. He co-authored the 2nd (1965) and 3rd (1973) editions of Understanding the New Testament with Howard C. Kee and Franklin W. Young (Englewood Cliffs, NJ: Prentice-Hall). He is the author of Biblical Interpretation in the Early Church (Philadelphia: Fortress, 1984) and many articles and reviews. He is a member of the Evangelical Lutheran Church in America and has served on regional and national committees, including the committees for the bi-lateral dialogue with the Roman Catholic Church and the Reformed Churches.

John Drew Godsey was born (1922) in Bristol, TN. He graduated with honors from Virginia Polytechnic Institute and State University (B.S., 1947), after serving in the U.S. Army (1943-46), worked in industry (1947-50), graduated from Drew magna cum laude (B.D., 1953), was awarded the Delaplaine McDaniel Prize and matriculated at the University of Basel (Switzerland), where he studied with Karl Barth and received his D.Theol. insigni cum laude (1960). His dissertation was published as The Theology of Dietrich Bonhoeffer (Philadelphia: Westminster, 1960) and was the first comprehensive study of Bonhoeffer in any language. In addition to authoring numerous articles, he edited Karl Barth's Table Talk (Richmond: John Knox, 1963), wrote the Introduction and Epilogue to Karl Barth's How I Changed My Mind (Richmond: John Knox, 1966), authored Preface to Bonhoeffer (Philadelphia: Fortress, 1965) and The Promise of H. Richard Niebuhr (Philadelphia: Lippincott, 1970), and co-edited Ethical Responsibility: Bonhoeffer's Legacy to the Churches (NY: Edwin Mellen, 1981). He edited Michalson's Worldly Theology for its posthumous publication. Godsey was ordained in The Methodist Church (1952, 1957). He returned to Drew in 1956 as a colleague of Carl Michalson, served as assistant dean (1956-59) and taught systematic theology (1956-68) before moving to Wesley Theological Seminary, where he was associate dean (1968-1971) and taught systematic theology until retirement in 1988. During the year 1964-65 he was a Fulbright Research Scholar at the University of Goettingen, Germany, and in 1985-86 served as president of the American Theological Society. He is a founding member of the International Bonhoeffer Society, English Language Section.

David McConnell Graybeal was born (1921) in Radford, VA. He earned his B.A. at Emory and Henry (1941) in Abingdon, VA, taught high school (1941-2), was Engineering Officer (1943-6), USN, on a destroyer escort in the North Atlantic during World War II. He received his B.D. (1949) from Yale Divinity School and Ph.D. (1952) from Yale University. He was ordained in 1939 and served in Wallingford, CT ('49-52) and then became Chaplain at Emory and Henry (1952-56) before moving to Drew (1956-91) where he is Professor of Church and Society in The Theological and Graduate Schools. Among his publications are The Christian Family and Its Money (Nashville, TN: The Methodist Church, 1960) and Can't

We All Be Rich? (NY: Friendship Press, 1966). In recent years, Graybeal has participated in the production of videos on social issues for use in congregations. He helped produce the film and video on the life and work of Nelle Morton, titled "The Journey is Home." He remembers with pleasure the courses which Carl Michalson allowed him to audit.

Howard Clark Kee was born in Edgewater Park, NJ, went to Temple (1937-8) and Bryan College (B.A., 1940), Dallas Theological Seminary (Th.M., 1944) and Yale (Ph.D., 1951). He is emeritus from the William Goodwin Aurelio Professorship of Biblical Studies and Chair of the Graduate Division of Religious Studies at Boston University and Professor of New Testament in the School of Theology (1977-86). Earlier he taught at Bryn Mawr (1968-77, Rufus Jones Professor of the History of Religions) and Drew Theological Seminary (1953-68, Professor of New Testament) where he was a colleague of Carl Michalson and (1951-53) at the University of Pennsylvania. Archaeological experience includes field work at Herodian Jericho, Shechem and Mt Gerizim, Pella, Ashdod. Dr. Kee and his wife Janet are now living in Philadelphia (though hardly "retired"). Among recent works is What Can We Know About Jesus? (NY: Cambridge University Press, 1990. v + 122 pp [Kee edits the Cambridge series "Understanding Jesus Today"]), Knowing the Truth (Minneapolis: Fortress, 1989. vii + 120 pp.), Medicine, Miracle and Magic in New Testament Times (NY: CU Press, 1986. x + 170 pp.), Miracle in the Early Christian World (Yale University Press, 1983. xi + 320 pp). In the last year, 1983, he received the "Professor of the Year" award at Boston University. He also held the Guggenheim (1966-67) and an AATS Fellowship (1959-60) and numerous lectureships, e.g., Lowell (1979). After co-editing Understanding the New Testament (Englewood Cliffs, NJ: Prentice-Hall) with Franklin Young (1957), and then Karlfried Froehlich (2nd, 1965 and 3rd ed, 1973), he completely revised the work for the 4th ed (1983; viii + 408 pp). In this he applied insights from earlier works, e.g., Christian Origins in Sociological Perspective: Methods and Resources (Philadelphia: Westminster, 1980. 204 pp), Christianity (Niles, Il: Argus, 1979. ix + 117 pp). Community of the New Age: Studies in Mark's Gospel (Westminster, 1977. xi + 225 pp; reprinted, corrected, Macon, GA: Mercer University, 1983), The Origins of Christianity (Prentice-Hall, 1973. ix + 270 pp. [rev, The New Testament in Context: Sources and Documents, xi + 239 pp, 1984]), Jesus in History (NY: Harcourt Brace and World, 1970. viii + 286 pp; 2nd ed, Harcourt Brace Jovanovich, 1977), Jesus and God's New People: The Four Gospels (Westminster, 1959, 92 pp), The Renewal of Hope (Association, 1959, 190 pp) and Making Ethical Decisions (Westminster, 1957, 96 pp). A festschrift was published in his honor, The Social World of Formative Christianity and Judaism. Essays in Tribute to Howard Clark Kee ed Jacob Neusner et al; Philadelphia: Fortress, 1988. xii + 368 pp. Complete bibliography [to 1 Sep 86], pp. 342-356. An accomplished musician, his libretto for New Land, New Covenant was a bicentennial oratorio set to music by Howard Hanson (NY: Fischer, 1976).

Kosuke Koyama is John D. Rockefeller Professor of Ecumenics and World Christianity at Union Theological Seminary in NYC. He was born in Tokyo (1929) and is a graduate of Tokyo Union Theological Seminary (1952) and came to The Theological School of Drew University to study with Carl Michalson and earned the B.D. cum laude (1954). He took his Th.M. (1955) and Ph.D. (1959) at Princeton Theological Seminary. A minister of the UCC of Japan, he was a Lecturer in systematic theology and Christian ethics in Chiengmai at Thailand Theological Seminary (1960-68) before becoming Director of the Association of Theological Schools in South East Asia and Dean of the South East Asia Graduate School of Theology in Singapore (1968-74). He was Senior Lecturer in Phenomenology of Religion at the University of Otago, Dunedin, New Zealand (1974-80) before coming to Union. His Water Buffalo Theology (London/Maryknoll, NY: SCM/Orbis, 1974. ix + 239 pp.) is considered a classic of Asian Theology but he has published many articles and books. Among them are Theology in Contact (Christian Literature Society of India, 1974), No

Handle on the Cross: An Asian Meditation on the Crucified Mind (London: SCM, 1976), Fifty Meditations (Orbis, 1979, 191 pp), Three Mile an Hour God: Biblical Reflections (SCM/Orbis, 1979/80. viii + 146 pp.) and Mount Fuji and Mount Sinai: A Critique of Idols; Orbis, 1985. x + 278 pp. He edited the South East Asia Journal of Theology from 1968-74.

Paul Sevier Minear is Winkley Professor of Biblical Theology emeritus (1971ff) of Yale Divinity School. He was born in Mt. Pleasant, IA (1906) and attended Iowa Wesleyan (B.A., 1927; LL.D., 1942), Garrett (B.D., 1930), Northwestern (M.A., 1930) and Yale (Ph.D., 1932). He has taught at the Hawaii [Honolulu] School of Religion (1933-4), Garrett (1934-44), Andover Newton (1944-56, Norris Professor of New Testament) and Yale (1956-71). He was Fulbright lecturer at the University of Utrecht (1958-9; Dr.Theol., 1962), Director of Faith and Order, World Council of Churches (1961-3), Vice-Rector (1970-72) of the Ecumenical Institute in Jerusalem and has held a number of Visiting Professorships. The University of Notre Dame awarded him an LL.D. (1966) and the University of Aberdeen awarded him a D.D. (1975). Among his many writings are An Introduction to Paul (Nashville: Abingdon, 1937), And Great Shall Be Your Reward (New Haven: Yale University Press, 1941), Eyes of Faith (Philadelphia: Westminster, 1946; rev, Bethany, 1966), The Choice (Westminster, 1948), The Kingdom and the Power (Westminster, 1950), Christian Hope and the Second Coming (Westminster, 1954), Jesus and His People (NY: Association Press, 1956), Horizons of Christian Community (St. Louis: Bethany, 1959), Images of the Church in the New Testament (Westminster, 1960), a Commentary on Mark (Richmond, VA: Knox, 1962), I Saw a New Earth (Corpus Books, 1968), The Obedience of Faith (SCM, 1971), Commands of Christ (Abingdon, 1972), I Pledge Allegiance (Geneva Press, 1975), To Heal and to Reveal (NY: Seabury, 1976), To Die and to Live (Seabury, 1977), New Testament Apocalyptic (Abingdon, 1981, 160 pp), Matthew: The Teacher's Gospel (NY: Pilgrim, 1982, 160 pp), John: The Martyr's Gospel (Pilgrim, 1985, 192 pp), Death Set to Music: Masterworks by Bach, Brahms, Pendericki, Bernstein (Atlanta: Knox, 1987, 173 pp) and The God of the Gospels: A Theological Workbook (Louisville, KY: Westminster/Knox, 1988, 128 pp). He edited The Nature of the Unity We Seek; Bethany, 1958.

Theodore H. Runyon, Jr. is Professor of Systematic Theology, Candler School of Theology, Emory University, where he has taught since 1958. He has also served as Chair of the School's Area II: History and Interpretation of Christianity, as Chair of the Department of Theological Studies in the Graduate School, as Acting Associate Dean, Director of Methodist and Ecumenical Studies, President of the University Senate, etc. A graduate of Lawrence University (Appleton, WI; 1952) and Drew Theological School (1955), he studied in Germany and received his doctorate from the University of Gottingen (1958). He has done post-doctoral studies at Gottingen (1964-65), Tubingen and Constance (1971-72); was a Fellow of the Institute for Ecumenical and Cultural Research at St. John's University (Collegeville, MN; 1979-80); was Visiting Professor, Methodist Theological Seminary (Seoul, Korea; 1985). The recipient of numerous scholarships and awards (Fulbright, etc.), he has lectured widely in colleges, universities, seminaries and church conferences across the U.S. and around the world. In addition to contributions to books and articles on Michalson, Gogarten, Tillich, Wesley, secularization, the "death of God," the sacraments, etc., he has edited What the Spirit is Saying to the Churches (NY: Hawthorne Books, 1975), Hope for the Church (Nashville: Abingdon, 1979), Sanctification and Liberation (Abingdon, 1981), Wesleyan Theology Today (Kingswood/Abingdon, 1985), and Theology, Politics, and Peace (Maryknoll: Orbis, 1989). Hope.. and Sanctification.. have been translated into Korean.

Lawrence E. Toombs, now retired as Professor of Religion and Culture at Wilfrid Laurier University (formerly Waterloo Lutheran University) in Waterloo, Ontario. Born (1919) in Prince Edward Island, Canada, he was educated at Prince of Wales College and Acadia

University. He received the B.Sci. (1941) and B.A. (Honors in Chemistry, 1942) and did post-grad study in chemistry at the University of Toronto and later in archaeology at the University of London (1961-2). During World War II, he was in the Royal Canadian Air Force as a meteorologist with the Department of Transport (1943-5) and then went to Pine Hill Divinity Hall (B.D. with Honors in New Testament, 1948). After his Ph.D. (1951) with John Paterson, he was Associate Professor of Old Testament at St. Stephen's College in Edmonton, Canada, and returned to Drew Theological School (1953-68) to teach and be a major figure in the excavation of Shechem (1956-68). He also dug at Jericho with Kathleen Kenyon, at Caesarea Maritima, and Tell el-Hesi. He taught at Union College of British Columbia in Vancouver (1968-9) before moving to WLU where in 1980, he was voted WLU's outstanding teacher of the year. He became chair of the Department in 1982. Among his many works are A Year with the Bible (Toronto: United Church of Canada, 1953), The Threshold of Christianity (Philadelphia: Westminster, 1960), The Old Testament in Christian Preaching (Westminster, 1961), Nation Making (London: Lutterworth, 1962), God's People among the Nations (NY/London: Association/ Lutterworth, 1963), Reader's Guide for Leviticus (Nashville: The Methodist Church, 1963), Excavation Manual (Wooster, Ohio: Wooster College, 1966) and Tell el Hesi: Modern Military Trenching and Muslim Cemetery in Field I (Waterloo, Ontario: Wilfrid Laurier University, 1985, xxii + 250 pp). The Tell el Hesi Series is ed Kevin G. O'Connell. Dr. Toombs co-edited with Norman E. Wagner, the Pottery Coding Handbook (Waterloo: Waterloo Lutheran University, 1971), with Norman E. Wagner and Eduard R. Riegart, The Moyer Site: A Prehistoric Village in Waterloo County (Wilfrid Laurier University, 1973), with Jeffrey A. Blakely The Tell el Hesi Field Manual (Cambridge, MA: ASOR, 1980, xix + 135 pp), with Leo G. Perdue and Gary L. Johnson, Archaeology and Biblical Interpretation: Essays in Memory of D. Glenn Rose; Atlanta, GA: Knox, 1987, xiii + 365 pp. A festschrift was published in 1984: The Answers Lie Below: Essays in Honor of Lawrence Edmund Toombs ed Henry O. Thompson; Lanham, MD: University Press of America. xxvi + 402 pp, with a partial bibliography, pp. xix-xxv.

John J. Vincent was born in Sunderland (1929) and educated at Richmond College, London University (B.D., 1954, First Class Honors), Drew University (S.T.M., 1955, summa cum laude) where he studied with Carl Michalson, University of Basel (D.Th., 1960, insigni cum laude). An ordained Methodist, he was a minister (1962-69) in Manchester and in Rochdale Mission. He has been Sheffield Inner-city Ecumenical Mission superintendent minister since 1970, where he has also been director of the Urban Theology Unit, where many Drew students have studied. Dr. Vincent was a Visiting Professor of Theology at Boston (1969), NY Theological Seminary (1970) and Drew Theological School (1977; and in D.Min. Summer Schools, 1978-83). Publications have included Christ in a Nuclear World (NY: Fellowship, Crux, 1962), Christ and Methodism: Towards a New Christianity for a New Age (Nashville: Abingdon, 1965; 2nd ed, Epworth, 1966), Here I Stand: The Faith of a Radical (Epworth, 1967), Secular Christ: A Contemporary Interpretation of Jesus (Abingdon, Epworth, 1968), The Race Race (NY/London: Friendship/ SCM, 1970), The Jesus Thing (Abingdon, 1973), Stirrings: Essays Christian and Radical (Epworth, 1975), Alternative Church (Christian Journals, 1976), Starting All Over Again (World Council of Churches, 1981), Into the City (Epworth, 1982), OK, Let's Be Methodists (Epworth, 1984), Radical Jesus (Grand Rapids/London: Zondervan/Marshall, 1986), Mark at Work (with J.D. Davies; Bible Reading Fellowship, 1986). In 1989-90, he was President of the Methodist Conference in Britain, in connection with which the Methodist Publishing House published a trilogy: Britain in the 90's, Gospel in the 90's and Discipleship in the 90's. A major work, A British Liberation Theology is expected in 1991.

## SOURCES

The Authors.

James T. Butler, Edgar W. Conrad and Ben C. Ollenburger, eds., Understanding the Word: Essays in Honor of Bernhard W. Anderson; Journal for the Study of the Old Testament Supplement Series 37; Sheffield: JSOT Press, 1985. 391 pp.

The Carl Michalson Society Bulletin

Contemporary Authors, First Revision and New Revision Series; Detroit: Gale Research, various volumes and dates. Cf. Cumulative Index, 1990.

Jacob Neusner, Peder Borgen, Ernest S. Frerichs, eds., The Social World of Formative Christianity and Judaism. Essays in Tribute to Howard Clark Kee; Philadelphia: Fortress, 1988. xii + 368 pp.

Hershel Shanks, Who's Who in Biblical Studies and Archaeology; Washington, DC: Biblical Archaeology Society, 1986. viii + 272 pp.

Henry O. Thompson, The Answers Lie Below; Lanham, MD: University Press, 1984. xxvi + 402 pp.

# TORONTO STUDIES IN THEOLOGY

23. Eric Voegelin, **Political Religions**, T. J. DiNapoli and E. S. Easterly III (trans.)

24. Rolf Ahlers, **The Barmen Theological Declaration of 1934: The Archeology of a Confessional Text**

25. Kenneth Cauthen, **Systematic Theology: A Modern Protestant Approach**

26. Hubert G. Locke (ed.), **The Barmen Confession: Papers from the Seattle Assembly**

27. Barry Cooper, **The Political Theory of Eric Voegelin**

28. M. Darrol Bryant and Hans R. Huessy (eds.), **Eugen Rosenstock-Huessy: Studies in His Life and Thought**

29. John Courtney Murray, **Matthias Scheeben on Faith: The Doctoral Dissertation of John Courtney Murray**, D. Thomas Hughson (ed.)

30. William J. Peck (ed.), **New Studies in Bonhoeffer's** *Ethics*

31. Robert B. Sheard, **Interreligious Dialogue in the Catholic Church Since Vatican II: An Historical and Theological Study**

32. Paul Merkley, **The Greek and Hebrew Origins of Our Idea of History**

33. F. Burton Nelson (ed.), **The Holocaust and the German Church Struggle: A Search for New Directions**

34. Joyce A. Little, **Toward a Thomist Methodology**

35. Dan Cohn-Sherbok, **Jewish Petitionary Prayer: A Theological Exploration**

36. C. Don Keyes, **Foundations For an Ethic of Dignity: A Study in the Degradation of the Good**

37. Paul Tillich, **The Encounter of Religions and Quasi-Religions: A Dialogue and Lectures**, Terence Thomas (ed.)

38. Arnold A. van Ruler, **Calvinist Trinitarianism and Theocentric Politics: Essays Toward a Public Theology**, John Bolt (trans.)

39. Julian Casserley, **Evil and Evolutionary Eschatology: Two Essays**, C. Don Keyes (ed.)

40. John Quinn and J.M.B. Crawford, **The Christian Foundation of Criminal Responsibility: Historical and Philosophical Analyses of the Common Law**

41. William C. Marceau, **Optimism in the Works of St. Francis De Sales**

42. A. James Reimer, **The Emanuel Hirsch and Paul Tillich Debate: A Study in the Political Ramifications of Theology**

43. George Grant, *et al.*, *Two Theological Languages* **by George Grant and Other Essays in Honour of His Work**, Wayne Whillier (ed.)

44. William C. Marceau, **Stoicism and St. Francis De Sales**

45. Lise van der Molen, **A Complete Bibliography of the Writings of Eugen Rosenstock-Huessy**

46. Franklin H. Littell (ed.), **A Half Century of Religious Dialogue, 1939-1989: Making the Circles Larger**

## DATE DUE

| | | | |
|---|---|---|---|
| | | | |
| | | | |
| | | | |
| | | | |
| | | | |
| | | | |
| | | | |
| | | | |
| | | | |
| | | | |
| | | | |